Sugar and Spice 2

Sugar and Spice

A Black Lace short-story collection

BLACK
lace

Black Lace novels are sexual fantasies.
In real life, make sure you practise safe sex.

First published in 1998 by
Black Lace
Thames Wharf Studios,
Rainville Road, London W6 9HT

Typeset by SetSystems Ltd, Saffron Walden, Essex
Printed and bound by Mackays of Chatham PLC

ISBN 0 352 33309 X

Contents

Introduction

❧ ❧

Our first short-story collection, *Sugar and Spice*, met with such warm approval that we immediately got working on the second anthology. With this batch of short stories we've broadened the boundaries and encouraged authors to go further; to look beyond romance and explore the no-holds-barred side of their imaginations. The result is an envelope-pushing collection of writings which dazzle and shock. While some stories, like *Party Piece*, are rooted in fantasy and take delight in opulent descriptions drenched with eroticism, a piece like *In the Gents* is as down and dirty as it gets, and the pared-down style is redolent of the transgressive writings of Lydia Lunch or Pat Califia.

I have tried to select stories that avoid the all-too-familiar clichés of erotic writing – both in terms of storyline and vocabulary. In *Absolute Trust*, for instance, power relationships are taken to the limit. Danger and fear are central to the story and there's not a whip in sight, which proves that one doesn't have to open the dressing-up box to explore SM relationships.

I want to continue this policy in terms of Black Lace novels, too. The series is five years old this summer and continues to be the UK's leading imprint of erotic fiction. Whenever TV and the press run features on erotic literature and women's fantasies, they come to us; they know we're the best. In order to keep the series fresh, we often review our editorial policy. In the early days at least half of the books had historical settings. Many authors felt it was necessary to eroticise history – to go one step further than bodice-rippers and romantic novels. One of our authors, Martine Marquand, has rightly pointed out that women's fascination with period costume is regarded as the quintessential embodiment of female fetishism.

Feedback from the readers indicates that contemporary settings are by far the most popular, however, and the majority of forthcoming Black Lace books will have present-day settings. Look out also for the first collection of our readers' sexual fantasies – *Venus 2000* – which is due for publication in May 1999. Having dealt with a huge amount of erotic material while working in Black Lace novels, I can assure you that this collection of genuine fantasies submitted by the readers are among the hottest things I've ever read. I hope you enjoy reading Black Lace stories as much as I enjoy working on them.

Kerri Sharp
July 1998

I'm always keen to see material from authors who write from the heart: women who aren't afraid to be bad girls and who want to translate their most outrageous fantasies into top-notch erotic stories. If you think you could write for us, send a large S.A.E. to

Black Lace Guidelines
Virgin Publishing Ltd
Thames Wharf Studios
Rainville Road
London W6 9HT

A first-class stamp is sufficient.

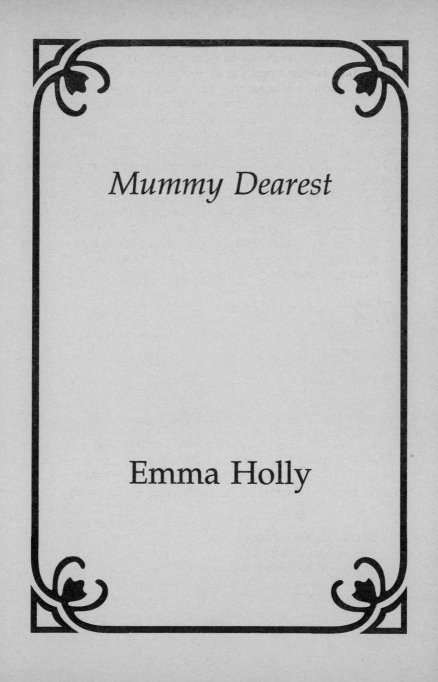

Mummy Dearest

Emma Holly

Mummy Dearest

❧ ❧

'*A*t last I find you,' he said in the beautifully pure Arabic of the Bedouins.

Of course, one might hear anything in Cairo: Japanese, gutter French, Swahili. But if one was an attractive Western woman alone at a café, one was rarely addressed so politely.

I looked up from my syrupy *qahwa ziyada*, my morning fix of sweet Turkish coffee. A young man stood before my table. He wore a long striped *galabiya* and a headscarf, worn loose rather than wrapped. Though his skin was desert brown, his curls were the colour of sun-struck caramel. His eyes – round with delight – were a bright amber-flecked blue.

'*As-salaam aleikum*,' I said, for lack of a better greeting. I have an excellent memory for faces and I knew I had never seen this striking youth before.

But perhaps someone had pointed me out as a buyer of antiquities for an American museum. No doubt he'd lead me to some dubious papyrus vendor where I'd be offered a likeness of Osiris, his staff of life erect, about to impregnate his beloved wife. If penises were involved in a forgery, I was invariably called to take a look. Apparently, the local gents believed I'd be too embarrassed to scrutinise their goods. They didn't realise a woman who'd survived a marriage as bitter as mine had lost her power to blush.

But I didn't take offence at their attitude, or their attempts to

3

dupe me. Though rich in culture, Egypt was poor in cash. The trade in bogus antiquities was a case of economic initiative – and part of the fun, I thought. None the less, I did not want this young entrepreneur to mistake me for a golden calf.

'Didn't they tell you I was a curator for a small museum,' I said, 'with a small budget?'

My accoster didn't seem to comprehend. His downy brows drew together. 'My name is Ahmed,' he said, his hands pressed prayerfully over his breastbone, his body bending forward in a bow.

'Chloe Sumner,' I responded, pleased as always to reclaim my maiden name.

Melancholy darkened his exotic eyes. 'Yes,' he said. 'I was told you might not remember. But you will come with me. I have wonders to show you.'

Such confidence was hard to resist. An air of adventure surrounded Ahmed. Perhaps he would lead me to an interesting find, preferably something small and scholarly which the authorities would allow out of the country, and which my employer would be able to afford.

The possibility sent heat pulsing to the crux of my thighs. My nipples drew tight with anticipation, making me grateful for the flowered smock I wore over my trousers. Bob the Bastard had been right about two things: I was an incorrigible gambler, and I did enjoy work more than sex. I tossed back the last hit of strong sweet *qahwah*, threw a few *piastres* on the table and stood. 'Lead on,' I said.

Ahmed flashed white teeth and waved me through the tables into the brilliant dusty heat of the Khan el-Khalili bazaar. Public contact between men and women was discouraged so he did not take my arm, though he did remain close enough to shepherd me past the stalls. Sidestepping a heap of carpets, he guided me on to the Sharia el-Muski where belly dancers, dressed even more modestly than I, haggled in rapid-fire Arabic over the price of sequins and gauze.

I'd walked these streets countless times and still the sights enthralled me. I was far more comfortable here than home in Philadelphia. These were my colours. These were my smells.

Under the blazing Saharan sun, my falseness melted away, leaving me naked and true.

One of the belly dancers laughed and wiggled her fingers at me, recognising me from a lesson I'd taken on a whim the week before. I had enjoyed her class more than I'd expected. Those sensual undulations had made sense to my long-ignored body.

'American Chloe!' the teacher called in heavily accented English. 'Shake that thing.'

Ahmed frowned and tugged my sleeve. 'Come. The master waits.'

A cool shiver tickled the back of my sweaty neck. I knew he meant his boss, but the words resonated strangely. The master waits. When we were married, Bob used to call himself my lord and master – a lame attempt at humour, considering he acted as if he really were. Even in our salad days, my skin had crawled at the words. But their effect in Ahmed's mouth was different. My chest tightened with a rush of adrenaline and my sex felt as if it had swollen to twice its normal size. Its folds slid wetly against each other with the movement of my legs, my pussy caressing itself, my clit a twitching pebble of sensation.

I told myself I'd gone too long without a good fuck.

Ahmed led me to an alley where a car waited, a Peugeot of indeterminate vintage repainted in flat Cairene turquoise. It listed half on the pavement, half on the dusty street. Another young man, this one in jeans and a cheap sports shirt, sat behind the wheel. Clearly pleased, he smiled warmly at Ahmed, then at me.

'This is Saad,' said my escort. He braced his sandalled heel on the side of the car, heaved the battered door open, and gestured for me to enter.

I hesitated. 'We're not walking?'

'No, no. We go a little ways.'

'How little?'

'Not far.' He shrugged in the vague Arab way that might mean one mile or a hundred. His eyes sparkled. I sensed that, whatever joke he was playing, he expected me to enjoy it.

What the hell, I thought. As yet, I had nothing to show for this buying trip. The chance that I'd find anything valuable today was remote, but I could afford a small adventure – or a large one, as the case seemed to be. Before long, we'd crossed to the opposite side of the Nile, leaving Cairo and the pyramids behind us.

'How far?' I asked.

'Not far,' said Ahmed, and handed me a bottle of mineral water.

Thus fortified, we drove south at maniacal speed, the Nile to our left, the desert to our right. We passed sand-coloured villages and lush green fields of berseem. Fishing boats wove between the wakes of tourist ferries. We wove between the potholes. At Asyut we stopped for petrol. I asked brown-eyed Saad if he wanted money to fill up the tank. He laughed for the first time and said I was their honoured guest. As the sun reached its zenith Ahmed offered me a *fateer* from his cooler, a delicious phyllo pastry and cheese concoction. When his hand accidentally brushed mine, his cock rose like a cobra beneath his cotton tunic, thickening and swaying. Neither of us said a word but our eyes met and held for a long, scorching moment. My stomach full, my ego gratified, I left my Western worry behind. *Ma'alesh*, I thought. Never mind. We would get where we were going when we got where we were going.

At sunset, I nodded off on Ahmed's shoulder. Gradually, surreptitiously, he shifted so that my breasts flattened against his ribs. His hand rested in his lap, hiding his erection from my shuttered gaze. Every so often I was aware of him squeezing its bulky length, his knuckles whitening, his thumb roving. This evidence of my feminine power must have gone to my head. I dreamt I was a pharaoh risen from my tomb to walk the streets of modern Egypt. Everything was a marvel to me: the buildings, the people, the crumbling monuments of my rule. Strange, what a happy dream it was; how it made the present seem as magical as the past.

I was smiling when I woke. Night had fallen and stars blazed against the death-black curtain of the night. The air temperature had dropped, but my body was warm and aroused as if, like sand, my flesh had the power to soak up and hold the sun. We had reached a small mudbrick village, twin to a thousand others along the Nile. I judged we were somewhere near the Valley of the Kings. Ahmed was shaking my shoulder.

'We are here,' he said. 'It is time.'

I shivered at his words, and again when he took my hand to help me from the car. The touch of bare skin was electric. It had been a long time since a man had held my hand. Too long.

'Where are the artifacts you wanted to show me?' I asked.

He made a shushing motion and pulled me into the nearest house. All within was dark and quiet but the back of my neck prickled, as if hidden eyes were watching, as if the entire village were holding its breath. We left our shoes by the door. A plush Turkish carpet surprised my bare feet. Still holding my hand, Ahmed led me through three darkened rooms. In the last I glimpsed an unattended computer screen which was scrolling the ticker tape from the New York Stock Exchange. Stranger and stranger, I thought. We reached what seemed to be a closet, until Ahmed lifted a trapdoor and revealed a flight of rough stone steps. Torches flickered in the space beneath, hissing anxiously as they burnt.

My heart beating in my throat, I descended. Like every collector, I'd heard stories of villages built over unregistered tombs; tombs looted treasure by treasure, generation by generation, guarded by blood-oaths from the jealous eye of the authorities. I inhaled deeply, trying to catch my breath. A peculiar scent filled my lungs. It was not the normal mustiness of the tomb, or the sooty spice-and-humanity that perfumed modern Cairo. This air was fresh and sweet, as if untouched by time or man.

But I could not puzzle out the mystery because I had reached the bottom of the steps and could see my surroundings. I was indeed inside a tomb. The chamber was small and square, perhaps five strides in either direction. Exquisite bas relief carvings covered the sandstone walls. I had not seen such workmanship since I'd toured the Temple of Seti I. The torches had left no carbon streaks and the carvings glowed with colour, as if the paint had barely dried. Such pristine preservation made me suspicious, despite the apparent absence of tourist depredation. I stepped closer to the wall.

A man, presumably the entombed, stood between Anubis and Osiris, receiving instruction for successful passage through the underworld. The style was clearly New Kingdom, eighteenth dynasty and very fine. If this was a forgery, it was the best damn forgery I'd ever seen. Something, however, hit me wrong. Though the quality of the carvings was royal, the dead man bore no signs of rank: no headdress or serpent uraeus, no staff, no double crown. More troubling yet, on his shoulder and breast the cartouche of the Queen-Pharaoh Hatshepsut had been inscribed – as if he were a civil servant. But if that were the case, how had he obtained the services of so skilled an artist?

I found the answer when I traced the hieroglyphs above the figures. 'Khaemwaset,' they said, 'beloved of Menena, sculptor to the great Hatshepsut. Your flesh shall rise up for you. Your bones shall fuse themselves. Your resurrected members shall be as strong as lions!'

So. The sculptor had decorated his own tomb. A warmth behind my shoulder made me turn. I choked on a shriek. Two grotesque figures loomed before me: a jackal-headed Anubis and a hawk-headed Horus. For a moment, I was too startled to think. Then I recognised the blue and gold eyes glittering behind one mask. Ahmed had donned an embalmer's headpiece. Our driver, Saad, was playing Horus. Together, they resembled tomb guardians come to life. My gaze slid down their slim bodies. Naked from the neck down, both their cocks were erect. The berry-brown heads shone with the juice of high arousal. As I stared, they vibrated with excitement. My own body quickened. I tore my eyes away.

'What's going on?' I asked, the last gasp of my rational American sensibilities.

'Come,' said Ahmed. 'Khaemwaset awaits.'

I followed, stepping into the dream this day had become. Ahmed led us from the first chamber past a series of small chapels, each dedicated to a different god, each lit by dancing torches. I saw no evidence that objects had been removed. Whatever benefit the village derived from this tomb could not have come from looting. We turned at the chapel of Min, the fertility god, depicted as usual with a massively distended phallus. The statue's shaft had been polished by admiring hands, probably village women hoping to be blessed with healthy children or attentive husbands. I touched the shiny penis as I passed and a flare of liquid heat surged through my body. Min was no dead god here.

A doorway led from Min's chapel to another chamber, this one dark. Preceding us inside, Ahmed paced its circumference, his torch illuminating the walls. Here I saw the same beautiful reliefs, the same vibrant colours. The subject, however, had changed from the instructive illustrations of the Book of the Dead. Here god fucked goddess in a mind-boggling variety of couplings. Bastet the cat lapped Khnum the human-headed ram. Anubis the jackal-headed lord of death buggered Nut the nightly swallower of the sun. Where the heads were human, I saw only two faces. Khaemwaset I recognised from the outer chamber and I presumed the woman was Menena. Certainly she did not bear the famous moon-face of the queen. I tilted my head to examine her. In all the carvings, Menena wore a charming smile: half sweet, half wry. I couldn't help thinking I had seen it somewhere before.

'Menena,' said Ahmed, confirming my guess. 'Beloved of Khaemwaset. Though he served the pharaoh-queen even in her bed, his heart belonged to Menena, who was a beautiful dancing girl. Hatshepsut kept them apart in life but not in death. Khaemwaset knew the secrets of the Great Sleep. When Menena died, poisoned by the queen, he swore to carry the memory of their love into eternity.'

'A pretty story,' I scoffed, though my throat was traitorously tight. When had anyone loved me that way?

'It is more than a story,' he said, 'as you will see.'

With no more explanation, he and Saad carried their torches to the centre of the room and lit a circle of alabaster lamps which sat on the floor around a narrow bier. As the light rose, I discerned a figure lying on the granite block. I gasped. It was a mummy, a freshly wrapped mummy. Its linen bandages reeked of precious unguents. I smelled cedar and myrrh and a fresh green scent which reminded me of ferns growing in a forest. It made no sense to me. If all this was meant to hoax me, the wrappings should have been crumbling and foul.

Ahmed stopped me before I could draw closer. 'Wait. Horus must consult with the master.'

'Consulting with the master' consisted of Saad in his Horus mask bowing over the mummy's head and waiting in motionless silence. It looked like some sort of trance. I shifted uncomfortably. 'The master told Saad where to find you,' Ahmed confided in an undertone. 'Saad is the heir to the secret of the Great Sleep. When the master wakes, Saad will be shown the hidden paths. He will be the village's new wise man. He will guide the fortunes of the next generations.'

'Um,' was all I could say, my head spinning at this outrageous disclosure. But something undercut my natural scepticism – perhaps the memory of the Turkish carpets and the computerised stock listings. A moment later, Saad distracted me from my doubts. He was cutting the mummy's wrappings with a long steel knife. Like the petals of a lotus they fell from the body beneath, a body that shone as white and sleek as marble. A statue, I realised, though it was far more naturalistic than any Egyptian statue I'd seen. The figure was life-sized, male, and perfect in every detail, from the veins on its neck to the thrust of its stupendous cock. It was tall and well formed, with the broad chest and narrow hips favoured by early New Kingdom artists. Stone curls spilt from a high elegant forehead and stone lips curved in a secretive smile.

What on earth? I thought – so far as I could think. I stepped closer, my hands itching to explore this beautiful male form.

'Yes,' said Saad, his voice distorted by the falcon mask. 'You must caress him, you must wake him. He has been sleeping a long time, longer than the white bear in the land of ice, longer than the fakirs of India. He needs a strong call to rise again.'

But first the men took my clothes from me. They set their masks aside and removed my modest smock and trousers. Ahmed's fingers trembled as he pulled my plain white bra down my arms. I knew what he saw. I was slim and firm, my breasts girlishly high, my hips womanly round. My skin tingled with awareness as Saad unbraided my thick chestnut hair and spread it across my shoulders.

'The master will be pleased,' he said. From the floor behind the bier he lifted a large faience vessel with a phallus for the spout. 'Now you must anoint him.'

He poured a stream of clear oil over the supine statue. The smell of ferns grew stronger, dizzying. Ahmed helped me on to the bier where the fallen wrappings, soft as the finest bed-sheet, cushioned my knees. I straddled the statue's hips. Its phallus

rose impressively, suggestively before my loins. A muscle fluttered deep inside my sex. For a second, I thought: what am I
doing? But the feeling faded as soon as I touched that cool oily
stone. It was meltingly smooth. I could not contain my purr as I
stroked up the lean broad chest. The mummy's stone nipples
were erect. Helpless to resist, I circled them with the pads of my
thumbs.

Saad uttered a low cry. I turned to find him massaging the
mummy's legs. His eyes were dark pleasured slits. 'Yes,' he said,
his voice husky. 'The master likes that. He wishes you to do it
again.'

I almost laughed, but then I felt a strange vibration between
my legs, as if a heavy lorry had rumbled overhead. Without
thinking, I gripped the mummy's shoulders. I blinked in amazement. The surface beneath my palms was warm. It did not give
like living flesh, but it was warm. I touched the marble face,
spread the oil over its sculpted planes. Not only did the stone
heat, but it was changing colour: a faint rosy tan that crept
everywhere I touched. I tried to explain this away as the effect
of the oil, but then the brows began to blacken, and the hair.

I covered my mouth with my hands, shaking with a strangely
sexual terror. My sex was seething, my cheeks cold. As if not a
moment could be lost, Ahmed grabbed the blue vessel and
poured more oil over the mummy's head. The hair softened as
he rubbed it in, unfurling until it spread in raven waves across
the bier.

'My God,' I breathed.

'Kiss him,' Ahmed said, tugging me forward. 'You must not
allow him to sink back into the dream.'

Trembling in every limb, I kissed the hard, still lips. Their
edges were parted. I could have sworn they'd been closed before.
I slipped my tongue inside and found stony teeth. This mouth
did not taste of stone, though, or of oil. I knew this taste. I
deepened the kiss, a memory hovering. Saad moaned, and it
seemed as if the statue moaned, as if the statue longed to kiss
me back.

'Khaemwaset,' I whispered. I knew then that I believed. However it had happened, this seeming-stone comprised a living
man, a man who must be seduced from his prison of sleep. I

kissed the closed eyes, the silent throat, the shallow groove that marked the central line of the torso. I circled the navel with well-oiled hands, and drew ten sleek lines over the carved curls of the pubic thatch. The curls darkened, dividing into separate silky strands. I caught my lower lip in my teeth and gathered the prodigious shaft between my fingers. Again, the body trembled, that low, rumbling vibration. I pulled upward. Saad moaned, the statue's voice.

I bent and let my breath wash over the priapic marble organ. 'Your flesh shall rise up for you,' I crooned. 'Your resurrected members shall be as strong as lions.'

With eager lips, I pulled the crown into the embrace of cheeks and tongue. This taste, too, echoed in my mind. I rubbed the shaft between my palms. This shape I knew, this curve, this twisting vein. Pleasures I could not quite recall fired my blood. I remembered a love so deep it was close to worship. He is so beautiful, I thought with some forgotten fragment of my brain. So wise. How can it be that he loves me?

The statue shuddered as if it sensed my doubt and wished it could allay it. The flesh within my mouth gave subtly, slightly and then I felt a pulse against my tongue, faint but palpable. Such longing swept through me my bones ached. I wanted to hold, to be held. Or were these his desires? Was I, like Saad, sensing the feelings of the being trapped inside the stone?

It did not matter. His desires were mine. I sucked the softly pulsing phallus, long patient pulls until I felt the throb strengthen, until I swore I tasted salt. Encouraged, I caressed the hard swell of the balls. The testicles seemed over-full, as if his seed had been gathering while he slept. A sympathetic ache knotted between my legs. I could not wait another minute. I had to take him. I rose and poised my empty sex above the cock that would fill it. I braced my hands on broad stiff shoulders, now stained a golden brown. I allowed the warm oily glans to part my swollen lips. I pressed down, feeling that thickness slide inside me, harder than human flesh but hot now, hot as coals. Oh, it had been so long since I'd felt a magic even close to this. Deeper the phallus glided, and deeper, stretching my grateful folds until my pubis kissed its root.

The mummy opened his eyes. His lids clicked upward like a

doll's – and, like a doll's, his eyes were glassy and fixed. Khaemwaset's irises shone blue with shards of gold – just like Ahmed's. It struck me then that my eyes were the same coffee-brown as Saad's. How strange, I thought, and yet it didn't seem strange at all.

I pictured myself through those frozen pupils: my flushed cheeks, my dark tousled hair. Hunger overwhelmed me; hunger and a desperate shredding patience that seemed to come from without as well as within. This last small wait must be excruciating for him. Finally, release was near enough to touch and he was powerless to draw it closer. Despite my remembered adoration, I knew I'd dreamt of taking him this way. Tonight I, a humble nobody, had the mighty Khaemwaset at my mercy. Tonight, his desire would humble him as mine had so often humbled me.

I smiled into the staring blue eyes. 'Welcome back,' I said and kissed him.

This time, the mouth closed slowly, slowly around my kiss. A tongue touched mine. Lips quivered infinitesimally. The body beneath me seemed to soften, to sigh.

'More,' Saad groaned and I pushed back on my arms. Like a belly dancer I rode his stony phallus, rolling waves of pelvic motion, the oldest dance, the sweetest dance. A quake shuddered through Khaemwaset's body. His arms twitched. His chest rose on a single halting breath.

'Menena,' he rasped on the exhalation. Chills raced down my spine. I knew the name was mine, though I remembered little beyond that sense of awe. My Khaemwaset. My love.

'Put his arms around me,' I said. Saad and Ahmed rushed to obey and soon those heavy softened limbs encircled my back. The young men stroked him, and me, their hands aiding and abetting our singular embrace. Fingers soothed his forehead; urged the rise and fall of my loins. Ahmed reached between us and plucked my nipples, drawing them out in long pomegranate buds. Saad cursed, as if he shared the mummy's jealousy. Khaemwaset's arms began to tighten. His hips shifted, lurched upward in a tiny rock. Our helpers cried out as one.

He was moving on his own: not much, but the effort brought a glaze of sweat to his struggling flesh. His eyes were alive now.

They searched my face, blazing with emotions: joy and love and the fiercest hunger I had ever seen. Moved beyond bearing, I hastened my pace. Our helpers pressed closer, one on either side. Their pants rang in our ears. Their cocks brushed our hips, then rubbed, then ground with the slippery, leaking, kill-me-now ardour of youth. But they were no more desperate than I. My climax rose like the strong hot wind of the *khamaseen*. Never had I felt such need, such pleasure. Hands clutched my waist: his hands. Strong and greedy they pulled me down that fiery obelisk, and down again and down again until my pussy clenched around his luscious piercing rod. His thumbs stretched lower, seeking the tiny red jewel of my desire. He found it wet and sleek. He rubbed. I tightened. His cock quivered and swelled and stretched. The pressure must have pained him. A ragged sob broke in his throat. He thrust deep.

I came with a wail of forgotten loss and rediscovered rapture. He moaned in answer and burst in a string of hard gasping spasms. His seed poured out in an endless flood, so warm, so forceful it seemed to breach my core. His neck arched. His face twisted with the ecstasy of a tortured saint. Watching him, I came again, convulsing tight and sweet until my arms no longer held me. I buried my face in his neck. A pulse beat there, strong and regular. He breathed. He rubbed my back with warm, pliant hands. He was awake again, himself again, and I – once again – could only be his slave.

'Hush,' he said, turning his head to kiss away my tears. 'Hush, Chloe. All is well.'

I started back and wiped my cheeks. He'd spoken in English. He'd said my name. 'How do you know who I am?'

When he smiled, his eyes crinkled at the corners; human, yet so much more beautiful than human. He touched the tip of my nose with his forefinger, a teasing gesture that seemed heart-breakingly familiar. 'You do not object when I call you Menena, but this surprises you? I dreamt as I slept, dearest Chloe. I dreamt of you and the world and these loyal servants of mine. That is the secret of the Great Sleep. It frees the soul to travel as it will, to learn as it will. Which is not to say I recommend sleeping quite so long!'

'Then why did you?'

He cupped my cheek. 'To await your return to this plane, beloved. To ensure that one of us remembered what we shared.'

I disengaged and leapt from the bier. I could not bear to hear him speak this way. I almost tripped over Saad and Ahmed, frantically grappling in their own quest for release. They were biting each other's shoulders, thrusting between each other's thighs. I did not stop to watch. With a groan of effort, Khaemwaset followed me. I was crying too hard to move quickly. He caught me in the chapel of Min.

'Tell me your fears,' he said, wrapping me in his arms and leaning heavily over my back. 'But please don't run, dearest. I am as weak as a baby.'

I gripped his enfolding arms, our bodies nestling together like swans. I sniffed hard. 'I'm just an ordinary woman. Not wise, not magical. Nothing compared to you.'

A sound rumbled from his throat, half sigh, half laugh. 'Oh, Menena. This is an old song you sing. I will tell you what I told you all those centuries ago. You do not know your own magic. Your art was every bit as great as mine. When you danced, time stood still and every woman felt her power rise inside her. Lovers smiled into each other's eyes and children laughed for the joy of life. The queen wept the first time she saw you perform, as she wept when she heard you had swallowed her poison. Her own jealousy broke her heart.'

I covered my face. 'I don't remember. Not any of it. I wish I could. You don't know what it would mean to me, to remember Egypt as it really was.'

'You remember more than you know, or I could not have drawn you here.' He turned me to face him. I was surprised not to find him taller, a giant; though every time I looked at him he seemed more beautiful, more dear. 'This time I will teach you all my secrets, even as I teach young Saad in thanks for his loyal service. I was wrong not to do it before.' He stroked my hair behind my ears. 'I revelled in your admiration, dearest Menena, beloved Chloe. I feared if you knew that, underneath it all, I was only a man, you would not adore me so.'

His confession floored me. How could he say he was only a man?

15

'You will see,' he said. 'When you know what I know, you will see.'

Could it be true? I touched his face, tracing the arch of his brows, the line of his aquiline nose. A door opened in my heart and an ancient hurt spilt free. 'I do not want a master, Khaemwaset. I want a lover, a friend – an equal.'

A tear rolled down his sculpted cheek. 'That may be difficult,' he said with a crooked smile, 'for you will always be my queen.'

The Ties of Friendship

Francine Whittaker

The Ties of Friendship

❖ ❖

*H*e retrieved his briefcase from its position by the rubber plant. And it struck him now, as it always did first thing in the morning, that Laura's sleep-freshened face looked younger, even innocent, with her short blonde hair tousled and damp.

'Let me take one last look at you. Turn around.' Grasping her by the arm he spun her round so that she stood with her narrow back towards him. 'Very nice, very nice indeed.'

She flinched as his fingers traced the weals that criss-crossed her pale buttocks. And somewhere in the kernel of her being, she felt the familiar flush of sexual arousal as he awakened her desire.

'Next time,' he said as he turned her round to face him again, 'we will try a more sensitive area.' He caressed her milky white breasts and felt her nipples stiffen beneath his fingers. 'Perhaps here –' he smiled as he ran his hand over the smooth flesh of her inner thigh '– or perhaps here.'

He made to go but she caught his hand. She stood on tiptoe and tilted her head up towards him. 'Goodbye, Brett.' She kissed him full on the lips.

He took a firm hold of her pale slender arms that entwined themselves around his neck like bindweed and choked all remnants of passion from his body.

This was the part he hated, he thought resentfully, this pathetic parting . . . and the drive home to his wife after a night's absence. The actual lies he found easier to deal with. Nevertheless, they were all necessary evils, for this was the only way to keep Laura's dependence on him alive: the only way to impose upon her the nature of their relationship. For theirs was no ordinary affair and he was well aware that he could never relax his guard for a moment. He knew that Laura met many men in her professional life and he could not, would not, permit someone else to discover the secret and erotic part of Laura that was his alone.

But, even as he extricated himself from her gluey embrace, he knew that whatever conditions he tried to impose upon her, it was he who was the real prisoner; it was she who had ensnared him long ago with her sensuous beauty. He just had to have more of her.

He opened the door. 'I'll ring you,' he whispered almost tenderly against the top of her head as he drank in the perfumed softness of her hair.

As he walked across the car park, he thought back over the events of the previous evening. A thrill ran through him as he remembered her ecstatic cries when he had wound her hair round his fingers and tugged, almost wrenching it from the roots. Then he had forced open her lips with his tongue, pushing roughly into the wet recess of her mouth while entering that other wet recess.

He recalled, too, how her hair had flopped over her face as, with her body bent forward over the back of the chair, she had raised her rounded buttocks so temptingly. He had secured her wrists to the front legs and her ankles to the back legs and taken her from behind. Then, at the very last moment, he had withdrawn and shot his creamy come over her back.

He unlocked the car door and slid into the driver's seat, with an erotic image in his mind of Laura, still bound to the chair, crying out in delicious agony as the crop fell across her tender flesh. And, with each stinging blow, he had loved her more than ever.

As he turned the ignition with one hand, he stroked his burgeoning cock with the other. He had loosened her bonds and carried her to the bed. He had lifted her head affectionately as, exhausted, she had sipped from the wine glass. He had allowed her to sleep for a little while before taking her again as tenderly as if she were a young virgin. And then he had bound her again.

Now he replayed in his mind the image of her naked body writhing on the bed. She had begged for mercy as she yanked frenziedly against the silken scarves, one at each ankle and wrist, that held her captive while he fucked her. Then he had withdrawn, leaving her securely bound while he retired to the chair to which she had previously been bound. With brandy in hand, he had watched her sensual struggles continue.

Her wretched sobs had shaken her beautiful shapely body; each time they had subsided, he had threatened to finish the affair and leave her for good. And then he had watched joyously as her tears returned. How she wept while she had begged his forgiveness. And how he had exulted in the debasement of such a jewel.

He had a bed like Laura's at home with the same brass bedstead, but had never put it to such use. He doubted his wife's submission would have given him the same satisfaction, for she was shy and unassuming and would set him no challenge. There was no compulsion to create a need for him within her as he had done with Laura, for it had existed within his wife from the moment they had first met.

But Laura was more complex. By day she was a highly successful career woman with a haughty manner and will of iron: a woman who systematically trampled male colleagues underfoot. Laura was something special. To dominate her and wring helpless cries from her subjection, that was the real passion.

Suddenly an idea came into his head, an idea almost too fantastic to contemplate. Maybe, just maybe, if he could find some way to put his newly discovered knowledge about his wife to some use, then maybe . . .

Laura came into the bedroom and placed her coffee cup on the bedside table. She breathed in the musky smell of Brett that still clung to the air and, putting her hand to her breast, she idly toyed with the nipple that he had bitten and left sore. Her fingers trembled as she felt it harden and, even as she felt the thrill surge through her, she was all at once overwhelmed by a feeling of emptiness.

Her hand dropped away to her side and she gazed mistily at the tangled sheets, damp and love-worn. 'Love?' she whispered into the emptiness of the room. No, Brett didn't love her. He had never promised her love.

She sank down on the bed and knew that she was a fool. She would never mean anything more to him than she did now. But she would die rather than give him up; she couldn't help herself. He had a mental hold over her that was stronger than any ropes or chains he could find to bind her physically.

But now in the cold light of day, the deprivations that she had revelled in just last night disgusted her. She had never understood how a woman, any woman, could get herself into such a crazy and sordid situation. She had believed all such women to be stupid, pathetic innocents. Yet she was no innocent and, being in her late twenties, she could hardly be described as a giddy schoolgirl in the first flush of love. She had more ex-lovers than she cared to remember, yet she had complied with Brett's command to drop them all. And, in her heart, she knew that she would be willing to play his sadistic games for as long as he wanted her – needed her – for she believed his need to be greater than her own.

She was nothing but an unpaid whore, she knew that, and while she hated him for what he had done to her and what he had turned her into, she knew she would always be there for him. For, in asserting himself as master, he had awakened within her a burning, wanton hunger and reduced her to a willing adoring slave.

Her thoughts turned suddenly to Beth, the wife he loved dearly, and she was torn between guilt and loathing. She knew that it really was love he felt for his wife and not the perverted desire that he felt for Laura.

The two women had known each other since university, when they had shared accommodation and they had become life-long friends. Though the Beth of those days had not been half so timid as the woman she had since become. Beth had always been a pretty, popular girl, though more with the girls than with the boys. A faint smile crossed Laura's lips at a distant memory of Beth as the honeypot to which all the other girls had swarmed.

Marriage had changed her, yet she had never been dominated by Brett, in any sense of the word. That he kept for Laura alone. Beth's love could never give Brett the sexual satisfaction that he craved, the way Laura's did. She considered that in a way it was she, his whore, who kept the marriage together. Beth would never have to be subjugated the way she had been; Beth could go on in her own sweet virtuous way, never knowing of her husband's double life and content in the knowledge that she was his wife.

Feeling unusually ill-at-ease, Laura spent the entire morning idling around the apartment, unable to settle. She was on leave from work but had so far not put any of her leisure plans into operation. Each morning she dressed, put on her make-up, and stayed in the apartment: hoping, always hoping, that Brett would come to her again. But until the previous evening there had been no sign of him.

After lunch, she settled down to read the newspaper but, unable to concentrate, she grew restless. And with her restlessness came a curious feeling of expectancy. When the doorbell rang, it had a certain inevitability about it.

'Beth!'

Like someone who has just witnessed an accident, Laura stood dazedly and stared at the woman who stood on her threshold and was unable to put feelings into words. Though she had shared her best friend's husband for so long Laura had never before felt pangs of jealousy – or such hostility – until now.

And contempt. How could the woman be so naive? The affair had been going on for years, right under Beth's nose.

'May I come in?'

'Yes, yes, of course.' Laura stepped back a pace and, as her friend entered, she was almost moved to pity at Beth's hunched shoulders and the way her head hung heavily. Yet the traces of her former beauty were still there. 'Go through to the lounge and I'll make some coffee.'

Five minutes later, they sat on opposite sides of Laura's • elegant over-priced dining table that she had bought with the bonus her boss at Bartlett and Putnam had given her last year.

'How have you been keeping?' Laura enquired dutifully: though the state of Beth's health was of no real interest to her, in her present mood of lovelorn agitation. Still, for the sake of appearances, she continued the ritual, fighting to keep the tremors from her voice as she asked demurely, 'How's Brett?'

Beth produced a sodden handkerchief from the sleeve of her mohair sweater and stuffed it against her nostrils.

'He's . . . he's fine,' she mumbled unconvincingly.

Laura sensed danger and swallowed hard, every muscle within her tensing.

As if she had suddenly come to some sort of decision, Beth drew in a deep breath and straightened her back, lifting her tragic grey eyes to meet Laura's.

'He's having an affair, Laura.'

Laura also straightened her back, determined to see the charade through to its conclusion.

'Brett?' She forced a little laugh that sounded false to her own ears. 'Oh, no, not Brett.' Her flashing blue eyes scanned the room quickly, checking for evidence the way she assumed Beth would. 'He loves you, Beth – I mean *really* loves you.' She wanted to scream at the stupid woman, 'He loves you but he fucks me!' Nevertheless, she continued, 'Brett would never have an affair.' Her eyes came to rest on the credit card lying on the coffee table; the card he had used at the swish new restaurant last night. 'Whatever makes you think he could ever be unfaithful?'

Beth's red hair flopped over her dull eyes. She made no attempt to tidy it as she began to wring the handkerchief between trembling hands.

'A wife knows, Laura.' She paused for effect, then continued, 'I used to believe that he really did love me and that he could remain faithful for ever. But not any more. He's found someone else.' She paused again and dabbed her eyes; they were devoid of any make-up. 'I know the signs, you see.'

Laura imagined that her guilt was scrawled across her forehead. But even as she squirmed, she thought of suggesting a shopping trip. Perhaps she should treat Beth to a make-over at Rosebay's Beauty Centre. That would at least divert any suspicions regarding herself. She felt a cold chill run the full length of her back and rose from her chair to cross the pink and grey room.

'What signs, Beth?' she asked as innocently as she was able. 'How can you be so sure?'

Laura reached the coffee table and slipped the offending credit card into the pocket of her jeans that moulded themselves to her well-formed buttocks: buttocks that still bore the red stripes from the riding crop that Brett had used for the first time last night. After all these years of having her bound this had been the first time that he had ever used anything other than a belt to mark her, though imprinting her white flesh with red criss-cross patterns had always been one of his greatest joys. Perversely, it always gave her great pleasure and a sense of pride when she examined herself in the mirror afterwards.

She came back to stand beside the woman who still considered Laura her best friend and was aware of a sickening feeling in the pit of her stomach as she watched Beth's heaving shoulders. She noticed, too, the barely controlled anguish in Beth's voice.

'It was little things, at first, like our evenings out together. We used to go to the opera or ballet. And Brett always enjoyed eating out. But now he says that he's too tired to go out. And he has to work late so often, these days.'

Beth paused while Laura returned to her seat and eyed the curvaceous blonde from underneath wet eyelashes. She raised her head and wiped away tears with the back of her hand.

Smiling sweetly, Laura looked into Beth's eyes and searched for some clue. Did she know? Was she playing a clever game that would finally expose the truth?

'He's changed his –' Beth searched in her bag for another handkerchief '– brand of after-shave lotion.'

'So what does that prove?' Laura said sharply.

'Nothing in itself, I suppose, though he always said he liked the one I buy him.'

'Perhaps he felt like a change,' Laura soothed, baulking slightly as she almost smelt the cloying sweetness that he had used all those years. In the end, she had found it necessary to buy him a large bottle of Dominion.

She felt no shame now as she looked her friend in the face. So what if she was being screwed by Beth's husband? As long as she could put Beth off the scent, there was no problem, as far as she could see. There never had been before.

25

It was odd how their friendship had survived through the years, despite their different hopes and dreams: perhaps even because of them. They had nothing in common, now . . . except Brett. She remembered now the church, the flowers, and the smiling faces; and her own joy at being one of the eight brides-maids to a truly radiant bride. And she remembered how horny she had felt while watching Brett as he stood at Beth's side. Laura had thought even then that he was too good for Beth.

Brett and Beth had thrown numerous dinner parties through the years. And the three of them had always indulged in good-humoured banter each time that Beth had invited some eligible male guest. But Laura had refused overtures from them all: the computer programmer, the photographer, even the actor that had finally made it to Broadway. She had had to; Brett had made his intentions, what he considered his rights, known long ago . . . She belonged to Brett.

There had been one time when she had been caught out, when Brett had called round the apartment unannounced. He had noticed at once marks on her wrists that proved that she had been bound: marks that he had not inflicted. He had found two men's leather belts lying across the chair. His vengeance had been swift and terrible. Never before, or since, had she seen him in a rage. Whatever cruelties or humiliations he had inflicted upon her had never been provoked by anger but by his all-consuming desire to hear her scream as she came, and to see her tug against her bonds and fulfil his wildest fantasies.

Beth's voice droned on, her whines punctuated by pathetic sobs.

'Brett seems so tired all the time. Too tired for sex. And he doesn't always come home at night; he spends an awful lot of time away from home.'

Laura swallowed. Hard.

'Have you asked him about it?' She flicked fine strands of shining blonde hair from her face. 'What does he say?' she queried in her most sympathetic voice.

'That he goes on business trips. But now I can't help but wonder who else is there. He's had promotion at work –' she bit into her bottom lip before continuing in a voice that wavered on the hysterical '– and I don't know where he is, half the time. It means more money, of course, but I get so lonely rattling about in that big house with only that damned dog of his for company. I'd give up the house, even the cars, to have things back the way they were. He went away for a whole weekend last month on some sort of management course in Scotland.'

Laura's mind recalled the beauty of Aviemore and how she and Brett had laughed when her attempt at skiing had ended with her lying in a snow-covered heap. And how they had drunk champagne in the jacuzzi afterwards.

And she could almost feel again the pain of the ropes that had bitten cruelly into her wrists that he tied behind her back; how he had thrown her face down on to the bed and called her a whore. He had sat astride her with his knee in the small of her back and pulled her head towards him by her hair. It was then he had used the gag for the first time, so as not to alert the other guests. Then he had removed his belt . . .

And then the feeling of shame she had felt the next morning when he had led her into the dining room. She had felt that the deprivation was there, written on her face for all the world to read.

'Then,' Beth sobbed, 'last night –' She broke off as her wails filled the room. She broke down and slumped across the dining table, her head on her arms and her shoulders heaving. She opened one eye and caught the smug look on Laura's face.

'What happened last night?' Laura prompted.

'He told me that he had an important dinner to attend with a client and that he might have to go on somewhere later. He said not to wait up as he would be late.'

Laura reached across the table and stroked her friend's head. The same way she had comforted her all those years ago when Beth had had a terrible row with her friend Abigail.

But now it was a feeling of guilt that mixed with the shame of what she had become; she had degraded herself and destroyed her friend. And she knew that she would go on doing it until Brett found a new toy to play with. And then what would she do? She needed to be dominated; she knew that now.

'Is that what you are upset about, Beth, that he didn't come home?' Laura didn't wait for an answer. 'It was probably too late and he didn't want to disturb you, so booked into an hotel for the night.'

Beth lifted her head and, for a fleeting moment, Laura felt compassion surface within her. She clutched at her stomach as the tear-soaked face looked into her own. But she determined not to let it get the better of her and drew in a breath to steady herself. She needed to think, keep cool, or she could lose Brett for ever . . . to his bloody wife!

'I know you're trying to help.' Beth's lips trembled pitifully. 'But you don't understand. I followed him in the BMW.'

Laura felt nauseous but met her friend's eyes resolutely, determined to bluff her way though it.

'Where did he go?' Laura had to know if they had been followed back here to her apartment.

'First he went to that new place on the other side of town, the restaurant that's run by that ex-footballer. And I was right. He met a woman. You know the type –' Beth laughed bitterly '– tall, blonde, all arse and tits!'

Laura baulked to hear herself described so bluntly. 'Did you get a good look at her?'

'No. But she was an expensive tart. You could tell that by her clothes.'

Laura's mind flashed back to the clinging silk trouser suit and she sighed at her own stupidity. She had seen the BMW, of course, but had had no idea. How could she? She shook her head slowly and adopted her most understanding expression. 'Did they leave together?'

'That's when I started to cry. I missed them when they left. All I know is that he didn't come home.'

Laura's heart was pounding. She had to think fast.

'Oh, poor Beth.' Her fingers toyed with the handle of her coffee cup. 'But I think you're worrying about nothing. I really do believe that she was a client. You seem to forget that these days a lot of company executives are women. I mean, look at me!' She noticed that Beth was looking at her, with an odd expression on her face. 'During his working week, a man in Brett's high-powered position probably deals with dozens of women. And of course she would be expensively dressed and probably had an expensive company car outside, too.' She curled her palm over her friend's hand and gritted her teeth as she felt the wedding ring beneath her fingers. 'Don't look so alarmed. I've told you, he loves you and has no eyes for other women.' Well, not eyes, she thought wryly, but he has plenty else on offer.

'He's bound to get tired,' she continued, but the sympathetic tone of her voice had been replaced by an impatient edge. 'He works damn hard to give you the things you've always dreamed of. Just look at your house. Barn conversions don't come cheap, Beth. And neither do exotic holidays. Look, if he has to attend a lot of business dinners, he's probably sick and tired of restaurants and would rather spend his precious evenings with you at home with real home cooking. Why don't you get that lovely housekeeper of yours to cook him something special, tonight?'

Beth's face began to brighten. 'Do you really think so? Could I have been jumping to conclusions?'

Laura stood up and cast her eyes around for a box of tissues. Retrieving them from the top of the TV, she pushed them across the table towards Beth.

'Here, dry your eyes.' It was beyond her how she and such an impressionable female could have been friends for so long. Beth was pathetic. At least she, Laura, had something to offer Brett. But Beth? It would be laughable if it wasn't for the fact that the man actually loved his wife.

'But there's still the matter of the after-shave, Laura.'

'Perhaps,' Laura continued kindly 'he just hadn't the heart to tell you that he was fed up with . . . what was it? Aqua Spice? He would never hurt your feelings and knows how sensitive you are. Now listen –' she flounced off in the direction of the kitchen '– you take it from me. Your Brett is as faithful now as he's always been.'

She stopped beside the coffee table and a secret smile curved her full lips at the memory of the holiday they had all spent together in France some years ago. One afternoon Beth had gone to bed with a migraine; Brett had been worried sick that Laura's frenzied cries would penetrate the hotel's thin walls.

'I'll make us another coffee.' Laura smiled sweetly.

Beth chewed thoughtfully on her thumb-nail. 'You're right, of course.' She gave a little laugh and dabbed at her eyes with a tissue. 'I'm so sorry I bothered you with all my troubles.'

'Not at all.'

Suddenly, Laura felt hate for the woman welling up inside her and wished Beth would go; she wished she would get out of her life for ever. Unable to endure the woman's whining any longer, she swung round to see Beth still dabbing at her eyes.

Her feet made no sound on the thick carpet as she came up behind Beth and said serenely, 'It's no trouble, Beth. What are friends for?' She raised her hand to strike her.

Then, all at once, she was aware of a wave of tranquillity that washed over her and she let her arm drop limply to her side. How could she hurt sweet, innocent Beth?

The moments ticked by as she became lost in her own conflicting thoughts and she was taken by surprise when she noticed Beth cup her own breast in her hand and begin rubbing it through her sweater, as if she were trying to eradicate a pain. And it was then that Laura remembered the incident that had sparked the row between Beth and Abigail, all those years ago. Perhaps she could even now save herself and turn the situation to her own advantage.

Slowly she opened her arms. 'Beth, come over here, love.'

Beth swivelled round slowly. Then, with a weak smile, she rose from the chair and melted into Laura's outstretched arms.

Laura's arms folded around her as her mind ran on. She kissed the top of Beth's head. 'Come and sit on the sofa. I know what will make you feel better.' She led Beth over to the sofa with its sumptuous cushions. 'Come, sit beside me.'

Once the two women were seated side by side, Laura began to ease up her friend's sweater. She was surprised to see that, like herself, Beth wore no bra. And she noticed at once how round and firm her breasts were. Fighting down the bile that was rising within her at the thought of the act she was about to perform, she took one of Beth's nipples between finger and thumb and worked it gently.

'Laura, I –'

'Shh. Just lie back and enjoy. There, now,' she soothed, taking hold of the other nipple and working it into a stiff peak. 'That's better, isn't it?' As her friend let out a moan and her head fell back against the cushion, Laura repositioned herself. Then she lowered her head and took one nipple between her teeth and began to nip gently at the hardened peak.

Beth responded by running her own hands over Laura's buttocks. Then, fumbling with the zip, she worked her hand inside Laura's jeans and stroked Laura's mound through her panties.

'Oh, Laura . . .' she mumbled. Then her hand was inside the scant panties and examining Laura's wet vulva. With an adept finger, she found Laura's hard bud of pleasure and began to work it rapidly.

Now it was Laura's turn to moan as sensual waves of delight washed over her, her words of desire lost against her friend's breast. Never had she been so intimately touched by another woman; never had she felt such wonder as two fingers slipped up inside her.

Suddenly there was a crack and a terrible stinging across her back. As she let out a cry of pain, she felt Beth's breast jammed into her mouth again.

'Suck it, bitch!' yelled Beth, who was now close to reaching her climax.

Again Laura felt a painful sting across her back and her body jerked against her friend as the blows now rained down on her.

All at once Laura knew what was happening. She turned her face to see Brett standing above her with a fearsome-looking whip in his hand as he raised his arm for another strike.

'You've done a good job, Beth, my darling. You –' he jabbed a finger in Laura's direction '– bring her off! Now!'

It was later when, naked and exhausted, Laura was dragged into her bedroom.

'Beth, secure her ankles to the bed,' Brett ordered. 'And make sure you tie them tight; she likes to struggle.'

Beth tied the ropes so tightly that they dug into her tender flesh and hurt her terribly. Yet even now, Laura felt her juices beginning to flow.

She lay spread-eagled on her back, naked, and bound cruelly by her best friend. There was confusion in her eyes. And she felt a sense of foreboding even as her sex burned with longing.

'Brett, I don't understand . . .' she began feebly.

'Don't you?' He threw back his head and laughed. 'Come here, Beth, and see this fine white flesh.' He drew his wife, now also naked with her hard nipples standing erect, to his side. 'See how, even now, the whore's nipples harden? See the glistening between her legs. She is truly a wanton; there is only one way to deal with her kind.' He brought the whip down hard across her belly. And, as she cried out with the searing intensity of the pain, he threw back his head and laughed. And he wanted her more now than he ever had.

He turned to Beth, who had watched the scene with her fingers inside her own quim.

'Let me,' she said simply, and snatched the evil whip from his hand. Then to Laura, she said, 'You have no idea how many years I've longed for this moment.' She lifted her arm and brought the whip down with a terrifying crack across Laura's splayed legs. She raised the whip again and this time brought it down across her breasts.

Now in a sexual frenzy, she beat her friend mercilessly.

Afterwards, when Beth had lovingly dried Laura's tears with the panties Beth herself had been wearing, Brett came and sat beside the still bound woman. She was beautiful, with her white flesh carrying the marks of the whip on virtually every inch of the front of her body, for he had given his wife a free hand. And she had wielded her new-found power joyously, watching Laura's body jerk with every strike and exulting in the cries of pain that were mingled with screams of passion as Laura's sweet juices flowed. And when Laura had come her release had been violent and intense.

Now, Brett motioned for his wife to sit on the other side of the bed. Then, together, they began to fondle Laura's full breasts and soaking sex.

And even now, with her body stinging from the cruelty of the whip, Laura felt the thrill of desire course through her and looked adoringly from one to the other. A whole new world had been opened up for her.

'Laura, my sweet,' Brett said as his dextrous fingers squeezed and teased her breasts, 'a few weeks ago I came home from work to find my beautiful Beth in bed with another woman. You can imagine my surprise, and delight. However, I did not tell her of my discovery until this morning. Then, when I told her how wayward you are and how I thought that you needed to be brought into line, she was only too pleased to help out. Though I warned her it would be a long, exhausting enterprise that could take months, even years, Beth was quite happy to go along with my little scheme. I understand that you were quite taken in by her little act of the deceived wife.

'It is true, she did follow us last night, and is now cognizant of all the facts of our true relationship. However, she has forgiven me and agrees with my assertion that a wanton like yourself needs a firm master –' he smiled up at his wife '– and mistress. Our house, as I am sure you are aware, is far too big for two people. So we have decided that it would be expedient if you were to give up your job and move in with us. That way, whenever I am unable to chastise you myself, Beth will be only too pleased to do it for me. You will have your own room, of course, though sadly, only boyfriends of our choosing. I see this as the perfect solution to all our problems.

'And always remember that it was not you who seduced my wife, Laura; rather, the other way round.'

Laura smiled, and arched her body against her bonds in a moment of sweet anticipation.

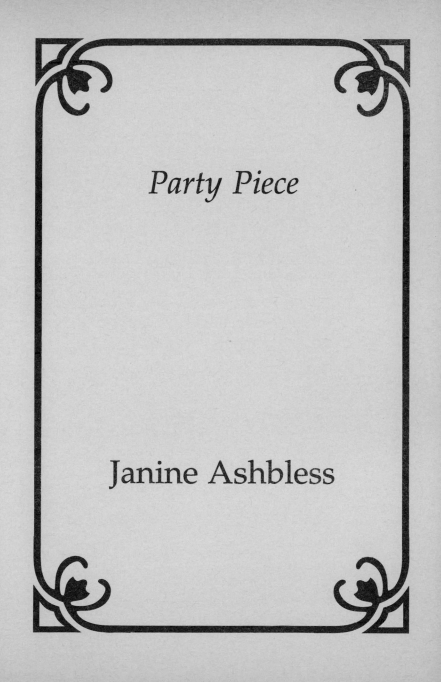

Party Piece

Janine Ashbless

Party Piece

❖ ❖

*A*s the last of the fireworks finished and late night became
early morning, most of the prince's guests moved below
decks into that part of the hold that had been converted into a
ballroom and applied themselves to the serious art of dancing.

She was the only woman in that great chamber who wore a
sword. It hung low from her left hip, the slim black scabbard
blending in with her dress, but the bright silver of the basket-
hilt caught the candlelight and shone. Though it was now the
fashion for young women of noble families to be taught fencing,
she was not wearing it out of affectation; she had earnt her right
to the blade on the battlefield. Soldier, courtier, heroine of the
Empire – she was the founding cause of the fashion. It was the
first time Leander had seen her in the flesh, and he could not
keep his eyes off her.

The ballroom was full; even on a vessel as large as the *Royal
Galleon* space was limited, and it was hard to pick out one figure
from the tight massing of bejewelled, corseted and painted
bodies that lingered at the edges of the room – easier to see
those in the centre where they needed more space to execute
their complex knotwork of dance-steps. There the long dresses,
the tight breeches, the bare shoulders and the elegant coiffures
could be shown off to their best effect, elaborate crystalline ruffs
could glitter under the fairy lights, long trains of costly satin
could be swirled like water across the beeswaxed floor, poses

could be struck and gems could be seen gleaming against pinned-up hair or plumped-up skin.

Leander had found a place on a stair-landing where he could see the throng to the best advantage. One of the prince's leopards drowsed next to his feet, chained to a pillar with golden links, and passers-by were careful not to barge into them. He watched her as she circulated through the crowd, pausing here and there to talk to some nobleman – she seemed to favour those in uniform – or accept an invitation to dance. She danced gracefully, with restraint, and never more than once with any partner. Leander watched her over the rim of his champagne glass in undisguised fascination. She was slender, very tall, with an olive complexion and a crest of black hair caught high in a silver net that nevertheless escaped to fall almost to the small of her back. Her midnight silk dress clung tightly to her figure. It was slashed up to the hips, then furled in an elaborate ragged skirt that trailed on the polished boards; between the curtains of material teasing glimpses of her smooth brown thighs could be seen. She wore high-heeled boots that reached to the bottom of those wonderful thighs, the glossy black leather of each bound tight around her leg by a dozen straps. Long gloves left her upper arms bare. She wore no jewellery, but for the silver in her hair and at her hip, and stood out in that bright and glittering company by the very severity and sombreness of her attire. A dozen gentleman poets were no doubt at this very moment, Leander thought, composing eulogies to the Lady Death embodied in their midst.

As the orchestra laid down their instruments to take a short rest and a castrato soloist ascended to the platform to entertain the guests, Leander took the chance to make his way down the stairs and across the room towards the object of his fascination. She was standing at the vast table on which was laid food to sustain hungry dancers, contemplating the fare spread before her. She seemed to be unaccompanied, to his delight. Leander wended his way between the guests who still clustered on the floor, trying to make as much speed as possible without giving any sign of hurry. Three naked gilded children scampered across his path, scattering rose-petals from wide baskets, and he had to stop to avoid falling over them. A couple of elderly noblemen, both bearing enormous powdered wigs teetering on their heads, blocked his way as they squared up to each other in what sounded like the start of an elaborate duel of vitriolic wit. He had to detour about the pair, masking his impatience badly, and they both paused long enough to sneer at him. Then a Junoesque woman in a dress composed entirely of peacock-feathers noticed him and forestalled his passage, laying a white-gloved hand upon his arm. A small turquoise dragonlet, coiled around her elbow, blinked sleepily up at him.

'Madame,' Leander said apologetically, 'please excuse me.'

The peacock-clad woman raised one eyebrow, glanced sharply over towards the direction of his quest and then shrugged, her flawlessly white shoulders rising and falling in elegant unconcern. She turned away, raising a fan of aquamarine feathers before her face; she would not look at him again.

Leander spared a moment to wince inwardly at his own boorishness, then pursued his course anew. He reached the table at the swordswoman's side. She was deep in consideration of the centre-piece, a roast phoenix stuffed and poised as if about to arise again from its nest of cinnamon twigs.

'Madame,' said Leander, drawing himself up to attention and clicking his heels together.

She selected a single gilded oriel's egg and brought it to her plate, looking sideways at him. Her lips curved in a secretive smile. 'You have been watching me.' The golden glow from the chandelier behind her caught the tiny fuzz of hair on the nape of her bowed neck.

Leander swallowed. 'Am I in the presence of the Ducina arl Guriemme?' he asked.

She straightened to look at him properly; saw a handsome young man in cavalry dress uniform – tight doeskin breeches, polished boots, a crimson jacket stiff with gold brocade – his face clean-shaven, his loose mouse-coloured curls offset by unusually black and heavy brows; a face full of pride and youthful aspiration. She gave a single nod of acknowledgement. 'Ducina Allisandra,' she said carefully.

Leander's heart jumped. She wore no make-up and had made no attempt to enhance her fine-boned face, or to hide the little lines that bloomed around her eyes and lips when she smiled –

which she did at him now. Her eyes were so dark that they appeared black in this light.

'Madame, I am Leander Brondam. My father is the Duc of Brondam.'

'Well,' she said easily, 'my father was a fencing instructor. Which regiment are you with?'

'The Fourteenth,' he stammered. 'Left flank, skirmishers.'

'Under Commander Marticus. Not a bad start.' She inclined her head. Shadow and light played across the cleft of her tawny cleavage. Leander tried his hardest not to look – not too obviously, anyway. 'Have you been in action yet?'

He cleared his throat. 'I was at Moriens. We took down a company of lancers.'

'Did you make any kills?'

'Three.' Colour was rising in his face; he had not anticipated this cross-examination.

'Very good,' she purred. 'Would you like a drink?' Trained baboons in red leather jackets were wending through the crowd, bearing gilt trays of drinks. Without waiting for an answer she turned to one of these and took a blue glass filled with peach brandy.

Leander scrabbled for what to say next. 'I have always wanted to meet you, Ducina,' he said awkwardly. 'I have heard so many stories. You are the hero of the Battle of Ront; you saved the heir's life at Fenvien; you held the Gate at High Tredas. You are the greatest sword in the Empire – I am honoured to meet you.'

She handed him the glass. She was no longer smiling. 'Thank you,' she said coolly. 'Is there anything I can do for you?'

'Ducina?'

'What is it you wanted from me? A transfer to my regiment?' She did not sound hostile, merely bored. She must have been approached this way a thousand times, he realised. He flushed, and clenched his fists.

'Dance with me,' he said through gritted teeth.

Her eyebrows flashed in surprise. She cast a glance back over her shoulder to where the orchestra were taking up their instruments once more.

'You are very bold, sir,' she murmured. 'An admirable quality in a soldier.' She extended one hand to him, sheathed in its black velvet glove to the elbow, and he took the fingers in his own, forcing himself not to tremble or to shout with triumph, both of which impulses warred within his breast. He could feel the warmth of her touch even through the cloth.

'Madame,' he breathed, bowing from the hips. Then he led the Ducina Allisandra out on to the dance-floor, taking up their place with the other couples.

The dance was a formal pavane, a slow measure performed by long ranks of couples facing each other. Leander, like all young men of his station, was as expertly trained in dancing as in swordsmanship and he led with confidence. He and Allisandra moved as a single unit when the music instructed, advancing towards each other and then retreating, turning about, sometimes coming so close that their hips were brushing, sometimes at arm's length – but never so far apart that they lost contact. The careful, deliberately confrontational movements reminded Leander of the wary circlings of duellists, and the ranks of men and women moving in synchronisation made him think oddly of the manoeuvring of troops as they entered a battle. But it was hard to think when Allisandra's gaze never released his and the little, knowing smile never left her lips. Hard to think of anything except how those lips might feel against him, and how lithe her slender body was, and how her eyes seemed to burn darkly. He could feel the heat of her regard kindling a terrible urgent pain in the pit of his stomach. They spoke not a word to each other, but they never looked away. It was as if they danced alone on a burning ship.

The music ceased, and the dancers pulled apart to laugh and applaud themselves. Leander could not clap or laugh. Allisandra inclined her head in that half-searching, half-mocking way of hers and extended her hand for him to kiss. He bowed over it, wishing that her bare skin could feel his lips through the velvet.

'I . . .' he began as he straightened up, but there was a movement at their side and her attention slipped from him. The prince's equerry stood there, resplendent in powdered wig and snakeskin breeches. Allisandra's hand pulled gently from his grasp.

'My Lady Ducina,' the servant murmured, bowing low, 'his Highness begs the honour of a few moments of your time . . .'

Leander coloured sharply and backed off. He had no desire to hear the rest of the message. Allisandra seemed to have forgotten his existence; she did not glance around as he retreated gracelessly from her side. The orchestra struck up a new tune and already dancers were regrouping as he made his way off the floor.

Leander climbed the stair through knots of gossiping guests and flirting couples on to the main deck of the ship; it was difficult to be polite and not to push his way too impatiently. Right at the head of the stairs, a thin figure in the yellow rags and pale mask of a jester blocked his path. It struck the posture of a broken-hearted lover, sniggered lasciviously, then grabbed at its crotch and groped itself with obscene relish. Leander clenched his fists and shoved the fool aside.

It was a relief to get out into the open under the stars. He flung back his head and drew a deep breath of the balmy night air, then snorted in disgust and strode quickly into the shadows, heading towards the prow of the galleon. There were few people out in the calm of the night; the party below was in its prime, the prince still present, and it was too early for more than the most amorous of couples to steal away from the lights and the frivolity. Leander walked the entire length of the deck without meeting more than a few people – and he greeted none of them, sunk as he was in his own thoughts. He was angry at his naivety, at the transparency of the face he had shown to one of the highest of the nobility, but most of all that he should have made a fool of himself for a woman who had probably had more stupid young gallants like him than he had seen summers.

He paused near the forecastle, jamming his fists against the wooden railing in frustration and staring out across the water. The lake was nearly flat calm and, though the fireworks had finished long ago, the lights of the harbour a few hundred yards away still gleamed and danced on the gentle swells, the whole city shining softly in the dark like a treasure-hoard of magical gems. In silver nets below the moored galleon, captured mermaids splashed softly in the lapping darkness; Leander knew that if he threw something at them he could probably provoke a sweet, eerie lament from their silver throats, but for the moment they were silent. He looked down at the lake then up at the blazing stars above, and suddenly he shivered. The many-storied hulk of the great galleon, decked now with streamers and lanterns and wreaths of flowers, seemed very small against such a backdrop of heaven and water.

He sighed, then swallowed down the lump of anger that choked his throat so that it lay, heavy but bearable, in his stomach. There was no point in blaming himself or anyone else. He had reached high and fallen short, that was all. It was said that the Ducina arl Guriemme had hundreds of noble lovers. It was said that she had the favour of the emperor himself. Perhaps one day Leander might attain such rank and fame that he could move in such circles – but by then the Ducina Allisandra would be an old woman, and not worthy of his attentions. He comforted himself with the thought that she was no more a part of his world than was the first empress of three centuries ago; however beautiful these two women might be, they were sundered from him by time and fate.

For a few moments he lingered to admire the moonlight of the rippling waves, then he turned away and continued his circuit of the deck, aiming for the main staircase once more. This time, he bowed politely to the next strolling couple he met, though the two young women in question answered him only with stifled giggles and clung tighter to each other. He turned to watch them, smiling to himself, as they hurried past into the shadows.

He was not prepared for the sight of Allisandra before him when he resumed his path aft. She was seated in a side-saddle attitude on the ship's broad railing, holding a small glass of liqueur and looking pensively down into the water. Despite his good resolutions, his heart wrenched painfully as he recognised her. The warm illumination of a cluster of fairy lights strung in the rigging over her head – each a tiny golden cage from within which a fluttering prisoner shed its gentle glow – turned her tanned skin to amber.

She smiled as she looked up at him. 'I've been waiting for you to come back.'

'I thought,' he said stiffly, 'that you had an audience with his

43

Highness the Prince.' Immediately he cursed himself for his ungraciousness, but she seemed not to notice. Her mouth curved lazily.

'I did, Leander; but it was only a very minor request he wished to make. He wanted me to do my party trick for his guests.' She touched the hilt of her rapier with one finger. 'I can throw two apples into the air, draw my sword and halve them before they strike the floor. Childish fun – but he found it entertaining. You missed it,' she chided him gently.

Leander let out a long breath. 'My apologies, Ducina,' he muttered. He saw the flash of her white teeth as her smile broadened.

'I had wondered whether you had come out here to meet some young woman,' she mused. 'No?'

He shook his head. His throat was dry; he had to clear it. He was very close to her. Her left thigh, the one highest on the railing, was completely exposed from the top of her boot to the tender crease of skin just below the hip. It seemed to glow in the gold light. He wanted very badly to touch it.

Allisandra did not seem to mind his undisguised gaze. 'So, you are alone. I am pleased; it means that I may talk to you again. I find your company tonight most congenial, Leander.'

He dragged his gaze back up to meet her dark eyes. 'You must forgive my lack of conversation, madame –'

'Allisandra.'

'Allisandra. Please: the honour of your own presence has gone to my head. Your beauty leaves me tongue-tied.'

Allisandra tutted. 'I'm not looking for flattery, Leander,' she said. 'Nor fine speeches. If my presence makes you feel . . . tense . . . then I must make amends. Drink this, for a start.' She handed him the small glass and he reached for it, not because he desired the liqueur but because he wanted to touch those velvet fingers once more. But as their hands met, the glass slipped; he grabbed for it and stopped it falling to the deck, but could not prevent the contents slopping out upon her bare thigh. Allisandra started.

'That is cold,' she sighed.

Leander bit his lip and stared down at the splash of dark brandy staining her leg. He felt light-headed and cold; his limbs

44

seemed to throb and buzz as if they were ready to explode. This was worse than the moment before the charge at Moriens. There was only one cure, and that was action.

'Ducina,' he said formally, 'allow me.' Without hesitating, he slid to his knees on the deck and pressed his lips to her inner thigh. He heard the soft intake of her breath over the sound of his own blood pounding in his ears. Her flesh was satin-soft and incredibly warm and he could smell her secret musky perfume. He kissed the sticky moisture from the smooth skin, gentle as the breath of spring, using his tongue to lap up the bitter spirit. He moved without haste, and it seemed as dreamlike and terrible to him as that first charge into battle.

When every last trickle of the pungent liquid had been erased, he rose before her again, his colour high, his jaw set. She gazed up at him; her eyes were bright and her lips softly parted.

'How gallant,' she purred.

He found he was still holding the useless glass. He tossed it over her shoulder into the sea.

'My pleasure, Ducina,' he said, almost with a groan. His scrotum was as tight as a clenched fist and his stones felt as if they were burning.

Her laughter was like the jingle of spurs. 'And so charming! You are wasted among rough soldiers, Leander. Did you come here with a companion? No? I think you ought to find a paramour tonight. It should not be difficult, with so many fine ladies here to choose from. It is such a beautiful night. And you are so very handsome. Hm. Did you know that?'

'Allisandra,' he grunted. His member had risen up and was rearing between his legs like a war-stallion, straining its long neck against the curb.

'Yes.' She began to play with one of the silver buttons on his open jacket, the one directly over his left nipple. Leander shut his eyes for a moment. 'You are a very handsome, lovely boy.'

His hand snapped shut around her wrist. 'Don't mock me, madame,' he said, eyes narrowed. 'I am no boy, for you to tease: I'm a man.'

His grip was harsh; it must have hurt her, but there was no sign of it in her face. 'Prove that,' she whispered, her lips describing brush-strokes of provocation.

He no longer cared for decorum. He took her imprisoned hand and laid it over the hard mound of his erection, and it leapt beneath her touch, stamping and bucking with an impatience that threatened to damage the fine doeskin of his breeches. Her eyelashes fluttered and her palm and fingers moved to clasp his bellicose flesh.

'Oh,' she breathed, her face drained of all mockery. 'Now you are teasing me, my Leander. Such a great promise cannot be made if it is not to be fulfilled.'

'I would fulfil it this instant, Allisandra,' he growled, leaning over her and bending to her throat. 'I swear you will never be able to forget the consummation of this promise, madame.' He took her earlobe between her teeth and she shuddered with pleasure; the response nearly drove him to insanity.

'Is – is there a cabin nearby?' she asked, her voice low.

He could not think properly. 'The forecastle . . . There is to be an entertainment there later,' he grunted, stretching his memory. 'There are seats. And mummers' props laid out. But there was no one there when . . .' His voice failed him. He pulled Allisandra to her feet. 'Come now.'

He led her back up the length of the ship. She clung to his arm as if she could not bear to release him from her embrace. They reached the small deck before the forecastle cabin and found it as he had half-remembered: set out with cushions and padded benches and musicians' instruments, but empty of people. In front of the steps up into the cabin was a tall screen, contrived so that players would be able to exit from the makeshift stage without being watched, and enter swiftly from cover. He pulled her behind this and towards the stairs, but she slipped from his arm and, when he turned, laughed and set her back to the mast there.

'No further, my gallant,' she said, holding out her arms to him. 'I would have you keep your promise right now.'

'Here?' Leander was surprised. They were concealed behind the screen from anyone walking the decks, but it was the flimsiest of shields, and there was neither surface on which nor room in which to lie.

'Here,' she commanded.

He grinned suddenly and went to her, pulling her roughly

into his arms. They kissed for the first time. Her tongue was savage and she bit his lips, but he pinned her by the throat and returned stroke for stroke. When she found that he would not be broken, she relaxed. He could feel the blood racing through her jugular. They were gentle then, exploring each other's hot mouths with the murderous delicacy of cats. She smelt of vanilla. He ran his fingers through her lustrous hair and chased the outline of her cleavage with his tongue.

'Take off your harness,' she hissed, digging her nails gently into the nape of his neck. He humoured her, tearing off his brocaded jacket and dropping it to the floor. She forced her hands up under his white shirt and he discarded that too.

'Beautiful,' she moaned, drawing her velvet palms across the smooth wall of his chest. 'Oh, you are beautiful.' She nuzzled the flat brown discs of his nipples and seduced them into erection with tongue and teeth. Leander had to brace one hand against the mast to keep his balance. Then she slid to her knees before him and rubbed her face against the soft leather that covered his tumescent crotch, and he thought he would faint with anticipation.

'Yes,' she murmured, more to his imprisoned member than to him. 'Oh, yes; right now, my lovely one. Let's see you now.' She unclasped his belt and pulled it open, then eased the tight breeches down over his narrow hips and tight muscular arse. His thick shaft, released from all constraint, sprang into the light. Allisandra hissed with pleasure and caught it in one hand, drawing back the tender foreskin. Her grip was firm. The smooth helmet danced in her black velvet-clad palm, thrusting out into the light between her fingers and thumb as she slid her hand up and down.

'Oh, you must have lied to me, Leander,' she crooned. 'You are no duc's son; you have the parts of a cart-horse colt – I've never seen a nobleman endowed like this!' So saying, she gripped the fingertips of her left glove between her teeth and tore the garment off, allowing her to cup his balls with her bare hand. Leander groaned, his head spinning. He could see her carnelian-painted nails; the two hands, one black and one white, vying for his swollen genitals; her tongue slipping out to lap at the shiny head of his lance. Tension was building in the puckered bag of his stones. From his toes to the tip of his cock was one unbroken line of rigid muscle, strained to breaking point.

'I'm about to let slip,' he warned her through clenched teeth.

'Oh? You told me you were a man, not a boy,' she said cruelly, probing the oozing slit of his knob with her darting tongue-tip. 'Can't you hold it?'

'Allisandra!' he snarled. He could not bear it any longer. He was forced to snatch her away from his ripe cock, dragging her to her feet and pushing her back against the mast again, for another few seconds of her torment would have had him spending his seed in great gouts all over her face. He was too proud to let that happen, though it cost him every ounce of will power to ignore his tortured charger. He pressed up against her yielding frame and kissed her ravenously. He could taste his own musk on her lips, smell it on her cheeks.

'Ready to ride?' he asked her.

'Oh, yes, my beautiful Leander,' she moaned. 'Please – now!'

He laughed softly and smothered her words with his lips. His hands groped for her sword-belt and loosened it; the hilt clattered as it struck the deck. He found the hook-and-eye fastenings down the front of her dress and released them one by one, each uncinching bringing more of her saffron flesh into the light. She wore nothing beneath the black dress. He stripped the silk from her as if it were rags and dropped it underfoot, then stood back to admire his work.

She was entirely beautiful: honed like a knife, slender as a maiden, tawny as a wild beast. Her breasts were small and proud, her belly taut with desire, her thighs hard as an Amazon's. Even in the excess of his lust he paused to let this sight imprint itself for ever in his mind; naked except for one long glove and her black thigh-boots, she epitomised everything he had ever desired. She reached out to him, writhing with impatience against the mast at her back, her eyes wicked and pleading.

They came together like a sword sliding into an oiled scabbard. He lifted her and she wrapped her long legs around his hips, and then the full thick length of his blade pierced her and she sheathed him to the hilt. They both gasped and clung to each other, shocked by their audacity, that mortal flesh might aspire to such perfection. Allisandra touched his lips gently with her bare fingers.

'Leander,' she said, with wonder in her voice.

At that moment there came a noise from the deck beyond the screen. They both froze. It was the sound of feet, and the murmur of voices, and the slurred laughter of several people. Chairs were moved. The voices did not fade.

Leander, caught at the apex of his desire, stared into his lover's wide eyes with horror. She looked to the screen; light was coming through the chinks, and shapes could dimly be seen moving beyond. Someone had brought new lanterns. Suddenly, but absolutely silently, Allisandra started to giggle; he could feel her shaking against him. It lasted only a few moments and then sobriety swept over her. With a mimed snarl she reached for his lips again, running her hot tongue into his mouth. He stifled a groan as heat washed over him, then grinned and pressed into her, pinning her against the mast.

Someone began to pick softly at the strings of a lute.

In absolute silence, only yards away from their unwitting audience, they danced the twisting dance of their desire. Leander slid his thick cock in and out of her wet and yielding purse, slowly at first and then with greater urgency. Their awkward posture, her legs wrapped around his hips, was a constraint that meant he could not ram into her as hard or as fast as they both would have liked; he dropped his hands reluctantly from her breasts to her arse, sliding one under each buttock to hold her up. The muscles stood out on his arms. She unwrapped her legs, trusting him with her weight, and this gave him the freedom to feint and retreat with renewed force, thrusting with the whole length of his glistening lance. Sweat bedewed her forehead and her eyes were rolling back under heavy lids. He kissed her throat, muffling his own little grunts. He knew he was going to climax very soon; even concentrating on her pleasure could not distract him from the fire roiling inside his balls. She clawed at his shoulders. Their short gasps of breath were coming in synchrony now, no longer inaudible. The wetness and the tightness of her, the hot and writhing length of her body, the open-mouthed vacancy of her expression now stripped of everything but a mindless awe – they were unbearable any longer. He felt the quickening begin at the base of his spine, felt his bollocks clench and force the first great spurt of semen up his shaft – and at the same moment felt Allisandra begin to shake. She arched her back and thrashed in his arms, her breasts jiggling wildly, her legs flailing.

He heard her boot lash out and strike the screen.

He was coming. He could not stop it. He could do nothing but brace himself against the wrenching fire within and the struggling body in his arms. He heard the world come crashing down about him, and did not care.

When she had ceased to shake, he opened his eyes once more. They both tried to still their gasping. The screen was flat on the deck, but there was no sound at all from their audience. Leander craned his neck and saw them caught motionless as a tableau; a score of beautifully dressed guests staring with speechless shock.

'You can put me down, Leander,' Allisandra said gently.

He lowered her to the floor and stepped back, absently capturing his turgid cock and tucking it back into his breeches. She pushed back a lock of sweat-dampened hair behind her ear and gave him one brief smile.

He wondered what on earth he should do now. The audience watched, transfixed.

Allisandra bent to pick up her sword-belt and fastened it around her naked hips with a swift easy motion. She faced the assembled nobility without the faintest trace of shame, her head high, her posture relaxed, clad only in sword-belt, boots and a single glove. The lamplight fell lovingly on the warm tones of her skin, on the sheen of moisture drying between her breasts and on her thick black pubic hair. She cocked one hip arrogantly.

Leander could not keep a smile from stealing on to his face.

Almost as an afterthought, she stooped to retrieve her dress, hooking it up in one finger. Then trailing it negligently on the boards behind her she strode past the assembled company, breasts and arse jutting proudly, hips swinging. She disappeared from view down the length of the ship.

Leander was grinning now.

The audience exchanged glances between themselves; then finally they began to applaud.

The Love that Stings

Maria Lyonesse

The Love that Stings

❧ ❦

*A*lex killed the engine of his vintage Norton and tugged off his motorcycle helmet. He ran a hand through his short but luxuriant hair. Behind him on the pillion Francesca took off her own helmet and shook out her chestnut mane. They were on the high moors. Miles from anywhere.

'Why have we stopped here?' she asked.

'Just this little place I know,' Alex replied. 'I think you'll like it. Come.'

He swung off the bike and began walking determinedly over the unfenced moorland. Francesca followed him, glad of the opportunity to undo the zip of her restrictive leathers. Alex had found the jacket at the back of the wardrobe in his spare bedroom. Whichever one of his previous girlfriends it had belonged to, Francesca mused with a hint of satisfaction, she couldn't have been anywhere near as well endowed as herself.

With the jacket hanging open, she loosened off the drawstring at the neck of her translucent Indian blouse. The cool moorland air licked its way down her cleavage. The feeling contrasted sharply with the heat that had been generated under the motorcycling leathers. It made her very aware of even the slightest tactile stimulation. It made her very aware she wanted Alex's impatient hands on her body again.

She had known him for less than twenty-four hours. They had met at a party the previous evening. The promise of unashamed

53

sexual intent she had seen in Alex's eyes had meant they'd both left early. The enthusiasm of his taut body to follow through on that promise meant Francesca was still moving with an agreeable rawness deep inside her.

They came to a small group of rocks – no, not rocks, she decided. They had been carved – worked into massive millstones then abandoned: a reminder that even these high moorlands once had an industrial past. Alex stopped and laid his motorcycle helmet carefully down on the largest stone. He turned to face her.

'I see you've made a start,' he said, gesturing at the unzipped leather jacket and the gaping neckline of her blouse. 'Take the rest off. I'll watch.'

Games, Francesca thought. I like it.

She wriggled her shoulders and let the jacket slide off – oh, so slowly. It made her feel sexy, the way Alex's dark gaze fixed itself unashamedly on the exaggerated bounce of her breasts as she did so. She loosened the drawstring of her Indian blouse as far as it would go, tugging the neckline right down, offering her deep velvety cleavage up to his face, teasing him. Alex was grinning broadly. He was obviously enjoying the show.

She pulled off the gauzy blouse and tossed it aside. Slowly she coaxed her breasts out of their stiff lace half-cup bra. Exposing them fully to the cooling moorland breeze was an incredible sensation. It felt as though thousands of tiny tongues were licking over her, pulling her nipples to tight eager points. Up until now her sexual adventures – though wholeheartedly and blissfully varied – had always been indoors. She just knew the first taste of it out here in the open was going to be something special.

Francesca kicked off her boots. She unzipped the flies of her borrowed black leather trousers with the slightest hint of reluctance; she had been enjoying the relentless clasp of the leather against her thighs. Her wispy G-string panties were the type that undid with bows at the sides. She tugged once, then twice. The panties fluttered to the grass. She was proudly naked in front of him.

Alex walked round Francesca in a slow circle.

'You're hard already,' she observed, admiring the bulge in his leather-clad crotch. 'Why not let him have a bit more room?'

Alex smiled enigmatically.

'Maybe he likes a little restriction. You know something?' he continued. 'You've got the most amazing skin.' He moistened a fingertip and glided it over the fullest curve of first one breast then the other. 'And I'm going to make your skin feel – I mean really feel – like it's never felt before.'

Quickly he shrugged off his own leather jacket and peeled off his T-shirt. His body was still a novelty and a wonderful playground as far as she was concerned. She enjoyed the sight of his tight tanned stomach and she knew already that stroking him around and around his navel was like dialling a hotline to his cock. As if aware of her scrutiny, Alex stretched up, cat-like, for her benefit. Then he put his black leather gauntlets on again and flexed the fingers experimentally. Francesca took a deep breath. What would that unfamiliar animal texture feel like on her skin? Alex obviously had something in mind.

'Turn your back on me,' he ordered – but with a mischievous smile playing at the corners of his lips.

She did as she was told. And found herself facing Alex's motorcycle helmet, which he had set down precisely on the millstone. She was becoming more and more convinced that he had planned this. Methodically. Perhaps he had even done this – whatever he was going to do – with someone else before. She knew that rationally this ought to pique her. It didn't. It intrigued her.

The deeply convex mirror of the visor reflected her breasts. Generous enough in real life, they were magnified by the visor into the sort of size normally only dreamt of by computer graphics wizards. Francesca was just basking in the thought of herself as some kind of sci-fi fantasy figure when she heard a rustling in the undergrowth.

'Keep looking forward,' Alex snapped.

Then the first lash fell across her back.

Francesca gasped. Acid pinpricks of sensation ran a fiery path from her right shoulder to her left buttock. Hot needles leap-frogged their way down her skin, quite literally taking her breath away. She'd had a lover once who liked to keep a knotted leather scourge – among other things – hidden under his bed and she had been more than willing to lie butt upwards and play his risqué games, but no cane or leather had ever had quite that intensity. When she had caught her breath again she twisted very slowly from the waist to look at Alex.

One gauntleted hand was resting on his leather-encased hip. In his other hand he grasped a single nettle plant, maybe three feet long.

'I told you to keep looking forward,' he murmured. 'And move your hair out of the way. I want you to feel every inch of this.'

She complied, tucking her long fall of chestnut hair over one shoulder to give him an uninterrupted view of her back. When the second lash came, she was waiting for it. This made the sensation completely different. Almost as soon as the trail of fire seared from shoulder to hip, it was cooled again by the fresh moorland air. She even stopped thinking of it as pain at all. After the initial shock of the stinging had subsided, her skin felt as though it had been opened up to a whole new landscape of possibilities. By the time the third lash hit her, smartly across the buttocks, she was loving it.

Alex clearly knew what he was doing. He had started slow to let her get used to it. As the quickening pace of her breathing told him she was becoming excited, so the rhythm of his strokes became more urgent. She thrust her buttocks towards him. He flicked their sensitive undersides with the very tip of the nettle – soft yet at the same time loaded with fire. Up until this moment, Francesca would never have believed how arousing that could feel. She was aware of every millimetre of her tingling skin as never before.

'Turn round,' Alex ordered; from the way he spoke, she could tell he was more than slightly breathless, too. 'And perch on that stone. Spread your legs.'

She turned and sat down on the millstone where he had placed that intriguingly mirrored crash helmet. The stone was ice-cold against her bare buttocks but that sensation of coldness was itself an intense reminder of the extremes her skin could enjoy.

Francesca leant back a little, supported by her hands, tilting her breasts provocatively towards him. She eased her thighs apart. She felt her slick vaginal lips pout open and the fresh moorland air licked its way between them, too. And she was more than ready. She couldn't wait to feel the hardness of his erection inside her again. The bulge in his black leather trousers was huge. Alex glanced down at it and grinned.

'So what do you think I ought to do with that?' he murmured.

'Set it free and fuck me with it.'

'How?'

'Fast and dirty – like you did last night and first thing this morning. Alex, I'm so horny. I'm nearly there. You don't have to go easy on me.'

Alex gave a low chuckle.

'Francesca, you need a few more lessons in discipline.'

He stroked the tip of the nettle in a very slow figure-of-eight – over the top of one full breast, under the curve of the other and around again – all the time just managing to avoid the ultra-sensitive tips of her nipples. She had been a rapid, eager convert to this new form of arousal. It didn't even occur to her, now, to think of it as anything other than sheer physical indulgence – the libidinous equivalent of the darkest, most expensive bitter chocolate. She tipped back her head and moaned as her whole awareness was focused delectably on her breasts.

The slow figure-of-eight slowed even more and then finally stopped. Her skin was blazing now. Her breasts had become so exquisitely sensitive that even the very slight movement of the fresh air across them was like the most erotic caress imaginable.

Alex tossed the nettle plant to one side. Then he pulled off his gauntlets and dropped them, too, on to the grass. He undid the heavy zip on his leather trousers, reached in and lovingly brought out his cock.

To Francesca there was something luxuriously kinky about the fact he wasn't quite naked. That his tight leather trousers were still clinging to his hips gave the whole thing an illicit sense of urgency. And his cock was so beautiful. The moist glans peeping like an acorn from its cup seemed so natural, so right out here in the open. She knew already that sex behind closed doors was never, ever going to have the same charge for her again.

She spread her thighs a little wider and tilted her hips, inviting him to enter her. But the roguish look in Alex's eyes told her that this still wasn't on the menu. She leant forward and parted her lips, ready to take the glistening tip of his penis into her mouth, if that was what he wanted. Alex grasped her shoulders and restrained her.

'Not yet,' he told her. 'Don't touch me yet. Touch yourself. I want to watch you playing with those gorgeous big tits. Squeeze them. Offer them up to me. Show me what you'd like me to be doing to them.'

She loved pleasuring herself. To do it in front of a lover suddenly gave it an extra piquancy. The type of men she normally attracted had been all too anxious to party with her breasts themselves. So, although a little self-conscious at first, she felt deliciously decadent as she cupped them, raised them up and began to tease both nipples between the very tips of her forefingers and thumbs. The grin of excitement on Alex's face encouraged her. Not taking his eyes off her breasts for a second, with exaggerated slowness he began to masturbate.

Francesca ran her own fingertips in a rippling arpeggio over the firm upper curves of her breasts. Even this light teasing touch was rendered extreme in the tingling afterglow of the nettles' caress. She could see that Alex, in spite of himself, was rubbing his cock more impatiently. Across his face the dilemma played itself out: the desire to spin this pleasure out as long as possible, battling against the rollercoaster urge to come.

She crushed her breasts together almost savagely, deepening her already pronounced cleavage. There was something so liberating about finding out, in front of a man like this, how roughly she could handle herself and still be turned on. In Alex's hands, his gorgeous thick shaft gave an extra little kick. Francesca tipped her head back, ready to luxuriate in the inevitable.

He came across the broad target area of her throat and breasts in quick forceful jets. She felt it hit her skin like a warm whip and her nerves' heightened sensitivity exploded into flame again.

Grinning that wolfish grin, Alex knelt down level with her. Such had been the intensity of his arousal that, despite having made furious love to her only a few hours previously, he had climaxed across her breasts as freely as a man who had been saving himself for weeks. Lovingly he began to rub it in.

She gave herself up wholly to the voluptuous, slippery sensation of his hands massaging his own semen into her highly sensitised breasts. He seemed lost in this garden of pleasure. Neither of them wanted it to end. He pressed his fingertips commandingly into her yielding flesh. He pinched and drew her dark nipples out to their fullest extent: a caress even more extreme than any she had tried, on the cusp of pain and pleasure. She loved it.

Without really thinking what she was doing, she reached for his penis. And she was amazed to find it semi-erect.

'You recover quickly,' she murmured.

'Because you turn me on.' He gave her breasts an extra proprietorial squeeze. 'These do.'

He stood up suddenly, bringing the tip of his cock to her mouth.

'Finish it off,' he told her. 'Suck me till I'm really hard.'

Francesca parted her lips willingly and moulded them around his glans. She ran her tongue up and down the velvety underside of his penis. He moaned. His shaft grew thick and hard, pressing her lips wider apart. Alex had an incredibly suckable cock. She would have loved to run her mobile tongue over and under and around his glans until he climaxed again. But there was an ache deep in her vagina; she was longing to be filled. She was relieved when, fully erect and virile, he pulled back from her.

'Stand up,' Alex ordered.

As she did so, Francesca saw him pulling on his black leather gauntlets again. With excitement tightening deep in her belly, she watched him choose another long nettle plant from the undergrowth.

'Turn round,' he told her. 'Bend over that stone again.'

Knowing what was going to happen made it even better this time. She tensed her buttocks in anticipation. The lash whipped once, twice, three times. It felt as if another layer had been peeled from her skin – and not in pain but liberating her to a range of tactile stimulation she could never have imagined. Alex drew the nettle for a fourth time very slowly over the fullest curve of her tingling buttocks. She was almost sorry when, from the corner of her eye, she saw him toss the plant aside.

He stood back for a moment. She watched him ease his leather trousers down over his hips. He was totally naked, then, except for his black gauntlets. He advanced on her.

'Keep looking forward,' he insisted.

Francesca felt one leather-covered forefinger part the lips of her sex and writhe its way in. It had an agreeable thickness. The idea of being penetrated by something leather definitely appealed. And the slight roughness of the seams in the glove against the sensitive walls of her quim was an incredible stimulation.

Alex worked his thick forefinger deeply into her. She gave her well-toned pelvic muscles a little squeeze: a promise of what she would really like to be doing right now to his cock. Finally he drew his finger out, slick with the clear honey of her arousal. This he massaged up and down her perineum.

When he reached the tight ring of her anus, he ran the moistened tip of his leather-clad finger round and round and round. After a moment, she felt him dip his little finger in her honeypot. When this was well and truly slippery, he penetrated her anus with it.

There was something so tantalisingly forbidden about the sensation of it. She rejoiced in Alex – the sheer range of his sexual appetite. She didn't know quite which gods she must have pleased so much for them to send her such an epicurean lover – but they had. Then she felt something else stroke up against her entrance. This time there was no mistaking the smooth swelling of Alex's cock. And he sheathed himself in her as fiercely as she had been aching for him to do all morning.

Then he concentrated on nothing else. There was only the sure animal thrusting – the intensity of his body plunging deep into hers. He had already come once; he could, she realised, probably carry on like this for ages. So she gave herself full permission to revel in the feeling. The friction of his penis – the headlong surge of honest lust – concentrated her awareness wholly on her lower body. She loved the sensation of his cock inside her. It was taking the fire she had previously felt across her skin deep, deep into her body. And yet it wasn't quite enough.

Leaning forward over the millstone Francesca was, of necessity, taking her weight on her hands. If she opened her eyes a crack, she could still see herself in the cleverly placed mirrored visor. Her heavy breasts were swinging in time as Alex relentlessly fucked her from behind. She ached to feel his hands on them.

'Alex,' she moaned, 'I want you to . . .'

'Yes?' he prompted.

She met his eyes in the mirror. She had the distinct feeling he knew what she needed and had done all along. But he was making her say it – he wanted to get a kick out of it – and as earthily as possible.

'I want you to feel my tits,' she gasped. 'Be rough with them. I just can't come unless you do.'

He reached round eagerly and cupped them. There was something about the sight of his black gauntlets against the yielding whiteness of her breasts. The musky-sweet scent of her own sex seemed to have fixed itself on the leather; together they made a combination that overwhelmed her senses.

Cupping and lifting her tingling breasts, Alex rolled and pulled at the berry tips of her nipples with a thoroughness that would have been painful if she hadn't been so intensely aroused. She didn't close her eyes again. Watching it happen in the albeit distorting mirror added a whole new kinkiness which she was really beginning to enjoy.

The rhythm of his fucking changed. Now his cock was barely moving inside her but its tip was stimulating just the perfect spot, high up on the front wall of her vagina. For a moment there was a divine balance between what his cock was doing to her sex and what his hands were doing to her breasts. The electric currents of desire swarmed through her body with a whole new intensity. Then they converged, flaming, on the fleshy mound of her pubis and blossomed deep into her body in an all-consuming, supremely satisfying orgasm. And Alex climaxed into her, like a single firework exploding in a dark November sky.

And afterwards they lay together in the long grass, saying nothing for a time until their frantic breathing slowed back down. Alex laid his head between her breasts and kissed them lovingly. There was still a little magic left from the nettles' fiery touch; even his light kiss sent prickles of sensation over her skin.

Eventually he raised his head and looked at her. His dark eyes were very sincere.

'I won't pretend you're the first woman I've brought here,' he began slowly, 'because you're not. But you're the first who's even begun to understand . . .'

'Alex,' she murmured, 'thank you. Thank you for showing me how much my skin could really feel. You keep doing things like that and you'll have one hell of a job getting rid of me.'

He grinned artlessly.

'Then let's show everyone how hopelessly you're mine,' he insisted. 'And let's show them here,' he added, running his fingers almost reverently over the upper slopes of her breasts.

Some days later, when the redness on her skin had totally subsided, they kept the appointment together that they had made at a certain studio.

The male tattoo artist – whom they had specifically requested – handled Francesca's large breasts with an evident pleasure that went beyond the strictly professional. She lay back on the couch and surrendered to the extreme sensations once more as he worked on her.

Alex stood close by and looked on as the botanically perfect image of a nettle appeared, twisting sinuously up from her cleavage and draping itself across the top of her left breast. Francesca noticed the swelling in his black leather trousers as his erection grew. She couldn't wait to find out just how he would use it on her this time when he got her home.

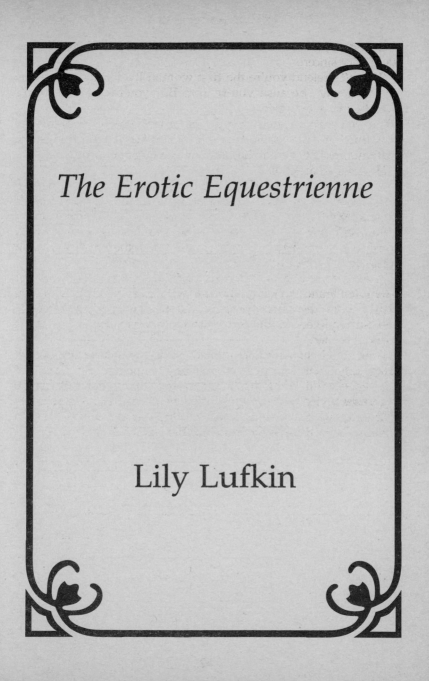

The Erotic Equestrienne

Lily Lufkin

The Erotic Equestrienne

❧ ❧

*L*ucy Lovegrove was a happy girl. She had been a happy baby, a happy child and now she was a happy young woman. Her general optimistic demeanour sprung from the knowledge that she was, indeed, a very lucky girl as she was able to indulge in the two great loves of her life – sex and horses.

The reason she could indulge in the former was that she was very attractive and had no lack of offers in that direction, and the latter was because she had just landed a job in a top competition stable yard – Priory Farm Stud.

At nineteen years old, Lucy had the looks which most girls her age would die for. She was petite, but her small frame belied her true nature. She was a girl who could look after herself and Lucy knew exactly what she wanted from life. With naturally blonde, long straight hair, a small waist, neat bottom and full round breasts, she was gorgeous. On rare self-critical occasions, although she was always light in the saddle, she cursed her large breasts and the way they bounced painfully when she took part in her favourite sport, showjumping.

She lived in her jodhpurs, moving gracefully like a young thoroughbred. Many male eyes greedily drank in the gentle swish of her hips and the soft rolling movement of her rounded buttocks, tightly encased in lycra.

Lucy had landed the job at Priory Farm Stud near Exeter and left her quiet, sheltered home in Wales to start the live-in position as assistant groom. The owners of the stables, Rod and Suzie Lamberton, seemed genuinely nice and had provided a small flat adjoining the stable yard. It may have been small but it was clean and tidy, with one bedroom (a double bed, she had noted gleefully), tiny kitchen, bathroom with shower and a cosy lounge. The pay was quite low but it was Lucy's first taste of independence and she intended to make the most of it. No more sneaking around, having sex in the back of cars, or behind the local night-club; now she had her own place and Lucy could indulge fully in life's little pleasures.

There were twenty horses at Priory Farm Stud; some were competition showjumping horses being brought on by Suzie and some were kept at the stables on livery, the owners paying for their keep.

Lucy loved the daily routine, getting up early to feed, muck out and brush off her four charges. After the grooms' breakfast at 8 a.m., all the horses were exercised around the narrow country lanes or across the rolling farmland nearby, where they were encouraged to stride out and strengthen their muscles.

As well as the road and hillwork, the horses were schooled twice a week, repetition increasing their balance and agility. The sleek creatures were meticulously groomed after their workout, their coats polished until they gleamed.

The yard was run like a well-oiled machine and Lucy felt proud to be part of the team which kept it so well tuned. The yard chores were shared between herself, Suzie, Rod and Jim, who was Head Lad.

Jim had been watching Lucy since she arrived and, from the moment he saw her, he was determined to have her. As they exercised the horses together, he had noticed the friction of her T-shirt rubbing at her nipples, making them hard, and he had imagined her wet pussy grinding away on the saddle. Getting an erection while riding was not a good idea, he decided, and many times he had to force his thoughts on to more mundane matters to avoid injuring himself. He longed to know whether her bush matched her long blonde hair and had bragged to his mates in the pub that he was going to find out 'if the collar and cuffs matched'.

One evening, he could not keep his mind away from Lucy. His prick seemed to have a life of its own. He watched as she bent over to prepare the night feeds for her charges, and he could feel himself getting harder as he imagined how it would feel to have the soft folds of her pussy around him. She stood up and turned around, and he was pleased to see her blush as she noticed the hardening in the front of his jodhpurs.

'What's the matter, Lucy? Haven't you seen a stiff one before?' he jeered.

He was not put off when she ignored him. As she made for the door, he blocked her way with his arm. When she tried to duck under it, he grabbed her by the wrist.

Jim had a high opinion of himself; he liked what he saw in the mirror and was generally very successful with the local girls. It was obvious, however, that Lucy was not going to give in easily, as she wriggled away from his grasp and ducked into the haystore, determined to continue her evening chores.

He followed her and, leaning against the doorway, watched while she filled the hay nets for the horses. It was a beautiful evening and the warm amber glow of the sunset made her hair gold and her face angelic. God, he wanted her! He longed to overpower her and force her to her knees; to jam his prick right down her throat and fuck her in the mouth until he came in hot spurts of creamy spunk all over her face. He forced his mind away from the thought and tried a few chosen compliments instead. In his experience, girls usually responded to that kind of stuff.

'You know, you are so pretty, Lucy. Why can't you be nice to me?' he wheedled. He stepped closer, drawing nearer to her sweet upturned face. He was so close that he could smell her scent, musky and alluring and so very feminine. He reached down for her hand and this time she did not try to pull away. He played lightly with her fingers, stroking and caressing; gradually he realised, as he murmured sweet nothings, that she was responding, just like a nervous horse. His hand crept up to her neck and he gently caught her hair between his fingers, pulling her head towards his. His lips moved closer to hers and, when they touched, he felt the electric shock of desire take him.

The softness of the caress was gone. His mouth covered hers

as he pressed her to him. He felt her yield to the insistence of his lust and his tongue ground deep into her mouth. His hand came up and sought her left breast, twisting the nipple between his finger and thumb. He heard her cry out and she pretended to pull away from him. So, he thought, as he held on to her firmly, little Lucy wanted to be persuaded. He was all for some play-acting, as long as he got what he wanted. He knew it would all be worth it just for a chance to fuck the sweet pussy that had tormented his thoughts for so long.

Entering into the spirit of her game, he grasped both her arms and twisted them behind her back, loosely tying her hands together with baler twine from the hay. He pushed her forward until she overbalanced across the bales, and then he was on her like lightning, pulling at her jodhpurs until they were down around her knees. She was a willing captive and, with her ankles trapped together by her trousers, she was exposed and vulnerable. He deftly unbuckled his trousers and unzipped his flies. His prick bounced up, hard and throbbing from its confinement. He could see that her pussy had flooded with wetness, which glistened around the lips pouting at him so alluringly. His fingers probed inside her; first one, then two and then three fingers were easily accommodated by her soaking depths, and he felt her pussy twitch involuntarily.

'No, no.' Vaguely he heard her token protest, but he did not reply. He knew she wanted him as much as he wanted her. Her hands, so delicately bound with twine, could easily slip their confinement, and she could escape at any time if she really wanted to. She was so wet that her juices were beginning to run down the inside of her thighs. His prick was huge and hot as he gazed down at the open sex exposed before him. Somewhere in the back of his mind he saw the blonde tufts of pubic hair around the tempting opening and realised that she was, indeed, a real blonde.

He could not wait any longer and, pulling his fingers out, he rammed his prick into her. In his eagerness, the glistening tip of his cock partly penetrated her anus and she squealed and bucked, forcing him to withdraw. The hard purple head urgently probed for a second time, spreading the delicate pink lips wide apart as he pushed his length deep into her pussy, the weight of his swollen balls banging against her tender clitoris.

As she lay across the hay bales, allowing him to pound away at her, the sight of her submissive form turned him on even more and his breath came in gasps. His prick slid in and out, faster and faster, feeling just the slightest resistance as her tight pussy felt the strain of his huge prick.

Abruptly he pulled out. There was still some pretence of a fight left in her and he knew what she wanted him to do. Reaching up, he grabbed a riding whip from a hook on the wall. He flicked the end across her plump rosy buttocks. She squealed like an angry filly and tried to kick backward at him. Down came the whip again, across her tender bottom with a sharp crack; a red mark rose like a burn. Again and again he swiped her, grinding down her token resistance until her arse was aflame and her face burning with desire. He realised that she was weakening and gently he flicked the exposed open lips of her sex. She gasped for breath as he flicked again, and then gasped even more as the end of the whip slid inside her.

Aware now that she had stopped pretending to fight him, he turned her over and laid her on a soft carpet of loose hay. Quickly he lifted her T-shirt, exposing her breasts. His mouth came down over her left nipple. It was huge and brown and teased up to a rock-hard point. He played his tongue over it and nipped gently with his teeth, while his hand roamed freely through her pubic hair. His forefinger slid wetly between her pussy lips and his thumb probed at her clitoris. She was soaking; her juices ran over his fingers as again he pushed them into her one by one.

With her ankles still anchored together by her jodhpurs, he pushed apart her knees and straddled her, his prick hugely erect. He entered her roughly, sliding easily into the hot wet hole, and he was encouraged as she cried out, begging him for more. He thrust deeply several times and felt the beginnings of her climax as she twitched gratefully, tight around his prick. He heard her moan and felt her moving with him. His breaths came in short gasping pants as his excitement grew. He gripped her hips firmly, pulling himself deeper inside her, pounding into the soft delicate flesh, as Lucy writhed in ecstasy beneath him.

Finally, her pussy spasmed and she came, crying out loud. Jim could no longer hold back; his face contorted as he climaxed with a groan. He lay inside her for some seconds, allowing his cock to subside.

'You bastard,' spat Lucy.

Jim just smiled and freed her from the twine loosely looped around her wrists. His filly was broken and he knew he would be riding her again soon.

Lucy managed to avoid Jim for a while. His constant knowing looks annoyed her and she was angry with herself for giving in so easily to her lust. Still, she was happy. She was surrounded by her beloved horses all day and had independence for the first time in her life. She was not about to let Jim get her down.

Lucy had been in her job for nearly a month. She had made good progress with her quiet style of riding, and the horses had begun to respond well, bringing Lucy success in some small local jumping competitions.

It was a beautiful May morning and she whistled as she brushed the gleaming muscled neck of Santa, the dark bay showjumper she had just exercised. He turned and nuzzled her back, breathing on the bare skin exposed between the bottom of her sweatshirt and the top of her jodhpurs. The aroma of horses was strong in the morning air and Lucy was in her own kind of heaven.

She glanced up at the sound of a horsebox arriving. Lucy knew Suzie had bought a new competition horse and that she would be looking after it. She let herself out of Santa's box and walked across the yard to meet her new charge.

The back of the horsebox swung down and out danced the most beautiful horse that Lucy had ever seen.

The mare was called Poeme. She was a light grey Arab with well-pronounced dapples on her hindquarters and a darker-coloured long flowing mane and tail. She stood haughtily in the yard, surveying her new surroundings like a queen looking down on her subjects, and blew disdainfully through her gently flared nostrils.

Lucy caught her breath and, at that moment, fell in love for the first time in her life.

The two became inseparable. Lucy spent hours with Poeme, talking to her and grooming her, and Poeme accepted the attention as her due.

Poeme may have been beautiful to look at, but she was a typical mare and difficult to handle. Some days she would not be bridled, some days she would not be mounted. The only rider she would tolerate was Lucy, which did not please Suzie at all.

Poeme had been at Priory Farm Stud for less than three weeks when Suzie made her first attempt to ride her. Unused to the different rider, the mare was a bundle of nerves, shying her way around the indoor schooling arena. Suzie fought for control over the skittering animal between her legs. A sudden gust of wind blew through the building causing Poeme to leap sideways in a move worthy of a ballerina. Suzie was unseated and dumped unceremoniously into the sand. The mare flew around the edge of the arena, bucking and kicking.

Lucy had been watching Suzie and Poeme with her heart in her mouth. Rod and Jim had gone to a competition on the other side of Plymouth and Lucy knew that she had to handle this by herself.

Eventually exhausting herself after her headlong race around the schooling ring, Poeme cowered in the corner, sweating with fright. As she stood with her head drooping, Lucy ran to comfort her. Suzie stalked off furiously, bellowing that the horse had to go, and Lucy burst into tears.

She led Poeme into her stable and unsaddled the nervous animal, soothing her all the time and telling her that everything would be all right. She ran her practiced hands gently over the quivering neck and scratched gently at the horse's withers, imitating the grooming motion of another horse. Gradually she felt the fear leave Poeme's body and the animal relaxed, beginning to pull at the hay.

Lucy let herself quietly out of the stable and ran around to the farmhouse to confront Suzie. She burst into the kitchen without knocking. Suzie was sitting at the table, waiting for her. Immediately, Lucy could see that her initial fury had died down.

'Sit down, Lucy,' she said softly. Lucy sat down heavily on one of the old oak kitchen chairs.

'Lucy, you are so young and I am very fond of you. You need

guidance and I hope you will always come to me for help. Poeme cannot remain in the yard – she is dangerous and I think she will hurt someone. I do not want that someone to be you,' soothed Suzie.

Lucy was weak with emotion and allowed Suzie's soft words to wash over her. She felt Suzie's hand stroking the light down on her bare arm as she spoke and realised that she was enjoying the caress. The hand moved higher up her arm, and gradually the fingers began to massage the back of her neck and toy with her silky hair. Lucy did not pull away as she felt Suzie draw closer and pull her into an embrace. Although her mind was telling her that Suzie was just being friendly, a part of her was responding to the caress in a different way.

She allowed Suzie to take her hand and, rising to her feet in a dream, was led upstairs into the bedroom.

'Sit down, Lucy,' commanded Suzie for the second time and Lucy obeyed, sitting down on the bed.

Suzie opened a drawer and took out a brightly coloured album. Sitting next to Lucy on the bed, she opened the book and gently ran her hand across a page showing photos of herself taken some years previously at a point-to-point event.

'I would have won that event, had I not had such a temperamental horse,' she said.

'As it was, I was thrown and fell badly. The injuries were quite serious and I was out of action for a year. Poeme reminds me so much of that pony and I cannot allow her to remain in the yard. It would remind me too much of that painful time.'

The tears which had been brimming up in Suzie's eyes fell heavily on to the photo in front of her and Lucy put her arms around the older woman.

'I'm so sorry, Suzie. I did not know,' she sympathised.

As Suzie returned the embrace, the two women remained locked together for some seconds. Lucy again became aware of the stroking on the back of her neck and she remained still, mesmerised, as Suzie's face drew closer to hers. She felt soft lips press gently against hers and she began to respond. This was new and a bit scary but she did not pull away. Suzie's hand crept beneath Lucy's T-shirt and cupped the full breast, teasing her nipple. Lucy grew braver with desire and returned the touch, gently manipulating Suzie's small breasts in her hands. More urgently now, Suzie pulled her own T-shirt over her head, exposing her naked breasts. Gently she drew Lucy's top over her head and unhooked her bra, then slid her jodhpurs down over her pert buttocks. Lucy shivered, suddenly aware of what she was doing, as she watched Suzie strip. The sight of Suzie, dark-haired and slim, in such contrast to Lucy's voluptuous curves, made Lucy go weak with desire.

She lay back on the bed and sighed as Suzie lay down beside her. She watched, spellbound, as Suzie's breasts crushed against hers and they kissed long and deep. Lucy felt probing fingers reach for the hot bud of her clitoris. The fingers moved, pushing harder and harder into her slickness. She moaned, aware that Suzie's lips were moving down her body, kissing, teasing, and licking, across her belly-button and down to the place that Lucy longed for her to be. She felt the expert tongue flick against the exposed nub, then the exquisite torture of her pussy lips being prised apart. Lucy writhed and squirmed with pleasure as Suzie's tongue plunged deeply into the wet warmth of her sex. She gave herself to the waves of sensation building in her, and cried out as she began to orgasm.

'Don't stop; don't stop.' There was no let-up in the insistent probing and Lucy called out again and again as her climax shuddered through her body.

She lay spent. She had never had such an amazing orgasm. So it was true. Only a woman knows what really pleases another woman.

As she lay on the bed, she watched lazily as Suzie opened another drawer in the chest.

'Now it's my turn,' she said, smiling.

Lucy sat bolt upright, her eyes widening as she saw Suzie strapping on a large black rubber dildo. It was not difficult to guess her intentions.

'Turn over and get on your hands and knees,' ordered Suzie.

Lucy obeyed and positioned herself in front of Suzie on the bed, her pussy and her tight round buttocks upturned and awaiting Suzie's attentions. The dildo was strapped around Suzie's hips and between her legs. Lucy could see it grinding on her clitoris as she moved.

As Suzie began to push the head of the huge dildo into Lucy's tight pussy, Lucy squirmed.

'It's so big,' she groaned, as Suzie invaded her from behind. Lucy had never been so completely and utterly filled, and she knew that Suzie was pushing the dildo in as far as it could go. The pain fought with the increasing pleasure as her breasts bounced with the continuing thrusts. Her pussy ached as the tremor of the coming explosion announced itself. She heard her voice begging, 'Fuck me, fuck me,' and Suzie responded, driving the rubber in deeper and deeper until Lucy orgasmed violently, spasming against the unforgiving black hardness.

Both women lay exhausted and spent on the bed. In their golden orgasmic mist, neither had heard the returning horsebox, nor the front door opening.

Tired horses had been unloaded and settled down for the night and Rod and Jim had come into the kitchen for a well-earnt coffee. The unmistakable sounds of sex coming from upstairs had, not surprisingly, attracted their attention.

Rod took the stairs two at a time, closely followed by Jim. Neither man could believe his eyes. The view was amazing. Suzie's back was towards the doorway, her boyish arse and pussy-lips spread wide from behind by the black straps of the dildo. Between her legs they could see the huge black dildo stretching Lucy's wet pink pussy as it pounded in and out.

Both men grew hard as they watched. Jim was the first to react, undoing his jeans, any embarrassment or reserve forgotten. He started fondling his cock, pulling the foreskin back and forth. He was hardly aware of Rod, whose hands had strayed down to his own hardening penis and achingly full balls.

As they greedily drank in the glorious sight of the two women satisfying each other, both men masturbated vigorously in the doorway.

What followed had to happen, Jim told himself later.

As the two women lay in their post orgasmic state, Jim started to pull off his clothes and bounded towards the bed. He was aware of Rod quickly following him. Neither woman had time to react as Jim flung himself on to Suzie and began fondling her breasts. Rod had joined in the tangle of bodies on the bed and was restraining Lucy, who was trying to get up. Both men were in a frenzy of lust: two hot hard pricks desperate for a pussy to fuck.

Jim gripped Suzie from behind and blindly poked at her. The strapping of the dildo created an easy entry and his prick slipped into the ready opening with the merest of friction. At first she fought but, as he pounded away, he knew she was his. His prick was large and insistent. He felt her stop fighting and push back against his hardness, aware that the dildo was grinding against the sensitive bud of her clitoris.

Lucy had managed to escape from Rod's clutches and was watching wide-eyed at the head of the bed. Rod had turned his attentions away from her and had begun to masturbate urgently, close to his wife's face. Lucy saw that Jim's movements behind Suzie were pushing her face closer to Rod's cock. She could see the temptation on Rod's face as he grasped the back of Suzie's head and pushed his prick between her willing lips. Lucy looked on with amazement at Suzie skewered between the two men, one in her mouth and the other in her pussy, both riding her in their different ways, and all three lost in their own selfish pleasure.

Unused to being left out, Lucy took a deep breath and dived in to join the action. She pulled Rod's cock out of Suzie's mouth and took him deep into her throat. His hands moved automatically around the back of her head and he held her there firmly.

Lucy's knees were spread for support, exposing her inner pussy lips and the sheen of wetness around the top of her thighs. Suzie reached for Lucy as she sucked greedily at Rod's prick. She manoeuvred forward and, with Jim still inside her, drove the black rubber dildo deep into Lucy's open pussy. Lucy gasped as Suzie entered her and she almost choked on Rod's prick as it was forced deeper into her throat with the thrust from behind.

They rode each other in a line, their movements coinciding for maximum pleasure.

Suzie was the first to climax, screaming out loudly.

Jim, with a pussy gripping his cock, could no longer resist and, groaning his orgasm, came violently.

As Suzie came, her own pleasure took over, and she could no longer keep the dildo inside Lucy. The slick black rubber slid out like a well-oiled truncheon.

Lucy, in pre-orgasmic throes, squealed in protest at the emptiness of her sex.

Rod saw his opportunity and pushed Lucy backward, lying on top of her, poking blindly at her wet open hole. His penis was too small and it slipped around inside her soaking cunt, the opening enlarged by the rubber which had filled her so well. He pulled out and lifted her legs up around his neck, forcing her to balance on her shoulders. His well-oiled prick poked urgently at the tight little rosebud of her anus. Holding her firmly, he pushed hard. The resistance of her virgin arse was deliciously tight around Rod's prick and he felt the spunk begin to rise immediately in his balls. Lucy fought and bucked like a bronco but Rod held her firmly with one hand, while the other competently manipulated the bud of her clitoris. He penetrated her deeply, groaning as Lucy's wriggling exaggerated the grip around his penis.

He felt Lucy begin to give herself up to the pleasure and pain as she allowed herself to be ridden roughly; fucked in the arse, while her clitoris sang with joy. As she moaned her orgasm, Rod could no longer control himself. He pulled out of Lucy's tight anus and spurted thick white semen over her stomach and breasts.

For a while there was an exhausted hush as their pulses returned to normal.

Suzie was the first to speak. 'Time to put the horses to bed, I think,' she said with a small embarrassed laugh.

Clothes were pulled on in silence, each person lost in their own thoughts and each hoping that there would be a next time.

Lucy got her way and Poeme remained at the yard. She alone rode and handled the horse, and jumped her to victory several times.

Priory Farm Stud grew in success and the winning team of Suzie and Rod and Lucy and Jim went from strength to strength both in the stable and the bedroom.

Lucy Lovegrove was a happy girl. She had been a happy baby, a happy child and now she was a happy young woman. Her general optimistic demeanour sprung from the knowledge that she was, indeed, a very lucky girl to be able to indulge in the two great loves of her life – sex and horses.

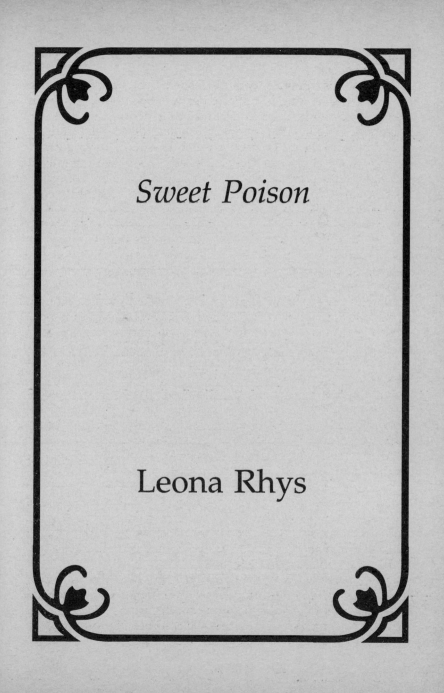

Sweet Poison

Leona Rhys

Sweet Poison

❖ ❖

She was walking near the woods looking for edible vegetation and berries; the snow was still melting on the ground and occasionally ripe flashes of cranberries and pink-orange salmon-berries peeked out from the dwindling clusters of snow. Her basket was far from full, but she still hesitated before entering the woods. The hush in the trees was whispering quiet as she picked her way through the bracken and the melting ice, searching for tell-tale bits of ferns she could dig for their coiled roots. She went on in this manner through the late afternoon woods, the sunlight hot against her neck; her feet were aching and wet from the cold. In some places the snow had melted entirely, leaving a damp flat tundra of grass tendrils and ripening moss. She thought she saw a clearing up ahead, so took a breath and continued deeper in the woods.

She did not expect to see what she found in the clearing: a dead young man lying on a bed of unseasonably green leaves. She walked closer, in her wonder forgetting her cold stinging feet and the gnawing in her stomach. The taut skin of his entire body was white but his hair shone red. His hair was the crimson of blood and currants. Past the pout of his lips and all the way to his waist flowed his hair. She wanted to touch his hair, eat it, swallow it down, rub herself in it. A beautiful man. As if still tensed with life, his cheeks were dimpled. His long eyelashes were strawberry-blond shadows against them; he looked as if he might raise his lids at any second. The early spring sunlight through the trees dappled the young man's face. A beautiful man. But he didn't breathe.

She drew still closer. She knew he was dead, but there was – yes, the wet of tears left upon his face; sweet poison was raining down from his eyes. It was poison that had killed him. She knew the signs and she could see them in his stiff limbs. On the green bed and near his lips, she noticed the broken shrub of mistletoe near his hand with its characteristic white berries. That had to have been it; that had to have been the poison. He lay prone – his face stilled into a smile despite his tears, the masses of his hair blowing in the forest breeze. The leaves were unspoilt green scallops around his bright body – like him, they looked to be hanging on to life's edges. It was poison that had killed him, and it felt like poison that ran trembling through her veins as she looked at his entire naked body.

And the whole of his body was perfect – his limbs, his cock, his neck and torso were all perfectly carved. A beautiful man. She dropped her basket and her spade. She bent her head down to kiss his cold lips, and she didn't feel the cold; she felt warmth, a warm current running through her, her cunt tightening. When she raised her head, she admired his nipples and their exquisite beauty on his bare chest. She bent her head down to gently suckle at one nipple and this time it was cold, ice-cold but soft against her tongue. She felt the brush of his hair against her neck. She drew back. She was as alone in the forest as she had been before, the birds still twittering in the trees. The sun beat down on the undergrowth, but there was no one but her and the young man there.

But she knew something had changed in the woods. There was a crackling around her but no source. She found herself breathing quickly; she listened to the trees, her senses heightened. There was a poison inside her. But by then the crackling had stopped and she heard nothing. She knew she ought to be heading back and her feet were beginning to ache again; she grew dizzy and light-headed. She looked down at the young man and again she felt the pulse inside her: she bent her head once more to his nipple and lightly sucked it. It turned hard in her mouth and she bit lightly at it before the implications of its rigidity hit her. She let her mouth release it and, though her heart quickened, without obvious haste she raised herself to face what was there. One of her hands remained on his bare smooth chest, and she felt the skin grow warm beneath her hand.

The young man had raised his lids. His eyes were green as the leaves on which he lay, and she was aware that he was observing her. Have I brought him back from the dead? she thought. But then the man reached for her; she closed her eyes and she felt him stick his tongue in her mouth. All of it, all that could fit deep in her mouth.

The lust that she felt was so heavy that her body reacted before her mind. Her mouth was sucking in his thickened tongue and pushing her own tongue under his before she was aware of it; her body had thrust her sex against his; her hands had taken his and pushed his hand under her shift, pushed his hand up inside her, where it was wet. Her sex had been drenched from the moment his thick tongue pushed between her lips. She wished his scarlet tongue were where his hand was, though at the same time she did not want it taken away from its wet swollen probing in her mouth. Stop, she thought, as his tongue traced circles in her mouth, painful circles she could feel all the way down in her groin. She wanted the young man to stick his tongue deep inside her, but this was impossible, she realised. Since the man does not live, she thought, as she felt him pushing her skirt up even higher over her hips.

She tore herself free and stared at him as they sat there on the leaves. A lovely venom was firing through her lower body but she told herself to calm down. Then he spoke; she hadn't expected that he would speak. His voice was low and came out slowly, but his words were precise. His expression was knowing. And, though his cock was thick and hard, he did not seem flustered in the slightest. She swallowed nervously; she felt sure she looked far less relaxed.

'You weren't supposed to kiss me; you got it wrong,' he said, tapping one finger against his dimpled cheek and looking at her, his eyes running down her body. The poison swam inside her. 'We'll have to change the story now, of course; it's not how it was meant to be. We'll say I kissed you instead.'

'But that's not what happened.' She looked around her, but in the woods there was only her and the pale red-haired man.

'But it will sound much better that way, won't it? You sleep lifeless in the woods, pale and beautiful, with the source of poison near your lips to indicate how your death occurred. Not the mistletoe no, that's too obvious. Something red and pretty, to match the colour on your lips. An apple. A poisoned red apple.'

'I would never eat a poisoned apple.' She stole an indirect look at his sex. His hair there grew tightly in copper curls. She wanted to finger and pull out the spirals.

'No?' His smirk told her he had seen her glance. 'But that's not how the story will be told. There will be a demure young woman in soft focus. Passive and soft and just your type – wandering through a picturesque woods. Someone will be jealous of you; someone always is. Do you understand jealousy? You'll be offered presents, secret gifts, bright apples as scarlet as my hair.' He touched himself where she wanted to touch him, buried his hand where her hand should be and stroked himself amid the soft curls. She understood jealousy. 'That's how the story will be told.' He got up lazily to lean against a tree, not bothering to stifle a yawn. He was irritatingly handsome with wicked eyes and, despite herself, she grew warm in the pit of her stomach.

She could already feel the poison. She felt her chest tighten and involuntarily her hands began to clench into fists. She was irritated. 'I'm the one who kissed you –' Her anger passed quickly and, as it abated, her voice softened. 'I woke you with a kiss, and touched your hair, and –'

'But that's not how it was meant to be.'

'And why not? All the tales I know have men smooching women they think are dead, and no one thinks anything of it and the story goes on from there and – how does it go on? Happily ever after?' she asked suddenly, both sullen and curious. Although she had been told them many times before, she couldn't remember how fairy tales were supposed to end.

'That's the last you ever hear of the couple, usually,' said the young man. 'I don't know about the happily ever after.' He raised one eyebrow and looked straight at her breasts until she began to feel uncomfortable.

'But you're dead,' she said. Her voice was abrupt. 'You were dead, weren't you?'

'Oh, bravo,' said the man. He stretched his body and rubbed his back against the bark of the tree. His hair rippled against the bark. Her mouth watered with poison. 'Give the girl a medal.'

'How did it happen?' she asked. Her insides were curling and extending, smooth like velvet. 'How did you die?'

He didn't meet her gaze. 'It wasn't how it was meant to be. Someone was jealous.' He twisted his red-gold hair in thought. 'And then I was offered poison. Beautiful mistletoe poison. And then I tasted it.' He fell silent.

'But that's practically the same story as the one you want to tell. Why do you want to change it?'

'Because it's not how the story is meant to be. There are important differences.' She turned away and picked up her half-full basket and spade to go, but the young man called to her. 'Isn't that right?' he said behind her. She turned round. He grinned at her and ran his eyes over her body, lingering between her legs.

She felt a hot slow flush begin to rise up through her body. 'No, it's not right. Not all the time,' she said. And then, more gently, 'But I could show you how it could be, if you want. I can kiss you, too.' She stepped forward and raked her fingers through the hang of his hair. 'I can kiss you; you don't always have to kiss me first. It doesn't always have to be like that.'

'Now you're teasing.' The beautiful young man smiled. 'But that's all right, that's how it's meant to be. You tease and seduce me; I take you when and if I feel like it.'

She gripped her basket harder. 'I'm just supposed to lie down in the snow and muck and let you have your way with me?'

The red-haired man smiled, his eyes glittering. 'That's why you're the one who should be kissed.'

'What type of person is kissed?'

'Oh, you know – pretty, soft, does what they're told.'

She came up behind him and dropped her basket and spade for the second time that afternoon. She pulled lightly on his hair; it flowed like warm ruby honey past his hips. She gripped him on both cheeks of his arse. She ran one finger over the tight flesh, and then ran it abruptly over the crack of his scarlet-ridged arsehole. She heard a moan from him, a very light moan, and then she knew what she was going to do. She reached around and felt each of his firm balls, weighing them almost gently in her palm, before she pushed him forward until he was on his hands and knees, bent before her. She heard him breathing heavily. She knew she was breathing heavily as well, but as her cunt throbbed she also knew she didn't care what she sounded like.

He, in any case, was silent now. She didn't know if this was how it was meant to be. But she was in it for her pleasure, so she ran another lingering hand across his slender masculine body and raised herself to walk around to face him. Her feet still ached in the slush, but she was beginning to enjoy the sensation – the constant stinging complemented her growing arousal nicely and was a delicious counterpoint. She faced the red-haired man again. His head was bowed, and she raised it up so he could look her in the eyes. She kissed him hard. The sugary poison lingered in her mouth. She was going to get what she wanted.

She let her gaze go down his whole body and his beautiful crimson hair again, just as his gaze had recently scraped over her. He watched her looking, and she read in his expression that it shamed and aroused him. She reached down and took hold of his cock. He was hard and he shook when she alternated a light pressing with a firm grip. She wasn't going to let him spill yet, though. She released his hard member and knelt in front of him, so that the tips of her breasts were more or less even with his eyes. Her legs were far apart as she knelt, and she slowly reached under her shift and reached up into herself, gripping herself hard. She didn't want this to be easy and soft, the kind of fuck he'd expect from the girl he thought she should be.

The eyes of the red-haired man glazed as he watched her touch herself, and she hitched her skirt up so he could see more clearly. She rolled her finger over the stiff and wet parts of her sex, enjoying the contrasts within her. Her finger lightly circled the little bud, until she grew so hot and trembling she made herself stop. She didn't want this to be over, not quite yet. She took her hand from her sex and thrust it in his mouth, and he sucked at her fingers so confidently and erotically that she felt half-tempted to test his skills elsewhere. But that wasn't what she had in mind for him, either.

'You like that?' she asked him. She removed her hand. 'Do I taste like I ought to?' He nodded, afraid to speak and break the spell of the woods. She had to feel herself quickly once more; she rubbed her hand once across her cunt and the feeling of sex rippled up through her. She could smell sex everywhere – on him and on her, and she didn't want to wait any more.

She walked with slow precision around behind the red-haired man; she didn't want to seem as if she were hurrying. She ran a hand under his body as she walked, from the sweat on his neck to his hard nipples, to the muscular furrow of his navel, all the way down to his hard cock. He was not insisting on keeping to the story now, she observed, and she felt both smug and horny. He didn't make a sound. She looked at him again from behind, the delicious sight of his splayed arse and the straining hollows of his hips. She pushed a finger up herself again and then spread her wetness over his hole, oiling his slender buttocks open for her and for her alone.

The moaning started again, but she realised it was her, this time. She couldn't wait to get started. He twitched forward and she gave him a light slap on one cheek. 'You're not coming before I do.' She picked up the spade from where she had dropped it previously and untwisted its wooden dowel-like handle, discarding the blade itself on the ground. The sun was even stronger on her neck and shoulders and she was beginning to think of it as an aphrodisiac. She could smell the ripe moss of the woods and she could smell the sex between her and the red-haired man.

She continued to make him wet with her own lubrication; she lavished his arsehole with her wetness. Then she reached forward and pressed on his upper back, so that he bent down with only his pretty arse in the air for her to feel and see. She stroked it admiringly several times, but then remembered exactly what her intentions were. She pushed the smooth dowel into his arse, and it was tight, so tight around the dowel that she felt her cunt tighten, too, as if the slick dowel were inside her as well. She gripped him by his hair and began fucking him slowly and, when he put his hand back to touch himself, she decided benevolently to let him. She liked the thought of him wanking while the smooth dowel entered and re-entered his arse, wet from her sex.

She made the dowel move slightly faster, and both she and the red-haired man were breathing heavily; they were in pace with each other. 'But I'm coming first, mind you,' she hissed at him and stopped the movement of the dowel momentarily as a little warning. He pushed himself back on to it. 'If you're wanting more,' she said, 'I'll do you with pleasure. Happily.' She still didn't move the dowel. But she knew in herself that his eagerness excited her, so she redoubled her efforts with the smooth wood, running her free hand through his beautiful hanging red-blond hair. 'Happily ever after,' she added, the tattoo beating a frenzy into him.

She couldn't wait; she pushed him flat on his stomach and climbed astride him. She mounted the protruding end of the dowel in his beautiful arse and rode it, circling her fingers hard through her slippery sex. She came and it was absolutely delicious; she gripped the waves of red-gold hair as it hit her, and she rolled into the boy, and all she saw was red and all she tasted was red and it was sweet poison in her body and she loved it.

She got up. She was staring at the prone body of a young man with long red-gold hair, lying on his back. Her unsevered spade was in her hand, along with her basket. The red-haired man lay calmly on a bed of green leaves as if waiting for someone to wake him with a kiss. She stroked his cheek and turned to go, but she bent to pick up a piece of a dark green plant with pearlised berries. She would have to leave the woods; it was going to be getting dark soon. But before she let the plant drop from her hand, she ran her tongue once along the edge of a single white berry and felt the tingling in her mouth. She knew it was poison, but it was so sweet. She wouldn't let its nectar get the better of her, though. That's not how it was meant to be.

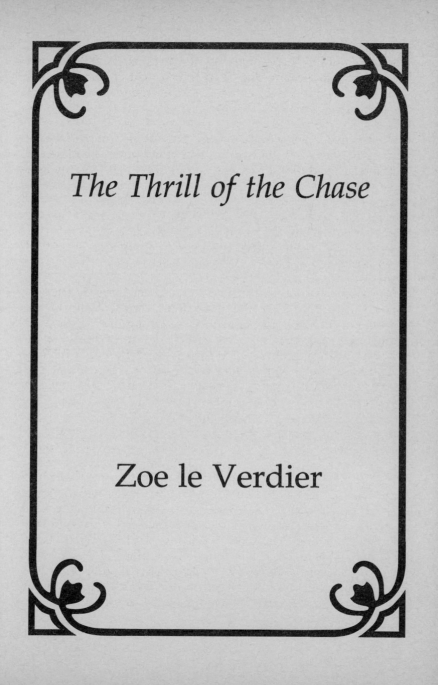

The Thrill of the Chase

Zoe le Verdier

The Thrill of the Chase

⸎ ⸎

H̲e wanted me the minute we met.

He turned to greet me and I saw it in his eyes, that flicker of surprise and hunger, quick as a snake's tongue. I sensed it in his body as he tensed almost imperceptibly, I read it in the curling corners of his mouth. I felt it in his hand as he shook mine, holding me in his grasp a moment too long. 'Pleased to meet you,' only takes two seconds. Another second, across the barrier between what we say and what we're really thinking, and it turns into something else; something far more primitive.

He wanted me, but I didn't want him.

It was my eyes that did it, I knew. My jaw-length straight hair is a nondescript brown, my lips are thin and my nose slightly Roman. But my eyes are fantastic. They're large, sometimes grey, sometimes blue, and framed with long dark lashes that reach my eyebrows when I frown. The irises are rimmed with a thick dark blue circle and, for some reason, my pupils are always dilated wider than is normal. Perhaps it's this, and this alone, that attracts people to me. Maybe they take this natural phenomenon as a subconscious signal that I like them more than I do – I'm not sure. But the feeling I get when I look at someone and they look back, and I hook their gaze and reel them in – that feeling is like the moment when a man slides down your body to your pussy and he parts your legs and you realise he's going to do what you wanted him to. And you didn't even have to ask – he wants to do it.

During my first weeks in the job, I met other men in the office who wanted me, but none as immediately and obviously as he did. He made no attempt to disguise his leer as I walked past his desk, his dark eyes burning holes in my back. I bought a short black skirt which I wore with stockings and I tormented him as he sat on the edge of my desk, crossing my legs high up to give him a tiny flash of pale thigh above the lacy stocking top. I loved to see him squirm. I began going to work without any knickers on, hoping that he would be able to tell by the glimmer of abandon in my eyes. I longed for summer, when I could wear skimpy dresses with no bra. He would be able to trace the edges of my breasts with his gaze, and he would see my nipples stiffen under his stare.

I didn't want him, but I wanted him to want me.

He flattered me, and I savoured his attention selfishly, like a bar of expensive chocolate scoffed in private. He was one of those men who loves women: they're called 'lads', these days, but they're just blokes who aren't afraid to be politically incorrect, to voice their lewd thoughts. Attention from a man like that is like a soft drug or a cigarette when you haven't had one for a long time: an instant, easy rush. Heady. Strong.

I heard him talking about me in the office kitchen as I stood outside, pretending to read the noticeboard. He said I had a gorgeous arse and a flush began at my neck as I imagined him fucking me from behind, his hands gripping my flesh and lasciviously parting my cheeks, his eyes feasting greedily on my tightly closed hole. But I didn't want him.

He was married, and I wasn't at all jealous of his wife. I met her several times at the office and I liked her laid-back manner. She knew her husband was an incorrigible flirt, and she didn't care. I like that in a woman – that happy self-assurance that comes when she expects nothing from her man. It takes many fine layers of confidence, built up gradually over time, to be that easy-going.

I didn't want him, but I began to enjoy the job. Every morning when the alarm went at seven, I'd curse and cocoon myself deeper under the covers: and then I'd remember that he would be there and I'd be wide awake, a tiny flitter of excitement like a hummingbird's tongue darting at my heart. Travelling into work on the tube, I'd watch myself in the black window as the train shuddered through the tunnels, my eyes smiling at my reflection as I jumped about in my bumpy Northern Line seat, and I'd imagine sitting on his lap with his cock inside me, letting the train's violent motion judder me up and down until he came loudly in front of all the bored businessmen, who wouldn't dare look up from their newspapers. At work, I couldn't see him from my desk but I could sense him; I could hear his voice and I laughed secretly at his vicious jokes, and he never knew whether I found them funny or not, but I did. And yet I didn't want him.

October, November, December. The Christmas party. Waking quickly, I poked my head out from beneath the covers and tasted the day, sickly with anticipation. Office parties are compressed with tension, the underlying sexual tension that filters through all workplaces like a soft gas in the air conditioning: all-pervading, creeping, the lustful yearnings of the year bubbling and simmering just beneath the surface of polite convention, until, with a resounding pop, someone breaks the skin that separates work from play – they light a joint, or kiss someone – and there we are, exposed, our guard dropped, more than just colleagues. He would want me intensely today. I dressed to please both of us, all in black: stockings, suspenders, G-string, push-up bra, a short dress that clung slightly – only slightly – in all the right places. The routine of getting ready – touching myself, business-like – aroused me. I turned my back to the mirror and looked over my shoulder. He would want my arse today.

But I still didn't want him.

Champagne and speeches at eleven, and he watched as the bubbles fizzed down my throat and gave me a faint headache. A procession of taxis to the restaurant and he sat opposite me and I talked to the woman next to me, ignoring him but intensely, insanely aware of his feet touching the tips of my shoes. Sitting at the table, he was opposite and to the left and it couldn't have been better – he had my best profile. He stared openly, and I talked and laughed, and every movement was for him.

I did not want him, but I loved that he wanted me.

He offered me a cigarette and he half stood and leant over to give me a light. His gaze fluttered over my cleavage and then I looked into his eyes to thank him. My fingers held the cigarette languidly as my lips closed around the filter and I pulled deeply. As I swallowed the stream of sharp smoke I closed my lips, then opened them in slow motion, as if my mouth were being filmed in black and white close-up and he was my audience, and I let the remains of smoke wisp and curl like a lazy come-on in his direction. Southern Comfort, its taste a sweet distraction from the bitter tobacco, pushed the dull champagne ache away and replaced it with a dazed euphoria. He watched and wanted me as my tongue slithered at the corner of my mouth and I ran my finger over my bottom lip.

Was that too corny? Maybe. I touched my neck and turned my head away and blinked slowly, feigning boredom. I assumed a tired look; a look that said the company was tedious and the conversation annoying, an unnecessary overture, and that at any moment I might lose patience with it all and pull someone up on to the table and fuck them right there, in front of everyone, because that was the sort of woman I was – impulsive, highly charged, on the brink of sexual abandonment. I looked at him as I moved a hand beneath the table and felt the satin of my naked inner thigh above a stocking top. He wanted me. I was wet between my legs. He wanted me. I lightly teased my clit with my sharp thumbnail and I looked at him, and he wanted me.

But I didn't want him.

After the meal, on to a trendy Soho pub for the hardy few who either had nothing to go home to, or didn't want to return to whatever was at home just yet. I sat with my back to the wall and listened as the conversation turned to sex. A young, overly earnest woman I'd never spoken to before was talking to me. I was so drunk I couldn't reply to her questions; alcohol answered from a strange distant land at the back of my head. My eyes deserted me and became someone else's – I was just borrowing them to look through. Her voice became a bee as she droned, and I scanned the heaving smoke-filled space to find him.

He was stood at the bar, buying a round, wanting me. I could see it in his eyes: impatient, ravenous. I sensed it in his body as he coiled himself, ready to spring. I read it in his mouth as he involuntarily licked his lips. I felt it in his fingers, touching *me* as he traced smooth elliptical circles on the sticky wooden bar while he waited.

He wanted me, but I didn't want him.

And then he was gone. He was back from the bar, he was sitting next to me, but he wasn't there. His back was turned, he was talking to another woman – a plain woman with freckles and large breasts. The pub went silent and, with alarming clarity, I heard only their voices. He was talking dirty. She was looking shocked. Giggling. Blushing. Laughing with her head thrown back and her white breasts jiggling under her low-cut cheap blouse. He was leaning closer to her, whispering now, smirking, sneering. She was touching her hair, shifting in her seat to face him, running a finger coyly around the edge of her glass. He was offering her a cigarette, lighting it for her, watching her. They were animals, baring their teeth, preening their feathers, fanning their tails.

He wanted her.

I wanted him.

She got up to go to the toilet and he turned to find raw aggression in my eyes.

'So you like to talk dirty?'

Half his mouth and one dark eye smiled. 'Yes. It gets me hot.'

I raised an eyebrow in contempt. 'Does *she* get you hot?'

'No.' He leant so close I could smell him. His breath was warm on my neck. 'Looking at you gets me hot,' he whispered. 'I'm dying to fuck you.'

The woman came back and tried to reclaim her conversation with him. But he was ignoring her now, and staring at me. Unflinching, I stared back. Disconcerted, the woman stammered and stuttered and tried to cover up the sexual tension which was smothering her.

He stood up. Without bothering to lower his voice, he said, 'I'm leaving. Are you coming?'

I shrugged, trying not to look too keen. My heart was racing so quickly I felt it in my throat.

'I'll wait outside while you make up your mind,' he said. 'Five minutes. Then I'm going home.'

I sipped my drink, taking four minutes fifty seconds, then went out into the thin sharp December.

He was gone. Shit. *Fuck.*

I walked around the corner and he pulled me into a doorway and tight against his body. We glared at each other for a moment, our eyes hard, hateful in our lust. Then he kissed me: a harsh kiss with the full force of a punch in the kidneys. Our lips crushed together. I felt the bones of his face against mine. His breath, hot and quick in my mouth, tasted of rum and tobacco. His tongue thrust its way between my lips, twisting with my tongue in a slippery, desperate wrestle. As we kissed and kissed and kissed, I took in other sensations and felt his powerful grip on my shoulders; I felt the muscles in his thick neck straining under my touch; felt the twitching hardness in his trousers pressing at my groin. His tongue stopped its exploration and he began to suck and bite on my lower lip, nibbling like a small, sharp-toothed fish, harder and then too hard, and as the pain became sharp I pushed him away.

'Bastard,' I snarled, touching my lip. 'You hurt me.'

'Please,' he said, desperate. 'Please ... you're driving me insane. Suck me.'

We swapped places and he stood with his back to the unlit street and a hand either side of the doorway as I slid down to a kneel. I unzipped his trousers and prised his cock out from between the folds of warm crumpled cotton. It unfurled before me, springing slightly as I touched it. My lips were wet with our saliva as I gripped the base firmly and my other hand delved for his balls, hairy and damp. My alcohol-soaked tongue traced the bulging vein that ran along his length and I breathed in deeply, inhaling his musty odour until it filled my lungs, coursed through my veins, traversed the electrically charged nerve-endings that sent scorching signals throughout my body.

I lapped the tiny bead of moisture seeping from his prick then sucked the purple head, my tongue flicking frenziedly as he grunted above me. With a thrust of his hips, his tender hardness reached the back of my throat, and I fought the desire to gag and I let him thrust. I tried to moan acquiescence, but there was no room in my mouth for sound – barely room for my tongue to lick and flicker. I sucked hard and squeezed his penis tightly at its wide base. I grasped his taut testicles and relaxed my throat to let him in deeper, my jaw aching sharply as I struggled to take his thick, fat meat inside. He came quickly, shuddering, moaning like a slowly dying animal as his salt slime filled my mouth and slithered down my throat, and I laughed to see him spent. Men are so easily pleased. A trail of his silver come dribbled down my chin.

He pulled me up and licked the juice away, tasting my mouth and claiming some of his come back before I could swallow it all.

'Jesus Christ, I want you.'

He didn't have to tell me that.

'I want to smell you, and taste you, and fuck you till you come, you horny bitch. It's been driving me wild, watching you at work all day then going home to my wife.'

We were the same height, and I held his eyes with mine and put my hands to his close-cropped black hair and enjoyed his shaven velvet neck.

He wanted me, and I wanted him.

He slid a hand under the hem of my dress and it went straight to my crotch. He pinched my pussy-lips together beneath the thin gauze of my knickers, as if he needed me tightly closed before he could savour his infiltration. He traced the edges of the material between my legs and up to my hip-bones, then he slid his palm beneath the material and cupped my mound, his other hand clawing at my shoulder as if to stop me from running away. A fat finger slid inside me, then another, and they hooked and twisted and explored as my inner flesh gripped him. I moaned but didn't close my eyes, and we stared at each other; contemptuous, challenging. He fingered me hard, the heel of his hand rubbing my clit until it felt like his whole arm was inside me and he was scratching the soft base of my brain and his elbow was in my guts. With a soft slurp his hand was gone and he was sniffing his glistening fingers and tasting me on his skin.

'You smell fantastic. You taste fucking fantastic.'

I grabbed his wrist and sucked his fingers, rolling my tongue around them, watching his eyes glinting, mixing my musky juice with his semen. We tasted of lust: dark, dirty, frantic.

Slow footsteps. A policeman. My lover took my hand and we stepped out of the shadows and found a taxi. I didn't hear his instructions, but I didn't care where we went. He wanted me, and I wanted him.

I didn't let him touch me in the taxi. We just looked at each other. I wanted to wait, to delay our abandon until we got wherever we were going. I savoured that journey – the last time we would flirt with our eyes, the last time he would imagine what my breasts looked like, what my arse looked like, the last time I'd wonder how he would fuck me. After tonight, we'd know.

The taxi stopped at our office. Of course. We'd met there, flirted there. He'd fantasised about me there: about taking me on my desk, on his desk, in the toilets. That was where he'd first wanted me.

We took the stairs two at a time in the dark, everywhere dark until we got to his desk which he cleared, turning on a small lamp that made the polished wood glow and lit up one side of his face.

'I've wanted you for so long,' he said, making it sound like a warning: as if the months we'd spent flirting had built up inside him like a dangerous gas, and he wasn't to be held responsible for the consequences.

He pulled me close again. He kissed and bit my neck and cupped and squeezed my swollen breasts. He moved his hands down over my waist and hips. He ruffled up the soft fabric at my thighs and his warm hands were grappling my buttocks, gratified to find them naked. Grabbing the thin strands of elastic at my hips, he pulled my G-string up, up until it rubbed the slit that ran from front to back, making me jolt and roll my pelvis back and forward, back and forward on the wet string that teased and bit into my flesh: a swinging tightrope between pleasure and pain. His hands came back to my waist and he lifted me up to stand on his desk. I fondled my breasts as he flashed cold steel at my hips and, with two swift cuts, he whipped away the wet rag from between my legs. I held up the skirt of my dress and he stared and stared like a hungry child. He held the heels of my shoes and licked my stockings, over my high insteps, my calves and up to my bare, inner thighs. He lapped each silky inner leg in turn and then his hands snatched at my hips and he pulled me hard into his face and parted my folded crimson lips with his tongue and licked the hidden surfaces. I stood with my legs wide apart and held on to his head as he lapped like a dog, opening me to him, and then he was squirming and poking deep inside me. He licked and bit and sucked and I gyrated to his rhythm, grinding into his face, three of his fingers inside me and, like a maniac surfer, I rode the crest of the orgasm that waved through my stomach and across my back and washed my brain.

My legs gave way and I fell. The hardness knocked my spine and my hungry pussy oozed and throbbed as I watched him undress. Then he was over me, shifting me into a sitting position with my legs dangling at the edge of his desk. He pulled my dress off – left my stockings and suspenders on, a dark surround to pale skin and curling wet hair. For a moment he slowed, and his fingers became soft as he caressed the curves of my cleavage, and brushed the dark areolae peering above the lace of my bra. He scooped inside the warm cups, lifting my breasts out so they poised, like delicate fruit, above their crumpled black cage. I flicked off my bra and they were free, and he buried his head between them and licked and fondled and nibbled and pinched my hard nipples as I held his shoulders and felt the sweat there.

He pushed me on to my back and lifted my legs, and my feet were on his neck. I felt the satin tip of his thick penis prodding between my lips, thudding against my clit on its way and making my neck muscles jump. And then he was inside me and I expanded to take him and contracted to keep him there. His eyes were dark cocks, violating me, and mine were greedy cunts, drawing him ever deeper. He gripped my breasts as leverage, tweaking their tips as he slowly withdrew to his tip and then hard, hard forward and I swallowed him in. Again and again, slowly, slowly out and hard, quick, deep in, pausing there to pulse inside me and feel me close around him, and then slowly out once more.

I wanted to feel his cock impale me, tear me in half, rip through my womb, my guts, my lungs and force itself into my mind. I wanted to open myself wide to him, turn myself inside out so that he could fuck my raw and bloody innards.

He wanted me. I wanted him so much it hurt.

As he began plunging quickly, my hips jerked up to meet him

and bring him further and further inside me. His hands were in spasm at my breasts as his buttocks clenched and drove. I reached down and felt the wet spot where he entered me with one hand, delighting in the lusty movement, and my other hand went to my clit and two fingers circled the hard knob of flesh, and fire flicked within. Harder, harder, harder, push deeper, rip me apart, fuck me, fuck me, fuck me . . . oh, *fuck*.

He juddered and held me still, spurting inside my clutching cunt as I drank him in. He muttered and burbled and I sighed, fingernails making dents in his glittering biceps as every muscle in his body contracted, and every muscle in my body relaxed.

He was out and his come was dribbling down my thighs; I felt clammy patches on my stockings. He flipped me over, face down on the desk, my breasts crushed beneath me, my feet on the floor, my legs wide apart; as wide as they could go. While he regained his strength he collected his come from my open snatch and lubricated the tightly closed flower of my arsehole, circling and prodding until I yielded and sucked his finger inside. Oh, God, that feeling: my moans were loud and wide. Fill me up. His touch was extreme, his thumb on my throbbing clit again; Oh, God, it's too much. He tormented and tortured, one hand working, kneading, one hand stroking my back, the sweat running down my spine. Then he was ready and he held my hips firm, stopping me from wriggling to search out his cock and it was there, pressing, pressing and then – Jesus, fuck – he was in. Sparks flew behind my eyes; my face was turned to one side and crushed to the cool wood, my hands were on my breasts as they were pushed and jiggled. His cock was so fat. The pleasure, the pain; oh, Christ, I'm coming. Oh, shit, I can't take it. Please stop, don't stop, slow down. He was shafting me quickly and it was amazing. My clit was humming, his fingers were in my juicy cunt. My body surrendered, I relented, he plunged. I came. I was crying. I always cry when I come that violently.

He collapsed on top of me, holding me, caressing my sides, stroking my hair. A flicker of stubble grazed my neck. He whispered, 'Jesus, you're amazing.'

* * *

On Monday, at work, he waited for me outside the ladies' toilet. When I emerged, he pushed me back inside and locked the door. He kissed me, and put his hand up my skirt.

'I missed you,' he sighed, gushing his hot breath into my ear. 'I've got to see you again. I've got to ... I can't stop thinking about you. Oh, God,' he groaned, as he discovered I didn't have any knickers on.

'I'd risk my marriage for you,' he said proudly, as if he were offering something irresistible.

He slid a finger inside me. 'Jesus ... Oh, Jesus ... I want you.' But I didn't want him. Not any more.

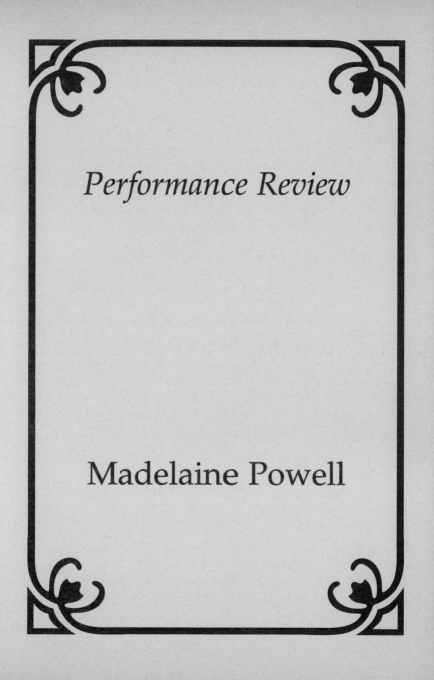

Performance Review

Madelaine Powell

Performance Review

❖ ❖

*S*ir,
   Further to my previous memo I have outlined below the
events of my performance review for your records.

   You suggested meeting the following day at a local hotel for
lunch to outline your expectations of my performance, and
assess whether I had exceeded, met or fallen below those targets.
You handed me the list of the key areas that were to be
measured. They ran as follows:

1. Time-keeping
2. Presentation skills
3. Ability to work on own initiative
4. Anticipation and appropriate reaction to needs of manager
   and subordinates
5. Good knowledge of equipment
6. Flexibility
7. Organisation skills

That evening, I pondered on how I would present and commu-
nicate the way I felt I performed in each area. In my experience
of working for you, I knew that you liked to handle situations in
a direct way, and always demanded facts and convincing dem-
onstration to back up opinions. With this, and each key result in
mind, I formulated a plan.

The next morning, I rose early to prepare for our meeting at midday. You had a prior engagement at the hotel and it was decided that you would wait for me in the restaurant. I booked a table, ensuring that it was situated in a booth to one side. This would offer us a little privacy for our discussion.

Laid out before me on the bed were the basic ingredients of my presentation – a bright red basque and suspender belt, black seamed stockings, black net gloves and a pair of high-heeled shiny stiletto shoes, finished off with a long strawberry-blonde wig. I decided on a rhinestone-studded necklace to round off the outfit.

Just as I was adding the last detail to my preparations, a knock at the door announced the arrival of my cab. Knowing we would drink over lunch, you offered the services of the company chauffeur; declining the offer, I decided on a cab. With a final check in the mirror I covered the creation with a knee-length black belted mac and made my way downstairs.

Sitting in the back of the car, I flicked open a hinged handbag mirror to check that the bright red lipstick and dark eye make-up had not smudged. I made sure the fringe of the wig partly covered my eyes and its long strands fell either side of my face and along the front of my mac. The effect was startling against the black material: so different to my natural dark-brown hair. Satisfied with my presentation skills I pondered on your reaction to the other key areas.

Once we arrived at the hotel I made my way into the Ladies' room to check that everything was in place. I was conscious of several pairs of eyes following in my wake. Then I crossed the foyer of the reception area to the entrance of the fish restaurant. I could see you sitting at the table, and noticed that you glanced up appreciatively for a moment before returning your attention to the papers in front of you. It was obvious that you did not recognise me. The maître d' had also spotted me as I entered and now approached. I explained I was here to meet you and then, much to my amusement, he asked if he could take my coat. I declined politely, trying not to laugh as I thought of his surprise if I had agreed. I watched intently as he then made his way over to you. You were never one to lose your cool, but I was delighted with your look of startled puzzlement as the maître d' pointed my way and then, after a few moments' consideration, your nod of assent.

The clock on the wall behind you chimed in time with my footsteps as I made my way across the room. Slipping into the seat opposite you, I crossed my legs, letting my ankle protrude from beneath the tablecloth. I could almost hear your mind working on the problem facing you. Lowering my false eyelashes demurely, I stared at your large fingers wrapped around a glass of whisky, a drop of which had dribbled down the glass and was slowly forming a damp patch on the starched tablecloth. Swinging my leg up and down, and pouting my red painted lips, I said, 'Well, shall we eat now or later?'

My voice confirmed my identity.

A bit of lace that edged the basque I was wearing began to scratch the skin on my left buttock as I moved my leg. As I wriggled to make myself more comfortable, I noticed you shift slightly on your seat. The objective of my plan was obviously succeeding.

'I will decide when and what we eat,' you replied.

Opening my eyes as wide as possible, I said, 'Of course, anything you say.'

From the look you shot at me, I knew that you suspected otherwise and that you were working as hard as possible to regain control of the situation. I let my leg fall under the table, placing it so my knee bumped against yours. At the same time, I brushed the top button of my mac which opened to reveal the top of the red basque.

I think I deserve an A for timing, I thought, as you inhaled sharply. Your pupils expanded and retracted like the lens of a camera as it captured the sight of my large breasts bulging from its restraints.

'Oops,' I said innocently, 'it's that top button again. I can never get it to stay done up.' I fiddled at it with my red-painted fingernails. You shifted in your seat again.

'I seem to have lost my appetite . . . for food, that is,' you said after a long pause.

Got you, I thought. Now it's time to reel in the rod.

Pulling at the collar of my mac, I said demurely, 'Well, I do know another place to review a few essential key areas.'

You kept your eyes on the button of my mac, straining to contain the situation as I stood up. The confused maître d' could do nothing as he was filleting a fish for another client at the time.

I felt your eyes on my backside as we sauntered across the large reception. Several people glanced our way and I smiled at the image of you holding your coat in front of you as you followed. I fiddled with the plastic room-key in my mac pocket.

One of my long false nails clacked against the plastic surround of the call button and the lift doors opened immediately. I stepped inside and turned to face you waiting to enter. With the third key area in mind, I grasped your standard red dotted silk tie and pulled you towards me. The lift doors clanged shut as my back hit the wall. I could feel the bulge in your trousers through the thickness of my coat. You were pushing so hard against me, I could feel my breasts nearly bursting from the basque. Your large fingers struggled with the knot in the belt of my mac.

Determined that we should reach our destination before you could undress me, but unable to reach the button with my hand, I lifted my leg. This movement caused your hands to work even faster. With surprising precision, I managed to stab at the appropriate floor number with the tip of my shoe. The bulge in your trousers was now resting neatly between my legs. The lift shuddered as it started to rise.

Just as the belt gave way and the front of my coat started to open, so did the doors of the lift. The sound of voices made you pull away quickly. As you turned round, I quickly straightened my clothes. Pushing past you, I said, 'This way, please,' and smiled sweetly at the small group of people waiting to enter. I flicked a long blonde strand of hair over my shoulder and then punched the plastic key into the lock. A loud click reverberated along the corridor and I pushed open the door.

I had booked a suite consisting of two large rooms. The first was furnished with a mahogany conference table and chairs with a bar and settee in one corner. Heavy velvet curtains hung at the windows. A double door to one side led to the second room. A king-size bed framed in a dark wood four-poster bedstead filled most of the room. The en suite bathroom featured a Victorian bath and separate shower room. Our feet sank into the thick carpet as we entered.

To demonstrate my skills with the key area number four, I had ordered a bottle of your favourite whisky, which stood with a cut glass decanter on the bar. I hoped that the other items I requested were also ready and waiting.

'Please make yourself comfortable while I arrange the paperwork for my review,' I said, pointing to the sofa, while I poured a glass of whisky. The walk along the corridor had sobered you up a little and you reluctantly did as you were bid. Undoing the top button of your shirt and loosening your tie a little, you accepted the proffered glass.

I went over to where you had placed your briefcase on the table. Clicking it open, I took out the few sheets of paper that you had prepared, one for each key area. Glancing at the comments with space for your final assessment, I spread them carefully over the table, making sure to stretch over the edge of the table. You watched intently. Every time I leant over, I noticed your legs widen a little. Your hand, which was resting on your thigh, moved upward a few centimetres each time you shifted position.

I took my time arranging the items until I knew you were on the edge of your endurance. Just as you quickly swallowed down the last of the whisky I said, 'Well, I think we are ready now. If you would like to sit here, I will just go and take off my coat.'

I pulled one of the chairs away from the table. It faced the double doors to the bedroom. As I disappeared into the bedroom, I saw you take off your jacket and hang it on the back of the chair. You had just sat down as I pushed the door shut.

Standing in front of a full-length mirror in the bedroom, I carefully straightened the seam of my stockings and ruffled up the lace on the edge of the red silk basque, adjusting the top to emphasise my generous cleavage. A quick glance in the mirror behind showed how the outfit gave me an hour-glass figure, my waist being pulled in by the laces that ran down the back of the basque. The rhinestone necklace glittered in the subdued light, highlighting the reddish blonde shine of the wig which lay over my shoulders and rested on the hill of my breasts. A quick daub of red lipstick and I was ready. Taking hold of the brass handle of one of the double doors, I opened it. Framed in the doorway, with the light behind me, I knew I must look stunning. This presumption was confirmed by the way your hand flew to the zip of your trousers as you stared, dumbfounded.

Before you could bring yourself to comment I said, 'Well, I think it's about time to review my key areas.'

I approached you slowly, placing one leg seductively in front of the other, with my hands resting on the exaggerated curve of my waist. You were sitting with your legs apart. Coming to a halt in front of you, I placed the tip of one of my red stiletto shoes on to the cushion. Staring at my foot between your legs, your eyes followed the shine of my stockings up along my shapely calves, over my knee and up my thigh to the clip of my suspender belt.

As your gaze continued to climb I gradually let my leg fall to one side. The sideways smile of my crotchless knickers met your delighted grin. Still with my foot on the cushion of the seat, I leant forward. Taking your hand from between your legs, I placed it on the arm of the chair. Your fingers gripped the wood as mine started to undo your belt. You watched my red finger-nails intently as they worked easily and efficiently. As I slowly pulled down the zip and released its bulging contents, I knew I would achieve a high mark for key area number five.

The long strands of my blond wig tickled you as I leant further forward to take hold of your equipment. Gripping it firmly, I stepped back. Having no choice but to follow, you stood up. Your trousers fell to your ankles. You had to shuffle as I turned you to face me with your back to the table. Your cock throbbed as I pushed you back on to the slippery surface. You were now sitting on the edge of the table with your legs dangling. I knelt slowly between your legs. You let out a cry as I placed my lips around you. As I worked, I undid the laces of your shoes and slipped them off, along with your trousers and underwear, leaving you in your shirt, tie and socks.

Glancing upward, I saw you staring down at the top of my blonde head between your legs. A red lipstick stain circled your cock, which was now disappearing and reappearing in a regular pattern. Not letting you go, I carefully stood up and pushed you gently back on to the table. Unable to speak, I put my hand between your legs, encouraging you to slide along the polished wood until I could kneel on the table between your legs, with my cleavage framing the scene.

I worked until I was sure I would get ten out of ten. At the appropriate stage of the exercise, I pulled away, leaving you hard and erect. Pushing my bottom as far up as I could in my kneeling position, I crawled upward, delighting in the feel of your hardness pressing against my breasts and stomach, until I stopped with it pointing upward between my legs.

My cleavage was now resting just above your mouth. Unable to contain yourself, you reached for the two proffered mounds, pulling at the red ribbon that held them securely in their containers. With a sharp tug you released them, and their contents spilt out, flicking their hardened nipples over your eagerly waiting mouth. As you continued to suckle at my breasts, which nearly covered your mouth and nose, I positioned your cock between the split in my knickers. Then I lowered myself carefully on to you until the whole length of you was inside me. You let go of my breasts for a moment as you gasped in appreciation.

I took the opportunity to sit up, pinioned on your cock. You tried to sit up to nibble my nipples again, but I pushed you down. As I sat up, my breasts rested on the frame of the basque, pushing their fullness up and pointing the large nipples towards you like a double-barrelled shotgun. Around your head lay your carefully prepared sheets of paper. Sitting comfortably with you lying underneath me, I picked up the first of the reviews. I had taken your thick fountain pen from your briefcase. With this between my fingers and your cock between my legs, I started to read the written points out loud.

As I read, I moved my hips, gradually getting faster and faster with each meticulously numbered paragraph. As we reached the final section, left blank for comments and a grade, I stopped with your pen poised.

'Don't stop,' you gasped.

'So, what mark do I get for time-keeping?' I asked, gripping the muscles that held you between my legs.

'Top marks . . . just don't stop!' you replied.

A drop of ink fell from between the gold-plated groove of the nib as I went to write in your comments. To demonstrate my agreement with your decision, I recommenced.

In this way I read out and marked in your comments on each of the first five key areas. Very pleased with the review so far, we came to number six – flexibility. At this point, I knew that the session would be coming to a head any time. With this in mind, I lifted myself carefully upward until I was just gripping the head of your cock. Frustration, mixed with curiosity, flickered in your eyes as you watched me lean forward again until I was on all fours. With practised precision I slowly rotated my body until I faced away from you with my head between your knees.

As you devoured this new presentation of my key areas, I lowered myself again until you filled me completely again. The stiletto heels of my shoes rested against your ears as I took up the sixth piece of paper. The rhythm of my hips rose and fell in time with my voice as I read out the next four paragraphs of comments. I felt your hands gripping the cheeks of my bottom stretched out before you, the tension in your fingers kneading the flesh harder and harder as your excitement grew. In this way, you assisted in finalising this particular session. Unfortunately, this happened before I was able to commit you to a grade out of ten but, from the volume and tone of your unintelligible comments, I took the initiative and gave myself top marks again. The urgency of your final movements shook my hand as I wrote, causing the ink to spurt and leave splodges on the paper. Although it was untidy, I thought it a fitting comment on my performance.

As your cries of pleasure died down and I felt you slowly soften between my legs, I took the opportunity to gather up the various pieces of paper, placing the final one on top. Satisfied that we had covered all the points, I slid off the table. Going over to your briefcase, I placed the papers back into the folder with your pen, which I had wiped clean before replacing the cap.

You moved to sit up with your bare legs dangling over the edge of the table. I could see the heightened colour of your neck resting against the immaculately starched collar of your business shirt and tie. These were still looking as crisp and neat as ever, except for the very end of your tie, which was now dangling in the moistened skin at the base of your stomach. I made a mental note to find you a dry-cleaning voucher.

Aware that you were looking at me, I smiled, the folder of reviews still clutched in my hand.

'Put the file in my briefcase and bring it into the bedroom,' you said suddenly, cutting into the thickness of the atmosphere that now surrounded us.

Your air of command was quite impressive, considering you were now standing before me in only your shirt, tie and socks. I wondered at the rather incongruous picture I must have made as I picked up the heavy black leather case and walked past you as demurely as possible in my red basque and stiletto shoes. Maybe this could be a start of a new image for the office, I mused, pushing open the double doors that led into the bedroom.

'Put the briefcase on the bed; I'll be back in a few moments,' you said, making your way into the en suite bathroom.

Doing as I was bid, I was checking my lipstick for smudges when you suddenly re-emerged, totally naked except for your tie which lay loosely around your neck. I felt the flush of heat between my legs get even hotter as I now saw your naked body looming large before me.

Without taking your eyes off me you pulled the tie from round your neck. 'Turn around!' was your next command.

My heart fluttered as I felt your body heat against my back. You were standing so close, the hairs on your upper thighs tickled the partly bared cheek of my bottom. Telling me, 'Put your hands behind your back – now!' you secured them with the tie. Then, turning me to face you, you left me standing while you lay down on the bed.

'Come over here,' you commanded quietly, flicking open the briefcase.

I stood obediently beside the bed while you glanced through each page of notes.

'Well, you obviously perform well in the individual categories. While I consider what overall mark you deserve, let's see the amount of rise you are able to achieve, even with your hands tied.'

The look in your eye gave me no choice but to obey, and I climbed carefully on to the bed beside you. You watched me intently as I balanced myself in order to tip forward at right angles to your body. I knew you would enjoy this particular approach to the situation and so raised my bottom as high as possible into the air as I leant over. My breasts spilt over the top of the basque, rubbing the hardened nipples on your thigh. I sidled up the bed until my breasts cushioned your cock between them, then I sat back on my heels. The split crotch of the basque was straining and pulling between my buttocks, making the ruffles around the edge stand to attention like the skirts of a ballerina's tutu.

As my lips approached your cock, it jumped slightly in anticipation. It jumped even higher as my lips closed around you, leaving another smear of red lipstick around its base. You called out in appreciation as my tongue went to work and even I was impressed at how quickly I achieved a rather outstanding rise.

Warming to my challenge now, I glanced up at your face over the hill of too many business lunches. You were looking again at the comments that I had penned, their contents making you clutch at your generously proportioned balls. I noticed that your cock hardened still further with each page that you turned. I knew when you read something that you particularly agreed with, as you would push your hips up, pushing yet further into my mouth.

Your appreciation motivated me and I started to feel an ache of want between my legs as your cock grew harder and harder. You were concentrating on watching my efforts now, your hands sliding up over the slippery smooth nylon of my stockings and on to the hot skin at the top of my legs. An excruciating tingle washed over my pussy as your fingers brushed against the split at the base of the basque.

A mental picture of your large fingers raced through my mind and I opened my legs wider in further invitation. My lips and tongue were doing their job meanwhile and I could tell that things would be reaching a climax soon.

Just as I thought you were about to come you suddenly pushed the papers you were still clutching to one side and said, 'That's enough. I think this is a good time to let you know what marks I have decided to give you.'

With your cock pointing the way, you moved quickly from the bed, pulling me with you until we were both standing in front of the full length mirror. 'Ten out of ten, I would say, wouldn't you?' you announced, gripping the back of my head.

Before I had time to reply, you bent me over and, with the flat of your large hand, I received my ten marks – five on each bare cheek of my bottom to be precise. Pulling me up again, you smiled at my flushed face; the smarting pain spread from my rear into my already heated pussy. Telling me to look in the mirror while you untied my hands, you enquired whether I thought it was a fair marking and one I thoroughly deserved.

The sight of your precisely placed hand marks clearly etched on my bottom sent a bolt of want through me, melting the soreness into a wanton tingling. Turning towards you, I started to undo the hooks along the front of the basque until it finally fell away, leaving me standing in just my crotchless knickers, stockings, shoes and rhinestone necklace.

'Would it be possible to have my rise now, sir?' I asked.

Turning to face away from you, I climbed on to the bed with my top marks raised in invitation. Needless to say, I got my rise.

A little while later, the clock on the mantelpiece in the adjoining room chimed three o'clock. I realised it was the time when you usually had your afternoon tea. Leaving you naked on the bed, I slipped your shirt on, which I found neatly folded over a chair in the bathroom. Going into the other room, I opened one of the cupboards where I knew the coffee and tea-making equipment would be stored. Nestled in amongst the selection of beverages, I noticed a packet of bourbon biscuits.

What a perfect way to finish off, I thought, unwrapping one.

113

In the Gents

Miranda Stephens

In the Gents

❖ ❖

They had fucked once. He had said, 'I want to fuck you in the gents. I want to fuck you to the smell of urine. I want to lick your tits with you sitting on the cistern. I want to fuck you.' Then he had turned away and made a phone call, but his cock was hard for her and he knew she could see it. He liked her looking at him and knowing that her empty cunt wanted him inside, fucking her because he was beautiful and he was hard for her.

She had been turned on because he was beautiful and crude. She said nothing but she went home and thought of being fucked in the gents where dozens of big cocks every day were handled by their masters. She wanted to smell the urine and feel their balls brushing against her as they peed and fucked her, and she wanted to be fucked there in manland where they hung out.

She pretended not to want his hands on her tits; pretended she couldn't feel him naked against her; couldn't feel the rub of hair curling around his cock and on his chest; pretended she didn't want him hard inside her; pretended she wasn't desperately empty for the hardness of this man.

She said in her bright voice,' Well, I'm off home, then.' And he had said,' OK, see you tomorrow,' without looking up from his computer.

She was walking out the door, longing for him to call her back and lick her tits and plunge into her, when he said, 'Come tomorrow.' She stopped in her tracks and stared at his dark eyes as they penetrated hers.

He said, 'Come tomorrow without knickers on. Come tomorrow without a bra. Come for me tomorrow with your nipples hard and rub your wet against me. You do want me, don't you?' She continued staring, her cunt screaming, 'Yes, fuck me now, here against the wall. Don't go home to your ghastly wife. I need you in me now; in the gents to the smell of men – now, now, now, you bastard.' But no. She smiled and said, 'Play your cards right,' and winked at him.

And she had glowed from his lust and had gone home and got that magazine out: the one with the story where the girls' tits touch each other as they kiss, and that got her started. She lay on the bed with her legs open to the mirror, and watched. She found her clit and worked it with her fingers as she thought of the bare arse and hips of the boy on the building site. He was hard for her; he was hard for all the girls. She thought of him, thinking of her tight little arse and tight little tits as she walked past him in her short skirt and high heels. She felt his eyes on her, and she loved being a girl so that she could do this to him: make him want to do it to her

He would have a big one. He would hold it, stroking it, hands sliding down the shaft of it, feeling his balls as he thought of having her against the wall behind the pub where they kept the beer crates. The wall would be rough on her back as he forced his way into her, making her do it, making her be dirty with him. It felt so good. He would make her come. She didn't want to; she knew it was dirty, fucking dirty, but she did it and she loved it and loved him for doing it to her with his hard strong body. Her hands couldn't get enough of him, till he unloaded his spunk into her. Then she imagined him sucking off the girls in the magazine, one of them riding his mouth while the other explored his hard cock with her tongue. That worked, and she felt the whole of her cunt explode with lights as she watched herself in the mirror.

She came gloriously, just in time to remember being fucked in the gents. She decided that was what she really wanted to happen tomorrow, so she would go to work without knickers or a bra. The man at work would put his hand on her thigh as she stood beside him, while he sat at his desk, all serious and busy.

She knew she had good thighs, strong and spare, and that would make his hand slide up her skirt. Then he would realise she had come to work without knickers or a bra, and be turned on, not just because of the feel of her, but because he had commanded and she had obeyed. And she would beg again to be fucked in the gents, her bare arse on the cistern, her legs around him, pulling him into her.

The next morning she had a bubble bath, which she used to think was like being sucked off by a hundred mouths, and she picked her red woollen dress to wear because the fabric was quite thick and it was cold out. She wanted her nipples to be hard for anybody who wanted to look, but she didn't want them to notice she was not wearing knickers or a bra, because that was her present for him. There were people on the tube who she hoped would suss her game and would want to fuck her, too.

Maybe one day she would like to give them their chance. But today she was being choosy, and wanted to be fucked to the smell of men in the gents. Fucked by his cock and his tight, heavy balls and the muscles in the small of his back, which drove his gorgeous bare arse, which she would feel with her hands as he thrust into her.

She was wet all day. Without knickers, her wet actually ran down her legs, and she let it. It wet the inside of her high-heeled red shoes, and she knew he could smell it, but he was really busy that day. So was she, but she fingered herself wondering when he would touch her.

He got off the phone and caught her in a daydream. He put his hand on her thigh while staring into her eyes. He slowly pushed his hand up her leg to the fullness of her arse and realised she had no knickers on. He then realised this was because he had asked her to not wear any. His eyes rested on her gorgeous full tits – full tits with the nipples suddenly quite hard.

His hand filled with one cheek of her smooth, bare arse. The realisation that she wanted him to fuck her made his cock fill to bursting. He knew she could see the bulge of his hardness and he wanted her hands to cup the weight of his balls. He loved to be hard; it felt magnificent. Sometimes he would stand sideways with his cock really hard, looking in the bathroom mirror. He would eye the line from his strong shoulders, across his broad chest, over his flat, muscled stomach, and down to the nest of hair from which his beautiful cock sprang. It curved up in an arc, culminating in the ridge below the head. It felt fucking wonderful to be so hard; it felt like he could take anything he wanted, and he knew she wanted him. Lucky girl – he would give it all to her in the gents, up to the hilt. He would fuck her hard; he might never stop.

With nothing in the way, his hand moved up under her dress to her back. It was exciting with no strap in the way, and with all her body given exactly as he had demanded. Both his hands moved under her dress to cup her breasts. Hard nipples, he thought; she's dying for it, he thought. She was his to fuck. She wanted his cock in her. She wanted to suck him off. Then he thought, fill her mouth with sperm; she would pass it, mouth to mouth, to another girl – a tall, skinny black girl – who would be watching them. Their tits would touch each other and then the black girl would slide down the white girl's body. She would use his sperm to wet this woman: the black girl's mouth at the white girl's cunt, pushing his sperm into her, sucking and tonguing, forcing his come up her and he, standing hard again, would open the black girl wide and lick her from anus to cunt and back before pushing just the head of his cock into her and gently exciting her, then ramming hard and deep into her, the electric shock of it making the black girl scream and bite the white woman she was tonguing. Then he would fuck her from behind, enjoying the hardness of her strong black body with his hands while she held his cock in her deep, tight cunt, pulling on him, caressing his balls with the curve of her arse, while she tongued the white girl's cunt. He would bite her gorgeous white tits into oblivion.

Now she could feel the heat from him, sweating out his fantasy. She breathed in his scent. 'Fuck me now,' she said. 'Fuck me in the gents. I want you in me. I want to be in there now. I want you.' But, she thought, I want more men. I want men all over me now. I want to be had by men I don't know and I want to be used in the gents by men with their hard, bare arses, and strong backs and shoulders and hairy chests and strong thighs, and they will serve me to the smell of men and shit and urine, but she said, 'Take me now.'

His hands were all over her. She loved it. She thought, he can't get enough of me. She knew the red woollen dress was turning him on. She knew he could feel the best of her, and her nipples were so hard. But her cunt was a yearning space she longed to have filled, by him or by other men, or almost anyone or anything. She wanted them so badly. I love to fuck, she thought. She wanted to be their whore; she wondered how it would be to kiss another woman's breasts; she was jealous because she knew he had.

Now, in the gents, alone, her hands were on his hard, round arse. It was nice under the jeans; it was nice to play with him beneath the thick material, and to be able now to enjoy his shape in his clothes – a shape she had thought of so often. Her hands were on the back of his neck enjoying the way his hair met his collar. His hands were under her dress – on her breasts and around her waist.

I must fuck her naked, he thought. I must see her, and have her totally submissive to me. So he unzipped the red woollen dress. A long zip, it went all the way up her back. She felt it slowly unpeel her. With no bra strap in the way, nothing between her and perdition, no protection, she was exposed. Fitfully, wantonly, in her mind she begged him to bare her; begged for her breasts to fall out of the dress; begged to see his devil's face as he saw her fallen angel look. The dress slipped off. She was naked; no game to play now, she wanted to see him, too.

The hard, merciless bulge in his jeans was her prize. She wanted to fuck it, suck it, that was her need. Unzipped, he wore nothing beneath. He had come ready; had obeyed his own command; come for her, hard, just for her. He sprang ready from out of the unzipped fly. She bent to him, and his cock slid between her full breasts. She then licked him, mouth slowly sucking him in, tasting him; tasting the pearls of want on his cock end – want for her ready, luscious cunt. But first she needed to savour his taste, to celebrate their fucking.

She rolled her tongue around the words: full up, fill me, full cock. 'Full cock,' she mouthed. Full for her; full with spunk to fill her up. Hands full of his balls, she took him in. Come in my mouth – no, don't, not yet! Suck on him, come in my mouth, no, too good yet to stop. Come in my cunt; I want the fucking – want to feel the muscles in the small of your back and your hard bare arse thrusting into me.

Then, with his hands on her breasts, he was pleading with her to want his cock; want it moving deep inside her – and so she opened to let him in.

Her cunt responded, drawing him into her while she marvelled at his strong shoulders. He found the angle for the hard shaft of his cock to caress her clitoris while filling her up. She held him tight, and only the lubrication of her juices let him move inside her.

Feeling her hold him hard inside her, his brain rioted. The black girl of his fantasies was now opening the white girl's arse, tonguing her anus, hands caressing her wet cunt and his balls. He thrust, harder and faster, the smells and sounds of the gents driving them to a frenzy that would not let them be. She felt him make her do it: no choice, no let up, hard inside her, moving, violating the space she would have let to three or more.

He forced her into it, and made her think of a rising tide of fantastic images: men's strong stomachs, hard chests, hair, hairy legs and arms, the smell of maleness, harder fucking.

His cock filled her as, in his head, the black girl writhed obscenely against the white girl's thighs. In her brain, meanwhile, the men came at her. No mercy. No let up. Coming to her, pulling her arse-cheeks apart, pulling her down on to them, coming over her, their strong bodies a seething mass of thrusting cocks and muscle, giving it to her hard as you like; making her do it. Then she felt the electric surge begin.

His balls rubbed against her and the coming rose in them. He felt the semen rise up his cock, and it was wonderful. No stopping now. The bitch would have to take it, spunk filling her as she sucked it out of him and took him to the hilt and made a sort of hard love to the smell of men and urine, shit and come in the gents.

Chocolate Kisses

Della Shannon

Chocolate Kisses

❖ ❖

*L*ucy breathed in once, twice, then began undressing, unwilling to delay the dreaded weigh-in any further. No, not 'dreaded'; negativity had no place in the battle to fight the flab. Battle? More like a war, a war she'd been fighting for longer than she cared to remember, but one in which she'd been gaining ground, and losing inches – at least, until recently. The scales hid beneath the bathroom sink, a predator awaiting its prey; they were the truth-teller, the unavoidable, undeniable arbiter of all her hard work, her denial, for the previous seven days.

Still, she paused to examine herself in the door mirror. Lucy was small in stature, with honey-blonde hair, cut short in a pageboy that brushed her round shoulders, and almond-coloured eyes, wide-set and sharp with scrutiny. Her breasts were round with thankfully no hint of sagging – yet – while below, her body rounded into that hated roll, before surrendering to a woolly bronze delta steepling her hips and thighs.

It had been an admittedly worse picture, months before, when she'd weighed an incomprehensible nineteen stone; her mother had thought she was pregnant, and Chris, in the well-intentioned but hopeless manner of men, had called her 'cuddly'. Ugh; she'd been a broad barrel of a woman, fit for a freak show. That was the reason for the mirror; here, she couldn't avoid the offensive sight every morning or evening, but she could remain determined to do something about it.

And she had – or so she thought. Walks, exercise, the right foods, and absolutely, positively *no* chocolates of any description whatsoever; for Lucy, they'd become a fix worse than any narcotic. And as spring crept into summer, then autumn, it had all started paying off. Jeans that had been consigned to the back of the wardrobe years before became wearable. Carting the groceries home was no longer an effort, and not because she wasn't buying cakes. And best of all was the shrinking tummy; now she could look at herself and see something almost human. But after an initial encouraging loss of six pounds in the first week, the subsequent reductions tapered off to a pound or two a week. And, last week, no change at all.

From nineteen stone to eighteen, seventeen, sixteen . . . closer every month to that magical goal of twelve stone. So close . . . Lucy must have dipped below the fourteen mark this week; she'd been particularly hard on herself lately. She *must* have.

Unwilling to prolong the agony further, she drew the scales closer with her toe and stepped on to them, watching with bated breath as the dial spun frantically, then settled.

Fourteen stone, eight. She'd *gained* six pounds.

Impossible. But there it was: the truth-teller, unavoidable, undeniable. She'd gained weight.

She'd *failed*.

With the compulsive dread of a driver unable to avoid staring at a roadside accident, Lucy gazed at herself again in the mirror, another truth-teller. Yes, there it was, she could *see* it. The roll around her middle was more distended than last week.

And with that dread came an acknowledgement, simple but no less convincing for it: that she'd been deluding herself all along. This wasn't some temporary aberration in her weight loss, but the start of a yo-yo rise back to hyper-obesity, the same yo-yo she'd ridden for most of her adult life. She was fat, and would remain that way: fat and ugly and defeated, no matter what her efforts.

It was an overpowering revelation. She wrapped her arms about herself and turned away.

Chris was planted in the living room, reclining on the sofa and watching the football match. He never moved when Lucy, dressed again, entered the room. He never said anything until she crossed his path, breaking the spell the television held over him as she proceeded to the kitchen. 'Get us a beer, love.'

She stopped at the kitchen doorway, gripping the frame as if for support. Over her shoulder, ashamed to look at him directly, she admitted, 'I've put on six pounds this week.'

She thought she heard him sigh, but nothing more. She stopped waiting for a more discernible answer and entered the kitchen. She needed chocolate, now: needed its sweet, reassuring comfort.

But there was none. At the start, she'd kept an 'emergency stash' of chocolate bars, to give herself a little treat every time she found she'd lost weight. But, after a while, she'd felt confident enough to give them all to Chris to eat. Her throat tightened; she hadn't felt such an acute craving in so long –

'Where's my beer, love?'

Lucy felt her face screw up, and her lips mouth silent obscenities. Like her weight, her relationship with Chris had had its ups and downs, and despite the improvement in the sex (when it happened), they seemed to have grown stale, vapid, with each other. The thrill, as the cliché went, was gone. Assuming it had ever been there in the first place; more delusions on her part?

'Lucy?'

She appeared at the doorway again. 'Did you hear what I said, Chris?'

He spared her a glance – there was an advert break – and furrowed his brow. 'Yeah, you said you were putting your coat on. Are you going out?'

Lucy's face grew taut. 'Yes, Chris. I'm going out.' Out of his view, she shook the tin of beer in her hand vigorously, then crouched and set it on the floor within his reach before rising and exiting, all with hardly a pause. 'I'm going out now.'

'Bring us back a takeaway, love.'

She sighed to herself in resignation; she should have known by now how he'd respond. But then what did she expect? 'Oh, Lucy, I *like* your love handles.' Vapid, insincere sentiment, worse than derision. She was slipping into her jacket when she heard the snap of the tin opening, with a whoosh of erupting gas just

preceding a strangled cry. It brought a slight smile to her face –
until she realised she'd be cleaning up the mess later.

The shops were closed at that time of evening, and she was
heading for the nearest petrol station to clear their stock of Mars
bars, until she saw the café: *Temptations*, whispered the pink
neon above the door. The property seemed small, yet when she
entered, Lucy found it all the cosier for its size, with an appropriate décor: paintings on the walls, tiny white enamel vases
with sprigs of dried flowers on the tables, burgundy tablecloths,
Spanish guitar from hidden speakers. A pleasing mixture of
coffee, sizzling meat and exotic spices filled her nostrils.

She was informed that, due to the late hour, meals were no
longer being served. All she wanted was a quick coffee, and a
sweet. Especially a sweet. But as she sat rigid, alone, barely
acknowledging the menu in hand, she found none of the
expected anticipation usually felt at such moments, at having an
abundant choice of delicious desserts at her beck and call, each
calling to her like puppies in the pound: *Please, Lucy, pick me!*
Nothing called to her now but her self-loathing; she felt sour
inside.

Lucy could feel the waitress's return, and set the menu aside.
'Sorry, I don't fancy anything now. I'll just leave.'

'I can't allow that, miss.'

It wasn't what was said that made Lucy's head lift in confusion, but that the voice was no longer the tired, feminine voice
of the waitress, but one deeper, heartier. She looked up to see a
tall, broad-shouldered black man in his forties, his skin the
colour of polished walnut, his head smooth-shaven, balanced by
a thick moustache and beard as black as his silk shirt and cotton
trousers.

'Excuse me?' was all she managed.

He moved to sit across from her with an ease that belied his
size. There was something about him that seemed too massive
for chairs, something beyond his muscular frame, beyond the
worldly lines in his face and the strands of grey in his beard.
Even when he smiled, the smile seemed too big for just his lips.
'I *said* I can't allow that, miss.'

He seemed friendly enough, but she wasn't in the mood tonight. 'And why should *you* care?'

His smile graduated to a grin. 'It's *my* café.' He laughed, a sound as deep and melodious as his words, with a Caribbean drawl. 'And people come to Temptations just for the desserts; if you left now, my reputation would be sullied.' He laughed again, making Lucy smile back helplessly, then reached his hand across the table. 'Isaac Dupere, at your service.'

Lucy extended her own hand. 'Lucy Stevens.' His touch felt hot, like a windowpane on a summer afternoon. 'And you'll have to excuse me for not ordering; I *had* intended to get myself a dessert when I entered.'

He leant closer, or so she imagined, his gaze intent, interested. 'But?'

He was a stranger. Handsome, undeniably; Lucy was attracted, something she hadn't felt in a long time. But did she really want to unload her troubles on to him? Then again, if she didn't, perhaps she shouldn't have left her last answer so open for further enquiry. 'I guess I lost my appetite.'

Then her stomach growled, very audibly.

She thought she could quite readily bury herself in the nearest pit. But instead Isaac ignored it, lifting up her menu, as if needing to read from it. 'Perhaps you just don't know what you want.'

'No.' She shook her head, suddenly feeling the need to be brutally honest with him, and end this embarrassment now. 'I just don't deserve it.'

Then he frowned over the menu, though without losing any of his good humour. 'We'll see about that.' He glanced past her, raising his voice. 'Chantelle!'

Lucy followed his gaze, noting that the café was now empty of customers, apart from herself; surely he wanted her to leave, so they could close up? But Lucy saw that someone was already locking the front door and switching off the outer lights, before approaching the table. Lucy hadn't noticed her before; the apron she was removing suggested she'd been in the kitchens before now. 'Isaac?'

He took the apron from her and cast it aside, then took her hand gently. 'My dear, we have a poor woman that needs some

129

enlightening.' Now he glanced back at Lucy. 'Lucy, this is my partner, Chantelle. Together, we make Temptations what it is.'

Lucy looked up; closer now, Chantelle was striking, her skin almost as brown as Isaac's, with prominent cheekbones, big blue eyes, and a neat bonnet of raven hair; the smell of a day's worth of cooking clung pleasingly about her. She also looked to be about Lucy's age, and current weight; perhaps she wouldn't have been considered traditionally beautiful, but there was a sassiness to her spirit that Lucy found appealing. Chantelle smiled warmly, her mouth full and naturally red, her voice laced with a more familiar London accent. 'Meaning I get the work and he gets the glory.'

'Untrue,' he assured Lucy, though Lucy guessed from their tones that it was a familiar banter between them. He leant closer to Lucy, as if in conspiracy. 'I help create the desserts.' Now his words directed themselves back to Chantelle. 'Desserts which this young woman believes she doesn't deserve.'

'Why ever not?' the woman asked genuinely, pulling up a chair and sitting down between them.

Suddenly Lucy felt under both their scrutiny, as polite and well-meaning as it was. It was obvious now that the two of them were an item, and that Lucy would have to curb any interest in Isaac. Still, what had she to lose by opening up to them?

'I'm supposed to be on a diet; I've lost nearly five stone already –'

'Congratulations!' They both beamed.

Lucy warmed to the compliment – more than she expected – but still felt twisted inside. 'But I'm starting to fail.' She looked away, ashamed. 'I'm going to be fat again, and ugly.'

Then she felt Chantelle reach out and take Lucy's chin between thumb and forefinger, drawing her gaze back. 'Who says?'

Her touch was warm, firm, lingering long after she'd removed her hand. 'Well, it always happens to me: I lose weight, then I put it on again –'

'No, I mean who says being overweight means being ugly?'

It was an unexpected question, one that made Lucy falter before answering. 'Look in the magazines, on television –'

Isaac hissed dismissively through clenched teeth, then raised an expansive arm. 'Shallow, trendy, stick-insect chic. Look around you *now*.'

Lucy followed the wave of his hand to the paintings: artwork reproductions from who knew how many centuries and disciplines, mostly of women, most clothed, some nude, but of all colours, shapes and sizes.

And she listened to the man's words that accompanied them. 'Big- and narrow-hipped, tall, short, dark, light, large-breasted, small-breasted; what some call "beautiful" changes with the seasons, more quickly than we may think, and we should not be bound by their capriciousness. Hell, look at *yourself*. There's nothing wrong with you.'

'And many things *right*,' Chantelle added. 'If you only believe it, too.'

Lucy listened to their words of support and encouragement, wanting to believe with them; she'd heard similar remarks in the past, but had discounted them. But . . . 'I can't even stay at my ideal weight.'

'Ideals are for gods,' Isaac declared. 'Not people. Are you happy with how you look *now*? Because that's all that matters.'

'Maybe that's really why she's here tonight?' Chantelle suggested to him. 'She deserves a special treat for all her hard work.'

Lucy knew the woman's words were really meant for her. If only Lucy could accept them. 'Chocolate's just a crutch –'

'Wrong,' Isaac cut her off. 'It's an occasion, to be celebrated; throw away your crutches.' He seemed to study her. 'And you agree; we can see it in your eyes.'

'And on my hips.'

Chantelle huffed in gentle exasperation. 'What's the point in denying oneself *for ever*, if you can't enjoy moments of indulgence on occasion?' She leant closer to Isaac. 'Maybe she needs to be shown how?'

Isaac grinned. 'Maybe.'

Lucy, caught up in the infectious merriment of her new associates, smiled back. 'What have you got in mind?'

'Chocolate.'

Isaac elaborated, his voice seductive. 'Chocolate hazelnut roulade. Marbled chocolate eggs. Perhaps even my special Chocolate Kiss Cake –'

'Enough.' Lucy could feel the inches being added on to her waist just from listening. But still she let them lead her away.

They lived in the flat above the bistro, a modest place decorated in Caribbean reds and greens and blacks, with an ornate cheval mirror in one corner, and a collection of low plush bean-bags instead of a sofa dominating the centre. The kitchen was larger than she'd expected for a flat of this size, busy-looking but immaculate; a waist-level counter separated it from the rest of the flat.

'Are you sure about this?'

Behind her, Isaac had put on a CD – Hot Chocolate, naturally – and was now pouring wine. 'They'd only be thrown out, or we'd be eating them ourselves.'

'And chocolate,' Chantelle added, handing Lucy her glass, 'like any pleasure, is best shared.'

Was Lucy imagining it, or was there a none-too-hidden meaning in the other woman's words, in her bright blue eyes? She'd never been attracted to other women before ... Lucy accepted the glass, surprised to find that her hand was trembling slightly.

Isaac held up his glass in salute. 'Here's to new friends, and shared passions.'

'I'll assume you mean the chocolate,' Lucy joked, sipping the wine tentatively, then more assuredly, liking the taste.

Chantelle finished hers and handed the glass to Isaac, then began unbuttoning her shirt. She smiled at Lucy. 'Would you excuse me if I take a shower first? It's been a long day.'

Lucy's throat felt dry, despite the wine. 'Of course. Go ahead.'

'Thanks.' The woman grinned again, reaching the last button of her shirt – she wore no bra – before turning away.

Lucy didn't mean to watch her leave; she was certain her face registered the quickening pace her pulse had taken. She continued to tell herself that this was all just some harmless sensual indulgence (if that wasn't a seeming contradiction). Then she started as Isaac reached out and took her glass, then her hand, leading her to a high stool by the kitchen counter.

'Sit.'

There was a casual but unarguable tone to his voice now; fun this might be, but this was also serious fun to him, and Lucy found herself eagerly complying. She perched on the stool, her feet resting on the first rung, her thighs parted and her hands resting between them. She watched him unwrap the packages he had carried from the café.

'Do you do this often?'

'What, bring unsuspecting women up to sample our delights?' He laughed, never really answering, setting a tray on the counter beside her: the feast of the world before her eyes, selections of a score or more of various desserts, all based upon or including chocolate. He grinned at her response. 'It's something new we're trying downstairs: A Little Bit of Everything. Like it?'

Lucy's mouth was shamelessly watering in classic Pavlovian style. 'I – I wouldn't know where to begin.'

'Then leave yourself in our hands; do what we say, and you won't be disappointed.' He appeared before her, sectioned a gooey piece of pudding with a fork and lifted it up invitingly towards her mouth. 'We'll start simply: open wide.'

She did. And it was absolutely delicious, the rush through her body as she tasted and swallowed like a leap from a cliff. She crooned to herself, feeling the smile stretch her face, then licked her lips.

'Wickedly delicious, isn't it?' he murmured, his voice a soft caress. 'Scientists tell us that cocoa contains phenylethylamine, which our bodies also produce when we're aroused. But Mama taught me how to cook, and she said chocolate was simply the Devil's Food, Sin With Substance. And a sin is only a pleasure we're afraid to enjoy.'

Lucy's eyes were closed. 'Your mother sounds like an intelligent woman.'

Isaac laughed, then continued with another sample, this time white chocolate torte. 'Now keep your eyes shut, let your mind focus on your senses of taste and smell. And *relax*. Enjoy yourself.'

She tried, and she did, relishing the soft velvet of the torte, then the firmer, crunchier delight of the chocolate chestnut meringues, then the sharp fiery freshness of the whisky mocha flan. Isaac was right; there was something, an innate decadence

to chocolate, an almost forbidden quality to it. Each taste satisfied her, yet also left her wanting more. And from the low
gravelly moans he made as he, too, sampled his works, Isaac felt
the same way.

At some point he'd moved behind her – she could smell his
cologne, feel the hairs on her neck rise at his proximity – as he
reached round to continue feeding her, his other hand warm on
her shoulder. There was a hard tight knot in her stomach; this
was innocent fun, she assured herself.

Moments later, Lucy's assurances blew away when he started
licking and nibbling on her ear; she could feel his erection
pressing into her lower back. A wave of heat washed over her,
and she felt faint. If this continued, there was no telling what
might happen next. After all, his lover was in the shower, only
metres away, not to mention *her* lover, such as he was, at home!
Wasn't this wrong?

Inside her dampening knickers, her pussy didn't seem to care.
She gripped the stool until she thought her nails would pierce
the seat, her protests aborted.

Isaac set aside the fork now, and let the freed hand reach
round and knead her left breast, making her gasp and shudder,
even as his right hand, promising more, snaked down boldly
beneath the waistbands of her leggings and knickers. Still silent,
as if Hot Chocolate's 'You Sexy Thing' did all his talking, he
cupped her pubic mound, gently squeezing, feeling her curls
press back.

Lucy gasped aloud and shivered in place, pressing her head
against his as his middle finger extended, tracing the groove of
her outer lips down, then back again, lubricating from the dew
collecting there.

When his finger pierced her, she parted her thighs further to
accommodate him. Isaac's expert manipulations – his fore- and
middle fingers diving and withdrawing, his thumb massaging
her stiffened clitoris with a circular motion – only heightened
the sweet torture. She drank in her own strong musk from
between her legs, letting the pressure build further and further,
as Isaac drew her to the inevitable –

'Delicious, isn't it?'

The song ended. Lucy gasped, her eyes shooting open to find

Chantelle before them, clad from breast to thigh in a thick pink terry towel. Still, Isaac continued, and Lucy didn't stop him; she sensed that the other woman was hardly jealous or angry at what was happening. This was all planned, after all, wasn't it? As if in confirmation, Chantelle lifted a piece of chocolate truffle cake from the tray to her mouth, bit into it, smacked her lips, and continued watching. Watching as Isaac quickly found the rhythm that was carrying Lucy before, carrying her now without shame or doubt.

For Lucy, at least, it was an experience separate yet shared, like the chocolate, and enjoyed all the more *because* it was shared. No animosity or possessiveness, simply an unspoken acknowledgement that a sin was only a pleasure she'd been afraid to enjoy – until now.

Lucy moaned aloud as she finally came to the tune of 'It Started With A Kiss', her pussy clamping on to Isaac's fingers, refusing release – how utterly delightful! Waves of dizzying heat ran through her like a wire, and she clutched her face, as if fighting to tame her breathing, her fingertips gathering sweat from her brow.

Chantelle was smiling; Lucy took her hands away to smile back as she felt Isaac remove his hand, heard him tasting her come, then started to undress Lucy. She helped him, kicking off her trainers and standing. Chantelle looked her over approvingly when she was naked, then said, 'Turn round.'

Lucy, her heart racing again, obeyed, now facing the cheval mirror. Isaac remained behind her, holding her arms at her sides in a token (and unnecessary) gesture of domination. Chantelle sided up to her and tugged her towel to the floor: the woman was as handsome naked as she was clothed, her skin smooth and warm, her breasts pendulous and budded with dark pink nipples that stood seeking attention. Her pubic hair was trimmed sable, the lips of her sex visible. In her middle lay a paunch much like Lucy's own, but she wore hers well.

Isaac released his hold on Lucy – she caught him in the reflection undressing behind her – as Chantelle snaked an arm round Lucy's waist and pulled her closer. 'Well, look at us, girl: are we ugly, or are we *beautiful*?'

Lucy didn't hesitate. 'Beautiful.' And she meant it, even for herself. She *was* beautiful, regardless of her weight. She felt proud – and, yes, aroused too.

Chantelle laughed softly as she drew Lucy into a kiss, their breasts pressing together as if in imitation; Lucy tasted chocolate on the other woman. Lucy could swear her heart had stopped, as Chantelle's tongue slipped between her parted lips and thrust into her mouth; shards of pleasure spread further through her as she sent her own tongue in reply. Their arms clasped each other, refusing to let go, as Lucy had refused to let go of the incredible new feelings running through her. Another woman . . . well, why not?

Somehow they made it to the bean-bags. Still aware of Isaac's presence, and wanting him as much as she wanted his partner, Lucy turned – and had a piece of chocolate truffle cake fed to her from his hand. She swallowed, then licked his fingers. His body was toned, yet showed signs of how much he enjoyed his own cooking, but like she did with Chantelle – and now, herself – Lucy still thought him handsome. She descended to her knees, took his cock – standing long and proud from black curls, its mahogany tip flaring, glistening – in her hand, then into her hot, willing mouth. He groaned, clutching her as she ran her tongue around the hot velvet rim of the head, then along the whole length of him, further than she expected she could.

Chantelle moved behind her now, kneeling to copy Isaac's earlier actions, kneading Lucy's aching breasts and cupping her mound. Lucy made her own groaning sounds, feeling her body move once again towards climax, wondering how long she would endure this.

Not long, as it turned out, as Chantelle pulled her off Isaac, making him moan and curse; Lucy could sense how close he'd been to his own zenith. But Lucy, her senses ablaze, felt hypnotised; she barely heard Chantelle whisper, 'Isaac, bring me some of your cake.'

Lucy's tunnel vision widened enough to acknowledge that Chantelle was leaning back on the bags, leaving Lucy kneeling on the carpet, a willing, eager acolyte to this god and goddess of sex and chocolate. Chantelle parted her thighs, revealing her open, waiting pussy, an exquisite oval shape of delicately frilled flesh covering the strawberry-pink of her inner sex, centred by the secret folds leading to her vagina, moist with milky dew; Lucy drank in her sweet and heady fragrance, so like her own.

Isaac set into Chantelle's hand a thick slab of the richest-looking cake Lucy had ever seen, painted in shades of brown and black she never knew existed.

Chantelle held the cake like Eve's apple. 'This is Isaac's Chocolate Kiss Cake: triple-layered chocolate sponge, six different chocolate frostings, chocolate chips, chocolate syrup.' Lucy felt her jaw drop at the sight of it; Chantelle grinned. '*You* provide the Kisses.'

Then she began smearing it over her own body, across her breasts, down her stomach to her thighs and pussy. Lucy was mesmerised by the sight, at how it clung to her, how the syrup crawled along her skin. But once Chantelle had finished, and began licking her own fingers, Lucy crawled up unbidden and buried her face in the other woman's full confection-covered breasts, licking, eating, wanting more.

As if from a distance, Lucy could feel Isaac behind her, lifting her up and parting her thighs. Warm fluid seeped from within, and she desperately craved to be stretched to capacity, literal fulfilment. Isaac kindly obliged; the lips of her sex swallowed the head of his cock, then almost the full stem as he pressed into her, enveloping him totally. His rhythm was slow at first, considerate, able to support himself without disturbing Lucy and Chantelle's own lovemaking; she felt his balls slap against her with every thrust, while his hands gripped her sides. But soon he was coaxing the rhythm into a more urgent gallop: lovely.

Lucy let the thrusts draw her down, down Chantelle's body, devouring all the chocolate she found, until she buried her face between the woman's thighs, lapping at the soaking folds of her moist sex, finally delighting in the novel, exquisite tastes. Chantelle's thighs reflexively closed against the sides of Lucy's head, her pussy wavering between taut reaction and supple submission to her bliss, ultimately becoming impotent to fight the exquisite sensations, the same sensations Lucy herself felt.

Soon Chantelle was going wild, the cries from her mouth inarticulate pleas and demands for Lucy to stop and continue and stop, her fingernails digging into the sides of Lucy's head. Suddenly she stiffened, her muscles contracting sharply against

Lucy's face; indeed, her whole body shook with release. Before she even realised it, Lucy's own climax followed, and her throttled cry was muffled into the sex of her new lover, as wave after wave of pleasure ran through her body, making her dig her nails into Chantelle's soft hot thighs.

Finally Isaac, too, came, letting himself succumb to that release of pleasure-pain, tensing as he climaxed within Lucy, fraught at first, his body spasming behind and inside hers, then diminishing until he was fully spent, then nearly collapsing on to her. She willingly supported him, and would have continued to do so, had he not subsequently withdrawn, leaving her feeling empty but immensely satisfied.

They clung together, Lucy and Isaac practically lying on top of an uncomplaining Chantelle, remaining like that for an uncountable time, silent, none willing to break the spell. Relishing her own dying post-coital embers, the warmth of spent lust seeping from between her clenched, still-shuddering thighs, Lucy stroked Isaac's beard as they kissed; somehow some of Chantelle's cake had managed to find its way there, as it had on her own body; or had he sneaked a slice for himself before delivering Chantelle's?

As if hearing her name in Lucy's thoughts, the woman manoeuvred her arms out to help herself to what chocolate remained on their bodies. Then, smacking her lips, she grinned at Lucy. 'And how do you feel now, girl?'

Lucy grinned back. 'I feel like having another slice of that cake.'

It was much later when Lucy returned home, but Chris was still awake, beer stains around him ignored, still watching television, still as attentive to her as ever. 'Hi, love. What'd you do?'

She stood in the doorway, unable and unwilling to remove the grin plastered on her face, as she was unable and unwilling to hide the truth from him. 'I met a couple, who made me feel good about myself, fed me, and gave me the best sex I ever had.'

'That's nice.' There was an advert, and he looked up. 'Is that my takeaway?'

Lucy held up the white cardboard box in her hands. 'No, it's chocolate cake. Want some?'

Honeysuckle House

Cyanna Rouselle

Honeysuckle House

❖ ❖

*T*he house fascinated me.

Fascinated and repelled me in the same way as erotic men's magazines had when I was ten years old. Covered with crude-but-titillating photos of women, I had found them irresistible. I remember pretending to browse the innocuous magazines at eye level. Then, heart pounding with suppressed excitement, groin aching in a way I didn't understand, I'd sneak glances up to those tantalising covers. It was a few years before I finally understood why my panties were always wet after a session at the local booksellers.

Sixteen years later, I, Samantha Sloan, had no need to peek at the covers of men's magazines. As a travelling sales rep for a distributor of erotic merchandise, I had access to much more explicit material, as well as the other goodies I enjoyed so much.

The house fascinated me to such an extent that I would go miles and miles out of my way, just to see it. I don't think I'd returned from a single sales trip without making a special detour. It was called Honeysuckle House.

Of course, it wasn't really the house that drew me, but the events that had happened there so long ago. They had, after all, changed the course of my life.

I was returning from my monthly swing through the Midlands and, as usual, had made a side trip to drive by Honeysuckle

House. The day was on-again-off-again rainy, not unusual for spring. Rhododendrons were coming to life along the road, buds emerging proudly, ready to bloom. I pulled into the familiar tree-lined lane, slowed, and prepared to let the emotions rush through me as I drove past.

But this time, there was a difference. It was for sale.

Twenty minutes later, the estate agent handed me the keys at the front door.

'There's quite a bit of furniture left, Samantha – it's all for sale. A few lovely antiques: an oak sideboard, a brass bed. The heating's coal – *very* inexpensive – but it could be upgraded to central gas *quite* easily. Don't you just *love* the garden? Even in this weather. Oh, look at that clematis climbing the stonework. And the azaleas! I just love the scent of azaleas, don't you? It's just *so* aggravating that I already have another client to show around this afternoon. I wish I could show you all the really *fabulous* features myself. But I'll ring you this evening, Samantha, to see how you got on. Say, about eightish? Oh, don't forget to drop the keys off at the agency office when you're finished. Bye, now!'

I fitted the key into the lock with hands that shook slightly. What would it be like after ten years? The only time I had been here was when it had been let for a two-week summer holiday to my family. But the details were etched into my memory as if with acid. I'd been sixteen, a determined-to-lose-her-innocence sixteen. I smiled to myself. I had achieved my goals even then.

The entrance was exactly as I remembered it: golden flagstones and a huge gilt-framed mirror. Even my image was much the same as it had been ten years ago, I confirmed to myself with satisfied pride, smoothing my hands over the curves of my breasts and snug waist. As tight and trim now as it ever had been.

I wore my usual navy-blue business suit: longish body-skimming jacket, very short skirt, massive handbag that also served as my sample case. A multitude of colourful silk scarves hid a neckline deep enough to dive into. Very useful things, scarves. No one would suspect that I wore my favourite black leather harness underneath.

My face was a bit pale, and tendrils of unruly flaxen hair escaped from a shoulder-length French plait; my blue eyes were wide. I looked frightened, but wasn't. Excited was more like it. Horny was even more accurate.

I moved into the blue-and-ivory living room. This was where I'd met the twins. University students from up north – down to visit their favourite aunt, whose back garden adjoined ours – they'd dazzled me with their maturity. Twenty years old, glossy black hair, deep-green eyes and emanating a sexual energy I had been eager to taste.

I couldn't have told them apart if I'd been paid a million pounds. Not until I'd realised that David was the shy gentle one and Damien was the ardent arrogant one. After that, it had seemed obvious.

The back veranda where it had all happened beckoned to me. Hesitating in the back doorway, I looked around, curious to see if anything had changed. The garden was full of fading daffodils and just-budding bushes instead of summer's blooms and lush greenery. Between the trees, I could see the upper floor of the house where the twins had stayed. Did their aunt still live there? Did they ever visit? The low brocade couch was still there in the corner, away from any prying windows.

Closing my eyes, I could again feel the warm sultry summer evening, hear the nightjar's call, smell the scent of roses.

Damien had been too impatient, too crude, had demanded my submission. So I'd played with fire that night, rebuffing Damien and blatantly flirting with David, the man I'd chosen to deflower me. Arrogantly, I had thought to teach Damien a lesson by showing him that it was I who would do the choosing, not him.

In spite of my open attempts to seduce him, David had been a gentleman, considerate of my inexperience, wanting to wait until we had more time and privacy, refusing to give in to my impatience. He'd whispered his seductive, sensuous plans for the following night into my ear, making me pant with desire, while Damien had watched and fumed.

Later that night, Damien had returned and silently, arrogantly taken what he wanted from me. My virginity.

My breath caught as memories engulfed me. Sweat broke out

on my brow and another, more shameful, dampness scorched the tops of my thighs between my stockings.

I fell back against the couch and attempted, with my fingers, to duplicate the feel of Damien rudely entering me, my maidenhood breached, my indignant cries and struggles going unheeded. Until they turned into gasps for more.

He'd had a huge cock – enormous, to my inexperienced eyes – which had seemed to pulse purple and curved maliciously to the left. He'd said nothing at all, just smirked at me with those green eyes.

I'd felt helpless, angrily but deliciously helpless, my hands tightly gripped above my head, my legs ruthlessly splayed. Sex exposed and vulnerable and throbbing with intense excitement between the edges of my ripped-open panties. Exposed to his lips, his tongue, his thick curved cock.

A shattering orgasm ripped through me. Was it real or just a faint echo of that night?

Sated for the moment, eyes closed, I lay on the couch and slowly returned to the present. It was cooler today than it had been then. Rain pattered against the roof. A door slammed nearby. The smell of wet earth proclaimed spring.

The sound of a step on the veranda startled me but I had no time to cover myself.

Good God! It was one of the twins. But which one?

He halted abruptly, emerald eyes wide, mouth open as if to speak words that would no longer move past his choking throat. I could understand why. My legs were spread wide, stockings slipping partway down my legs. My skirt was tangled around my hips, exposing a tight, a very tight, crotchless leather thong, through which my labia protruded. My nipples, rigid and rosy, thrust brazenly through displaced scarves.

What was Damien doing here? Or was it David? My nemesis or my cavalier? I couldn't tell. It didn't really matter – they both figured in my fantasies.

His black hair was untouched by grey and he radiated casual sex-appeal in his jeans and plain white Oxford shirt. Relaxing slightly, I slowly and sensuously began to rearrange my clothing. A strip-tease in reverse. Raising one leg to the couch to pull up

144

a stocking, my labia pouted even further out with a little wet sliding sound, rubbing against my still-swollen clit.

'Which are you? Damien or David?' Did he recognise me? I pulled up the other stocking and slowly stood.

'Damien.' His voice was hoarse.

My nemesis! The only man who had ever dominated me.

A thick bulge was forming behind the zipper of his jeans. I watched it grow. A deep gnawing ache coiled low in my stomach as indelible images of that swollen erection flooded into my mind. 'Do you remember me?' My breasts wobbled from side to side and spilt out of the low neckline as I tugged my skirt down to the tops of my stockings.

'I . . . Yes. You're Samantha.' His voice firmed, became low, husky, seductive. 'I've never been able to forget you. Or how you tormented us.'

I'll bet! I thought derisively. 'I've never forgotten, either.' My fingers caressed and pinched my breasts before slipping them back into place. 'What are you doing here?'

'I've lived here for the last couple of years. In my late aunt's house.' The bulge in his jeans grew larger. 'I saw you from the window and had to check if it was really you.'

'And David? Does he live here, too?'

'No. He still lives up north.'

I was disappointed. I'd always wished that David and I could have carried out those seductive plans he had whispered into my ear.

I rearranged the scarves, allowing some gaps to remain, and sly inspiration hit. I wanted sweet revenge. I wanted to dominate Damien as he'd dominated me. I wanted to finish what he'd started that night, but on my terms. He wasn't to know that I felt indebted to him for the experience. After all, it had driven me to the discovery of how exquisitely pleasurable domination could be. Especially domination of arrogant cocksure types.

And, I'll be honest, just the sight of him was turning me on more than most other men were able to.

Hadn't that estate agent said something about a brass bed? I smiled at him. I would 'reward' Damien for the inferno he'd ignited in me that long-ago night.

'I haven't seen the upstairs yet. Why don't you show it to me?'

145

Without waiting for an answer, I picked up my bag and entered the house.

I found the room with the bed and slowly pulled off one colourful scarf after another, gradually revealing the cleavage between my breasts. Damien watched silently, his breathing fast and shallow.

My jacket fell unheeded to the floor, exposing the leather body harness which tightly bound the under-swells of my breasts, forcing them up into circular mounds of sensitive flesh. I played with my breasts, lifting them, offering them, flicking the nipples with my nails, running a blue scarf around and over them. The silk tantalised my hard little peaks and I moaned.

His erection would no longer fit below the waistband of his jeans. It bowed outward, straining to break free. I was mesmerised. Finally, he pulled at his waistband, loosening it. The purple head of his cock shot up and out, and flexed once.

I had only partially put on the harness that morning, leaving the upper straps to hang, discreetly hidden under my clothing. I pulled them up into place now, fitting the too-small leather cups tightly into place. The hook at the back of the neck could only be done up after forcing part of each breast through the nipple openings. I pulled each breast through the holes so that the nipples and a surrounding expanse of flesh bulged out like two ruby-red plums, ripe and juicy, ready for the plucking. The harness bit into my skin, filling me with pleasure-pain. With every movement, my nipples felt like they would burst with pleasure.

The effect on Damien was electric. His cock pulsed strongly and the head engorged, glowing bluish-purple against his white shirt. Thickening and elongating, it extended even further out of his jeans. My clit hardened in response.

'Like what you see?' I taunted, flicking silk at his thick knob.

He came towards me, greedily grasping. 'Come here.'

I evaded him with a cynical smile, breasts bobbing. He was still crude and impatient. I would have to teach him patience, control.

'Tease!' His hands shot out and grasped my breasts, held on. I gasped at the delicious addictive pain flooding from my nipples. 'You're just the same. You drove me crazy that night.'

Was he trying to justify his actions? Fat chance!

I could see a shining drop of fluid beaded on the tip of his erection. I bent over and laved, carefully, thoroughly. Hips thrusting, he clasped my head and pressed down, trying to force his swollen cock deeper. But I had no intention of allowing him to dominate me as he'd done before. It was my turn.

I twisted free and slipped a scarf around the exposed head of his cock. Back and forth, back and forth, I tugged on the silk, caressing the sensitive ridge as I drew Damien towards the bed. His hands returned to my nipples. My groin ached unbearably with desire and anticipation. I tightened my thighs but there was no relief.

'Why did you leave the next day?' It had bothered me, not knowing. 'Couldn't face the morning after?'

'David needed to leave – said he'd received an urgent call. I've always regretted not finishing what you started.' He leant over and mouthed a swollen plum, enclosing it in wet warmth, stabbing at the nipple with his tongue.

'We can finish it now.' But on my terms, I thought as a rush of power thrilled through me. He was no longer dealing with a naive girl, but with the experienced dominatrix I had become. He would enjoy learning how vulnerability could intensify his sexual pleasure. And I would enjoy teaching him.

Again he tried to take control. But I was prepared and garrotted his erection to keep him compliant.

I unfastened his jeans and shoved them down his legs, leaving the head of his cock to protrude from a pair of silky boxer shorts. The jeans caught around his ankles and he tried to free himself. A quick shove and he was on the bed, sideways.

He seemed to relax, to accept what he thought was coming. One by one, I tied his wrists securely to the bed frame with one scarf each – useful things, scarves. His arms were drawn wide, one tied to the head of the bed, the other to the foot. I pulled one leg free of his jeans and tied it to the foot of the bed so that the knee was bent and the leg outspread. This time it would be *his* genitals that were exposed and vulnerable.

His green eyes, darkened with desire and perhaps some

uncertainty, watched me as I secured his other ankle to the headboard. 'I've never been tied up before.' He yanked the silken bonds, testing them. But they didn't loosen.

I disposed of my skirt but left the stockings on. The leather thong which bound me produced a wicked burn between my legs with every undulation of my hips. A burn that needed some relief.

'Well, big boy,' I said, scratching his knob with delicate fingernails, 'it's your turn to beg.'

'Make me.'

'My pleasure.' And it would definitely be my pleasure, I thought as I unbuttoned his shirt.

Damien was smiling, relaxed, perhaps feeling confident that he couldn't be made to beg. But I knew that before long he would be pleading with me for release. A release, as I knew from experience, which would be all the more explosive – for both of us – because he would have to beg me for it.

I trailed another silk scarf over his legs, over his belly, through the dusting of black hair on his chest. He continued to watch me with those emerald eyes, just as he had all those years ago, saying nothing but betraying himself by breathing heavily. His skin twitched like a horse ridding itself of a fly as I played the scarf over his body, over every inch of exposed skin. When the scarf reached the top of his boxer shorts, I reached into my bag and pulled out a small pen-knife. His shorts were in my way.

'Hey!' He swallowed and yanked violently against the bonds, hips bucking.

I smiled, enjoying his instant of understandable fear, but reassured him. 'Keep still. I wouldn't want to accidentally nick your balls. Or your sweet arse.' He held himself motionless as I pulled the crotch of his shorts away from his body.

A quick flick, a loud rip and his shorts were slit from arse to scrotum. Framed by the cut edges of the silk, his tightly furled arsehole looked like it was being offered to me, to do with it as I wanted. And I wanted! Oh, how I wanted!

I ducked down to rummage in my bag of tricks. What could I use today? A short crop, nipple clamps, an anal vibrator, condom; these would be for him. The anal plug for me. We could share my latest toy: a large vibrator with a hollow tip. Special ice packs, the kind that doctors use, the ones that go icy cold once an inner capsule is broken, were shaped to fit into the tip. I hadn't yet had a chance to try it. I readied the ice vibrator, since it would take a few minutes to chill.

I tossed everything on to the bed with condoms and a large tube of lubricant and straddled him, allowing my sex to nuzzle the base of his shaft.

I dragged my breasts over his chest and clutched the two pairs of nipples together fiercely. Mine were rigid, swollen. I gouged the erect tips into and against his, the rough sensations shooting into my belly. In imitation of how my breasts were severely constrained, I grasped his nipples, one by one, pulling them away from his chest as far as I could, and attached the nipple clamps. The clamps bit deeply around his nipples, forcing them into puckered bulbs. I flicked the clamps and he groaned.

I exulted! He was as vulnerable as I had been. Power coursed through my veins. It excited me more than any physical touch. And I could tell he was just as excited, by the powerful flexing of his silk-covered cock against my sex.

I lubricated the anal plug and, shifting so my arse hung just above his face, inserted it into my tight rosebud which peeked out from its special opening in the thong. The plug was big, and I had to bear down to get it to go in. But, oh! The fullness, the delicious pleasure-pain. My internal muscles clenched and released spasmodically, sending shudders through me. I pressed the plug in slow circles, gasping and moaning, excited beyond awareness.

Damien's head darted up and he bit my protruding sex like a pit bull, hanging on tight despite my sudden writhing. His lips and teeth clamped down hard on my outer lips, squeezing my clit between them. Pain flashed through my genitals, both from his bite and the plug, which I hadn't stopped rotating. Glorious! Daggers of pleasure shot outward, down my thighs, up into my belly. I writhed and gushed, the fluids creaming his face, and he released me to lap at the secretions.

'You'll pay for that piece of disobedience,' I hissed as I got off his face.

The crop whished through the air, slicing the silk boxers and leaving a red streak where I struck him across his arse, just below his scrotum. He recoiled and struggled against his bonds, but said nothing. Maybe he was familiar with this game.

I smiled and struck again, a little closer this time.

Again. Closer yet.

And again.

He stopped flinching and held perfectly still. Smack! The crop barely grazed the sensitive skin of his tightly drawn-up testicles. A slow angry flush spread outward from the reddening stripes.

'More?' I enquired, tracing his perineum with the tip of the crop.

He didn't make a sound, although his cock was dripping, ready to come. I wanted him to beg as I had begged. For that was what shamed me about that long-ago experience: I had begged him for more. And more.

I changed my approach and gently rubbed lubricant over his reddened arse cheeks. I slid my fingers down to his anus, massaging and relaxing the tight muscles, lulling him. He looked like a virgin. Tight, so smooth and tight.

A virgin for a virgin. That was fair, I thought.

I delicately slid one fingertip, then two, into his now well-oiled arsehole, stroking in and out, in and out. Gasps escaped from him, despite his rigid control.

I greased the stocky head of the anal vibrator, never stopping my tender ministrations to his tight rectum. Moving it into position, I slid my fingers out and the tip of the wonderfully thick vibrator in. He grunted and his rim tightened reflexively but I pressed harder, forcing his sphincter muscle to expand. And expand.

My eyes were fixed unblinkingly on the junction between anus and vibrator, watching it slowly widen. My sex clutched convulsively in sympathy.

When it was a third of the way in, I stopped and played a bit. I rotated it, spun it, inscribed circles with the protruding end.

'Ready to beg yet?'

'Never!' The word sounded like it had been forced through gritted teeth.

I smiled, flicked the vibrator on and then, without warning, shoved it in as far as it would go, as he had done to me. A loud gasping groan, this time.

And then I resumed my efforts with the crop. I was very skilful with a crop; had perfected my aim so that I could strike within a hairsbreadth of any object. Nipple clamps, scrotum, the head of his cock jutting out of the boxers, the end of the anal vibrator. I just, just missed them all. His body twitched uncontrollably with each stroke.

And I twitched uncontrollably, too. My efforts had set my breasts to bouncing painfully and, every so often, I couldn't resist giving them a light flick with the crop. The anal plug shifted inside me with each movement I made. I played with it, encouraging the muscle spasms.

He finally gave in. 'Enough! No more!'

I dropped the crop and immediately began sliding the vibrator in and out of his arse while pressuring his perineum. His hips lunged, his cock flexed, seeming to beg for release. But I needed to hear it from his lips. 'No more? You want me to stop?'

'Ahh! No, dammit.' His breath came in short gasps. 'More! Harder! Faster!'

I slowly began withdrawing the vibrator from his rear. 'Say "please"! Beg for more!'

'Bloody hell! All right! Please, Samantha, please fuck me!'

Triumph! The words alone were almost enough to make me come. 'You'll have to wait your turn.'

No longer able to hold back, I straddled him. Damien's eyes flicked between my nipples and my sex pouting out from between the leather strips of the thong. His cock strained towards my dripping sex but I only allowed a little rub. I had other plans.

The ice vibrator felt blue-cold against my palm. I ran it caressingly over his face so he would know what I was feeling and then shoved it into myself. My labia were pinched tightly between the edges of the tight thong and the vibrator; they pulled at my clit with each stroke of the vibrator.

God! It sent shivers of pleasure through me. I angled it back against the anal plug and turned it on. The vibrations shook me so that my breasts bounced and my stomach muscles clenched. I could barely kneel over him, I trembled so.

I twisted around and lay on his belly in a sixty-nine position.

My clit was desperate for relief and I rotated my hips, grinding it down hard over his tongue.

'Lick me,' I ordered. 'And don't stop until I tell you to.'

He licked and laved, slipping his tongue between the inner and outer lips, swirling it around my clit, sucking me with his lips. My back curled. My buttock muscles clenched tightly around the anal plug, pressing it against the vibrating ice-rod in my cunt. In seconds, a shuddering climax rocked me, but didn't drain me.

I slid my hands down inside his shorts alongside his cock and fondled his tightly knotted balls before ringing the base of his thick cock with my fingers.

One wet lunge and his swollen erection was deep down my throat, throbbing, the shreds of the boxer shorts pushed aside. My fingers tightened relentlessly. I couldn't allow him to come just yet. His licking slowed for a moment but I pressed my clit back down against his mouth. He obeyed, groaning, and stroked harder.

My throat muscles convulsed about his cock and I moved up and down just enough to shift the knobby head past the tightest, smallest constriction. I've always loved the feel of a thick cock deep in my throat. The salty masculine smell of him fizzed in my nostrils like champagne. Tighter and tighter I squeezed the base of his cock; faster and faster I forced his cock-head past the ring of throat muscles.

The tension coiled deep within. I felt full to bursting from every orifice, ready to explode again from the wild pressures building. My stomach muscles were reflexively clenching, simultaneously forcing my clit down harder on to Damien's mouth and his cock deeper into my throat. A final thrust, my mouth almost swallowed my fingers, and I climaxed again, powerful spasms rocking my body from both my throat and my cunt.

He continued teething and laving, torturing my suddenly over-sensitive clit and my hips bucked with aftershocks.

Dazed, in triple slow motion, I slid his cock from my mouth. Resting my chin on his hard belly, I made an inspection. And smiled. His erection pointed, throbbing and thick, straight at me. My improvisation had worked: he hadn't been able to come.

His cock pulsed, reaching out for my wet lips which just

grazed the tip. 'Goddamn it, Sam! Don't stop now.' Damien rotated his hips, trying to grind the anal vibrator further into his arse and his cock into my mouth. 'More, please, more!'

I was becoming exhausted but felt like a junkie in need of an ever-higher rush. I had thought that his subjugation of me so long ago had brought out my highly sexed dominant nature. But this triumph over Damien, my nemesis, the man who haunted my sexual fantasies, was making me insatiable. I wanted more.

I pulled out the anal plug and the ice-rod with a gasp at the sudden emptiness. Straddling Damien again, facing his feet, I lowered myself over his sheathed cock, positioning my well-prepared arsehole on to the thick head. His erection hadn't shrunk; if anything, it was bigger than before. I grasped it with two hands full of lubricant and lowered myself on to him, slowly easing his cock into my rectum.

Would he fit? God, I felt as if I were being split in two.

My breath caught and I had to stop for a minute to let my muscles expand to accommodate him. I moved the head in and out a little, massaging the inside and sending spears of pleasure-pain through me. When I thought I was ready, I tilted my pelvis just so and impaled myself the rest of the way.

My vision dimmed with the red-hot pain. All else faded except the inferno burning through my arsehole. Gasping for air, I became aware that Damien was gasping just as loudly. He'd probably never had his enormous cock in anything so tight! I know I'd never had anything so big up me before.

I waited, perfectly still. Slowly, the feelings of pleasure increased until they became irresistible and my rectum began to clutch at his cock. I slid the ice-rod vibrator back into my vagina and held it there, savouring the new sensations. It was large and, with Damien's cock up my rear, I couldn't have been any fuller.

I pressed the ice-rod against the thin barrier separating it from his cock, hoping that he'd be able to feel the coldness. The anal vibrator was still in Damien's arsehole and I moved it in and out with my other hand. His hips twitched violently under my weight, urging me to move.

So I did. As I raised and lowered myself slightly on my knees, his cock grated in and out, rubbing against the ice-rod as it moved. His hips flexed and he began to pound into me. We fell into a rhythm: I slammed the vibrator up his arse and he forced his cock into me. I left the ice-rod fully embedded but frantically manipulated my clit with my free hand, in time with our mutual thrusting.

All awareness of the room, the house, fled. Consciousness shrank to concentrate on the shards of pleasure and pain lancing through my body. Excitement rose in me, coiled tighter than anything I had ever felt before. We continued our pounding rhythm.

My back curled, every muscle in my pelvic region clenched spasmodically. Orgiastic waves swept through my out-of-control body. And kept on coming. I shuddered with the force of the orgasm. And kept on shuddering. I felt like an erupting volcano, spewing molten lava while the earth shook and rolled. I could feel my inner muscles grasping, clutching, at his cock, but had no awareness of anything else. The ice-rod slipped out of my vagina.

Aeons later, exhausted, I lay, panting softly, on top of Damien. He was gently kissing, nibbling, the back of my neck. The room smelled of salt and sweat and sex. The rain was still falling on the roof.

On the drive home, exhausted but content, I thought back over the afternoon with satisfaction. I knew I had finally resolved my obsession with Honeysuckle House and the events from long ago. I could go forward now, stronger than ever, free of the past.

Fragmented memories of the afternoon drifted through my mind: Damien, lying vulnerable before me, genitals on offer. Begging. The power and control that had filled me with exultation. The amazing final orgasm that had seemed to last for hours.

Memories of that other night floated in and intermingled with the others.

Damien gripping my hands and ankles in an iron-hard grip. Damien struggling futilely against the bonds that I had placed on him.

The violent thrust of his enormous, wickedly curving cock as he took away my virginity. The image of his virgin anus being forced to expand for the thick bulbous head of the anal vibrator.

My angry cries of protest changing to pleas for more, more. Damien, begging me for more.

The feel of his tongue on my exposed sex. His cock lying wet and glistening in front of my face, pointing ramrod straight at my lips, just after I had deep-throated him.

I frowned. The images were wrong.

In one, a cock, with a pronounced malicious bend to the left, seeming huge to my innocent eyes. And in another, a truly enormous shaft, perfectly straight and true, looking me in the eye.

And as my memories of that long ago night shifted to reveal the truth, as cavalier and nemesis exchanged places, I realised that my fascination with the past, with the house, wasn't yet finished.

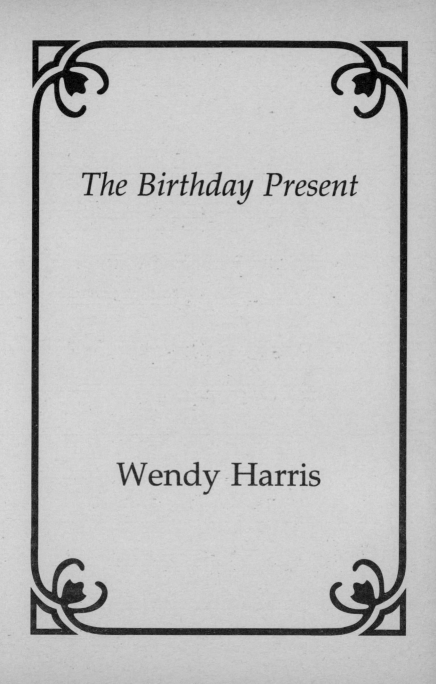

The Birthday Present

Wendy Harris

The Birthday Present

❖ ❖

Jayne smiled to herself as she tipped the contents of a shiny black carrier bag over the candy-striped duvet. Tonight's the night, she told herself. Shit or bust.

A chuckle gurgled at the back of her throat as she plucked a black basque from the scattered garments on the bed and dangled it from her fingers by its slender straps for a moment, before clutching it tightly to her body. Her cheeks burned with embarrassment at the daring of her purchase. Her stomach fluttered with excitement. Wait till he gets a load of this, she thought, now giggling like a pubescent teenager. If this doesn't make his dormant dick leap to attention, then he might as well join a monastery.

It had been almost a year since their last fuck and, after so many months of sexual famine, her body craved sustenance. She was desperate for sex. Gagging for it, as her teenage son would say. Yet how could she tell Dave without hurting his feelings?

She loved him. She couldn't just blurt it out and she wasn't the type to discuss the matter in a caring and sensitive way. She didn't know how to speak in a measured voice or stop her questions from turning into accusations. Her temperament was too volatile. If he pushed the wrong buttons, she'd simply explode and he'd be wounded in the fall-out. Deep down, she knew that she was angry with him. Angry with the fact that he'd chosen to ignore her needs; behaving as though his absence

159

of desire was infectious, like a disease that he'd caught and passed on to her. He didn't seem to realise that she was immune. That her own sex-drive was alive and kicking like a cornered mule.

Desperate women, she persuaded herself, must resort to desperate measures. She looked at the weapons of seduction on the bed: black stockings, crotchless knickers, stiletto-heeled ankle-strap shoes. It was her arsenal against an enemy of indifference. What would he make of it? She had never worn anything this raunchy before. Could it trip the switch and turn him on? Her stomach lurched but she steeled herself and shrugged out of her bathrobe.

Squeezing her freshly scrubbed and scented body into the rigid confines of the basque was more difficult than she had supposed. She puffed and panted as she grappled with the hooks, her face contorting as she twisted the unyielding garment into position. But, finally, the battle was won. It felt strange. Like a man's strong arms gripping her tightly. The feeling excited her and, without hesitation, she reached for the split triangle of silk that comprised the panties and slipped them over her hips. Draughty and rude, they felt even stranger than the basque and the sight of her pubic hair peeping through the lace trim sent a warm flush tingling through her body. Panting, not from exertion now, she tore at the wrapper of the stockings and drew them out carefully, caressing their sheer silkiness between her fingers before sliding them slowly up her legs. How long had it been since Dave had run his hands up her legs like this?

She fastened her shoes and strutted boldly towards the full-length mirror. She didn't know what to expect. Would she look ridiculous?

'Good God,' she uttered, catching her breath as she absorbed her reflection. The basque had remoulded her. Flattened her tummy bulge; narrowed her waist; pushed up her breasts to form two luscious orbs of pale creamy flesh. Her legs, extended by four-inch heels, looked sleek and sexy beneath the clinging black silk of her stockings.

Her sex clenched as she spread her legs to reveal the bush of dark hair between her thighs. She couldn't resist stroking it with her fingers, shivering as she parted the lace lips of her panties. Christ, it was a long time since she had felt this horny.

Closing her eyes, she started to burrow with her finger. But suddenly the front door slammed and Dave's voice called up the stairs, 'I'm home, Jayne!'

'Don't come up!' she shouted, snapping out of her sultry daydream. 'I'm wrapping your birthday present.'

She wondered briefly why she had bothered to warn him. He was a creature of habit and would never have broken his daily ritual by coming up the stairs. He always went into the lounge as soon as he came home, routinely plonking himself in his favourite armchair and burying his head in the daily paper. There would be virtual silence for the half an hour that it took him to read it, broken only by the occasional grunted comment or an enquiry after his tea. Yet she didn't want to take any chances. She couldn't risk him spoiling her surprise. She had planned everything to the last detail.

She opened her wardrobe and withdrew a filmy black negligée – the last piece of gift-wrap – smiling as she watched herself in the mirror putting it on and draping it into position. After a final brush of her long fair hair and a dash of lipstick, she was ready. She swallowed and plumped up her breasts. 'Torpedoes loaded,' she advised her reflection. 'We're armed and ready for action.'

As she glided down the stairs, her confidence soared. It was all working out just as she'd planned it. At the doorway to the lounge, she saw that his head was immersed in the newspaper, just as she'd known it would be. Taking a deep breath, she leant against the doorframe in a practised pose and murmured softly, 'Darling, here's your birthday present.'

He glanced up and, like a bad actor, delivered the wrong lines and ruined the take.

'Very funny,' he chuckled, turning his attention back to the article he was reading. 'Did you know our bloody shares have gone down again?'

If he had slapped her in the face or thrown a bucket of cold water over her, he could not have humiliated her more thoroughly. Jayne tried to speak but a lump the size of an apple was clogging her throat. With tears stinging her eyes, she backed numbly into the hall and retreated up the stairs. Once inside the bedroom, she closed the door behind her and let the lump in her throat burst out as a sob.

'You stupid fool!' she hurled at her reflection, ripping off her negligée. 'You should have known this would happen.'

But her image stared innocently back at her. How could she have known that his rejection would be so cold, so callous? Anger swelled inside her as realisation dawned – he'd done it deliberately. The bastard wanted to make her feel as inadequate as himself.

He wanted her to think that it was all her fault. That she was undesirable, unattractive. 'Liar,' she raged, lifting her chin and thrusting out her breasts as she turned in front of the mirror to examine herself from all sides. She didn't look ridiculous. She looked sexy. The verdict of Dave's disinterested prick was unacceptable.

Seething at the memory of his comment, she snatched a sleeveless button-through dress from her wardrobe and threw it on over the basque. Her fingers fiddled with the buttons as she clomped angrily down the stairs. As she entered the lounge, only three of them were fastened.

'I'm going out,' she snarled at Dave.

'Like that?' He stared at her accusingly but she saw a flicker of fear in his eyes.

'Why not?' she countered. 'It's fucking funny, isn't it? Perhaps I'll give someone a laugh.'

Remorse showed in his face. 'Don't be daft,' he said. 'You can't go out like that.'

She grabbed her car keys from the table. 'Your dinner's in the oven. It's your favourite. Happy birthday, sweetheart.' She turned on her heel and strode from the room, muttering, 'Fuck you' as he shouted after her. Then she smothered his voice with an explosive front-door slam which made the next-door neighbour glance up from his gardening. His mouth dropped open as Jayne flew past him in her half-buttoned dress and flung open the door of her car.

Too angry to drive, she sat for a while, staring at her white thighs above the glistening black stocking tops, trying to imagine a strong male hand inserting itself between them. Not Dave's hand, now, but a stranger's. The idea sent a slither of excitement rippling down her spine. Reluctantly, she shook the thought from her mind and buttoned up her dress. Firing up the engine, she crunched into first gear, stabbed her foot on the accelerator and screeched down the driveway with screaming wheels.

She had no idea where she was going or what she was looking for. She drove for hours, for miles, searching for an answer to the hunger that gnawed inside her. As darkness fell, she pulled into a petrol station beside an old cinema. It was a seedy run-down place but her eyes were constantly drawn to it as she filled up her tank. Handing over her credit card to the attendant, she found herself enquiring if he knew what film was showing at the cinema.

'A bluey, I expect,' he told her. 'It's a wanker's paradise in there. Not your cup of tea, I should think.'

'No, I suppose not,' she agreed.

But after she'd driven a mile from the station, her mind wandered back to that shabby little cinema. A porn movie. It reminded her of the time that Dave had hired a video and they'd watched it together curled up on the couch, laughing at the grunting, writhing bodies and spurting cocks. It hadn't turned them on but it had given them a couple of novel ideas and they'd experimented for days afterwards. He'd wanted her all the time, back then. Just a look or a touch from her could bring a misty yearning to his eyes. How different now. She had all but prodded his loins with a poker but still the ashes stayed cold while the fire in her own raged on unattended. Could a blue film put it out? She steered the car into a three-point turn.

The man in the booth looked at her strangely but made no comment as he handed her a ticket. Clutching it tightly, she walked through the grubby curtains. Bland, tuneless music crackled from the speakers as Jayne picked her way down the aisle. It was gloomy but not pitch black and she could feel eyes boring into her as she passed by shadowy figures hunched in their seats. Men, sitting apart from each other, isolated in their own sordid fantasies. The place stank of sweat and stale semen.

Jayne found an empty row and worked her way to the middle. After she had sat down, she stared blankly at the screen without watching it, wondering why she had come. Surround-sound couldn't make a fake orgasm real and there was nothing erotic in a man's buttocks eight feet wide. So, why had she come?

Minutes later, Jayne had her answer as someone began shuffling towards her. Her breath clung to the back of her throat and she clutched at the fabric of her dress as the seat next to her creaked under the weight of the man who sat down. Long legs encased in black trousers positioned themselves and a large callused hand slid over one knee. A labourer's hand, she guessed. Strong, blunt-fingered. Neither young nor old. She imagined the face of its owner but did not lift her eyes to check the accuracy of her guess.

She felt no compulsion to move, even as the hand began rubbing the trousered thigh in a lewdly suggestive motion. He was breathing heavily now and she sensed that he was peering down her dress, feasting his gaze on her cleavage. The idea fascinated her and she could feel her nipples hardening under his scrutiny. Suddenly, she knew that she wanted the hand to touch her. But how could she deliver her message without breaking the spell?

Inhaling, she crossed her legs so that the hem of her dress slithered upward. Her fingers trembled as she continued to pull inconspicuously on the fabric until the dark line of her stocking top appeared.

She knew that she had lured his eyes to the bait of her legs when his hand suddenly stopped moving. She heard his sharp intake of breath and then he gripped his thigh until his knuckles gleamed in the darkness. Her heart was thumping with expectancy as the hand disappeared from her field of vision. A moment later, she opened her mouth in a silent gasp as she felt its warmth against her shoulder, resting lightly against her, as if by accident. Perhaps waiting for a protest that did not come.

Encouraged by her silence, the hand moved slowly over her shoulder, pausing an inch above her breast. Jayne tensed; the agony of waiting triggering a throb of anticipation in her pelvis. She trembled as his hand fluttered over her breast like a butterfly, teasing and tormenting until she could hardly breathe with longing. At last, it closed over the dome of her breast, and as she thrust herself forcefully into the cup of his palm, his fingers dug into her, kneading and caressing through the material of her dress.

She could hear him panting softly and, out of the corner of her eye, she could see him stroking his groin. With shaking hands, she unfastened the buttons of her dress and gasped as his fingers lunged into the opening, forcing their way into the lace of her basque to ravish her eager flesh. She groaned as he grasped her nipple and massaged it between his fingers; the thrill of his rough callused skin making her feverish with desire as he moved from one breast to the other. Exalting in his touch, she almost cried out when he suddenly withdrew his hand and could taste her relief when, a moment later, his palm slid over her knee.

Her eyes grew hazy with lust; she watched his circling fingers snagging her stockings as they worked slowly up her thigh towards her naked flesh. There was an excruciating pause as he toyed with her suspender. Then, at last, his fingers connected with her skin and the electricity of his touch jolted through her body, forcing pent-up air from her lungs.

His own breathing was laboured and heavy as he began to explore her thigh, forcing his fingers under her buttock to grasp and fondle the cheek of her bottom. She heard the sound of his zip opening and her eyes were drawn to the rigid column of his erection as he pulled it from his trousers and gripped it in his hand. She felt a buzz of achievement. She'd done it. She'd given him a hard-on.

Uncrossing her legs, she parted her thighs, allowing his probing fingers access to her sex. He groaned as he discovered her damp pubic hair through the open split of her panties. Laying his hand on her mound, he waited, letting the weight and the heat of his palm drive her wild with hungry yearning.

She twitched and strained uncontrollably, clinging to the edge of her seat, a scream of frustration mounting within her. But just as she thought it would escape, his fingers delved into her crevice and pressed the swollen nub of her clitoris. She tossed her head and moaned aloud as he rubbed it slowly to the rhythm of her thrusting hips.

She was conscious of him wanking himself now but felt no desire to look at him or touch him. His clever fingers knew exactly what she wanted. They spread her lips wide, sliding over her sex before moving back to tease her clitoris. He varied his tempo, changing the pressure of his fingers: roughly buffing her one moment, slowly circling the next. He tormented her with heart-stopping pauses which set the muscles of her flanks twitching as she thrust her pubis against his palm.

Masterfully, he steered her into a euphoric state of absolute desire until his fingers became the centre of her universe. They must not stop. They must not stop.

Her legs began shaking and as she started panting, his fingers worked faster and faster. Someone was groaning. Was it him? Was it her? Her eyes flicked open and, through a daze, she saw faces in front of her. Men were peering over the back of their seats. Where had they all come from? They were staring, drooling. Feasting on the sight of her quivering body. But it didn't matter. She spread her legs wider. Let them see. Let them all see what he was doing. Nothing mattered except the rising volcano of passion inside her. Their leering faces blurred as her juddering climax erupted.

The feeling peaked and waned but he wouldn't let it subside. Pushing his fingers deep into her throbbing wet sex, he worked them in and out, steering her back to the precipice. Oh, God, she didn't want this to end. It felt so good. Hands reached over the seats and lifted up her legs. Countless fingers clawed at her stockings, groping her calves and thighs. Others descended on her shoulders from behind, ripping at her dress, tearing at the cups of her basque, grasping and squeezing her naked breasts as the swimming sea of nameless faces looked on. She was burning up, shaking with desire as his fingers pumped in and out of her.

Then, abruptly, her pelvis went into spasm and her second orgasm thundered out. A savage cry broke from her as she arched her back and grasped the man's leg, digging her nails into his thigh. Then oblivion descended and, for a moment, she floated in blissful unawareness. But, as rational thought returned, she grew conscious of the hands still frantically pawing at her body. The faces of the men surrounding her swam into focus. Businessmen in suits; teenage boys with gleeful grins; grey-haired men in macs. Horrified, she struggled free and staggered to her feet. There were men everywhere. She pulled her dress together and started moving down the row.

They grabbed her, pulled her on to their laps. Hands went up her dress, pinching and squeezing and violating her as she was passed along like a sex-doll. Someone shoved her breast into his mouth and sucked at her nipple as she fell on top of him. Another forced her hand into his open fly. Then an outstretched leg tripped her up and, as she sprawled over it, her dress was lifted over her head and hungry hands tore at her panties. The string snapped and her bare backside was fondled and stroked.

Jayne knew that, if she stayed there a moment longer, someone would take her from behind. Her head swam. Why couldn't she move? What was keeping her there? Although their hands were lifting her rear and pushing her head down until she was jack-knifed over a pair of muscular thighs, she was not being forcefully restrained.

Then a voice uttered urgently, 'Give it to her. Let her have it.'

She clawed at the carpet but her body seemed welded to the legs of the man who had tripped her. As rough hands parted her buttocks, a flicker of panic and fear made a scream well up inside her throat but, at the same time, the muscles of her sex clenched in eager anticipation. When the sound came, it was more like hysterical laughter than a scream, bursting out of her in rapturous relief as the probing helmet of a cock slid into her labia, searching for its target. Now she knew why she couldn't move. This is what she'd come here for. This is what she wanted.

'Oh, yes,' she whispered. 'Give it to me. Give it to me.'

As the first thrust came, she flexed her back, gasping for breath as the anonymous prick drove into her. Hands clamped over her breasts and the man's pelvic bones slammed against her flesh as he plunged his cock home, again and again. The thrill of his ramming shaft after so many months of emptiness made her squirm with pleasure as she jerked her hips to meet his violent thrusts.

'Go on, son,' jeered a voice. 'Fill your boots up. She's loving it.'

The words jolted Jayne to her senses. What the hell did she think she was doing? Letting a stranger fuck her while all these voyeurs watched and wanked?

'Get off me!' she cried, and wrenched herself out of his grasp. His cock squelched out of her as she twisted her body. Somehow, she got to her feet and, striking out viciously at everything in her path, fought her way to the end of the row.

She stumbled into the aisle and, with tears of shame streaming from her eyes, ran out of the cinema and fled to the sanctuary of her car.

Once inside, she locked the door and slumped against the steering wheel, trembling, tearful, bitterly ashamed. How could she have let those nameless, faceless men touch her? She looked down at her torn dress, her laddered stockings and remembered their grasping, groping hands. It crossed her mind to report them. But how could she? She'd have to tell the truth. That she'd loved it. God help her, she'd loved every dirty minute of it. The thrill of those anonymous callused hands. The excitement of exposing herself to a bunch of sex-starved strangers. The thrust of a turgid cock between her thighs. Jayne shook her head. No, she couldn't tell the police.

When she got home, Dave was waiting for her. He was shocked by her appearance and leapt to his feet. 'What the hell has happened to you? Please, God, don't tell me you've been raped.' She started to cry and he gathered her into his arms. 'What is it, Jayne? For Chrissake, what is it?'

She let him steer her on to the couch. 'I'm so sorry,' she sobbed, as he knelt down in front of her. 'I don't know what possessed me. I feel so ashamed.'

'Tell me about it,' he prompted her softly.

At first she couldn't speak but, with gentle persuasion, he coaxed the story out of her. And as she described each sordid detail of her experience, he listened in silence. When she had finished, she buried her head in her hands, waiting for a torrent of angry words. Instead, he gripped her shoulders and croaked a question. 'How many of them touched you?'

Surprised by the tone of his voice, she looked up. There was something in his expression that surprised her even more. 'I don't know,' she murmured. 'A dozen, maybe twenty. Their hot clammy hands were all over me. Clawing at my flesh like ravenous animals.'

Dave's hands slid down to her breasts. 'Did they touch you here?'

She nodded wordlessly as his fingers trailed down her body until his palms were resting on her thighs. She noticed that they were damp with perspiration. He scraped his cheek against her silk-covered knee and repeated his question. 'Did they touch you here?'

'Yes,' she whispered.

He prised her legs apart and her head bobbed guiltily as he grabbed her pubic hair.

'Yes,' she breathed. 'They touched me everywhere.'

'Jayne,' he uttered urgently. 'Something's happening.' She lifted her face and saw that his eyes were misty with desire. 'Tell me again. Tell me everything. Everything they did to you.'

'You're not angry with me?' she asked him.

'No.' He took her hand and pressed it to his groin. She could feel his stiff cock straining against the fabric of his trousers. 'Sweetheart, this is the best birthday present you've ever given me,' he told her.

With a sigh of relief, Jayne threw her arms around his neck. 'In that case, my darling, I'll start at the beginning.'

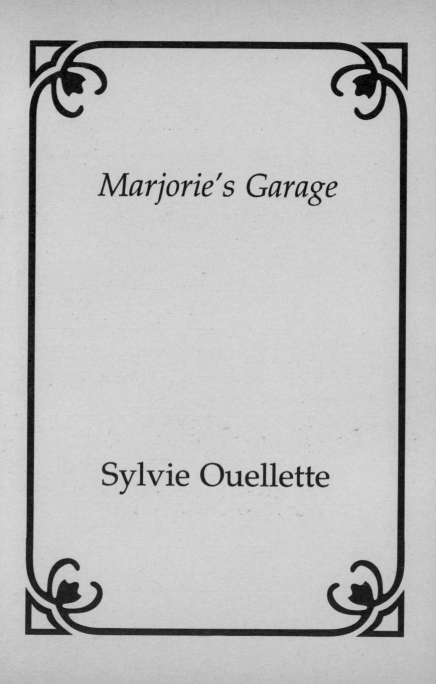

Marjorie's Garage

Sylvie Ouellette

Marjorie's Garage

❧ ❧

Sitting behind her desk, Marjorie had a clear view of the car showroom. The place was completely deserted in the middle of the afternoon, which made it easy for her to notice the man just as he entered by the side door of the garage. He hesitated for a moment, as if stepping into foreign territory, then decidedly headed for the service counter. It took Marjorie only a fraction of a second to assess his type: embarrassed, yet trying to appear bold. Easy to manipulate, she hoped.

She found him incredibly attractive. Quite tall with strong features, he was obviously the kind of man who took good care of himself. His pale cropped hair was perhaps a tad too short for Marjorie's taste, but it gave him a boyish appeal she rather liked. She was disappointed not to be able to see his hands, which he kept deep in his pockets. He went and stood by the counter, waiting for someone to notice him.

Majorie sprang to her feet and quickly checked herself in the mirror behind her, on the only wall of her office that wasn't glass. She smiled contentedly, reassured that her face looked exactly like all the photos framed and mounted next to the mirror. Seven nearly identical visions of herself smiled back at her, lined up at eye level: SALES REP OF THE YEAR, 1991 through 1997. It was amazing – and gratifying – to see how little she had changed in all those years. Not a single grey hair in view; not a single wrinkle either. Her flame-coloured hair bounced around her head in untamed waves. Perhaps it would be wise to change her hairdo eventually, but Marjorie didn't want to take that chance. She considered her image a lucky charm and feared that any modification would jeopardise her success.

She quickly reapplied some lipstick, gave a broad smile to make sure she didn't have any on her teeth, then went to meet the man who was patiently waiting at the counter. He started and turned when he heard her coming from behind him.

'Welcome to Spencer Autos,' she said in a sultry voice as she extended her right hand. 'I'm Marjorie Spencer. Is there anything I can help you with?'

She purposefully held on to his hand a bit longer than necessary, squeezing it firmly but not too tightly, wanting him to feel her warmth. Her keen eye didn't miss how he swiftly looked her over from head to toe. She was used to men being impressed by the sight of her – not only by her beauty but also by her assertiveness. And this time wouldn't be any different. Just as she had thought, the man blushed, sheepishly stared at the floor and put his hands back in his pockets.

'All I need is an oil filter,' he said in a small voice. 'It's for a series B Ford Escort.'

'I'm afraid our receptionist is on his tea break at the moment,' Marjorie answered as she casually stepped closer. 'We'll have to ask our mechanic, Giovanna.'

She called out to a woman who appeared from under the open bonnet of a car at the far end of the garage. As Giovanna approached the counter, Marjorie kept a close eye on her client. She could easily see how impressed he was by the young Italian mechanic. Giovanna was quite a sight even in simple street clothes, but she was unusually beguiling dressed in her dark blue overalls. Her long, dark curly hair floated freely in coils on her shoulders. Her rolled-up sleeves revealed the bronze skin – albeit sprinkled with grease – of her taut arms. The thick gold chain around her neck contrasted with her soft, tanned skin. The medallion hanging from it shone against the dark fabric of her overall, drawing attention to her generous breasts which bounced softly underneath as she walked.

'I'm not sure we have oil filters for that make of car, any

more,' Giovanna answered after Marjorie told her what the client wanted.

'Well,' Marjorie replied in a condescending tone, 'perhaps if you had a good, thorough look in the supplies room . . .'

Giovanna sighed and turned round. 'I'll see what I can find,' she muttered as she walked away.

Noticing that the client still hadn't taken his eyes off Giovanna, Marjorie slipped her arm around his shoulders and turned him to face the showroom. 'Why don't you come this way and have a seat?' she suggested. 'We'll be more comfortable while we wait for her.'

The client followed her silently, never taking his hands out of his pockets.

'A series B Ford Escort, did you say?' Marjorie continued. 'That's quite an older model. Is it still in good running order? Are you planning to do this oil change yourself?'

'Oh, no!' the man protested. 'My wife will be taking care of that.'

'I see,' Marjorie said. 'So it's her car, then?'

'No, it's mine, really. She drives a Mercedes.'

'Lucky her. What model?'

'I couldn't tell you,' the man admitted. 'I can never remember the exact number. I'm not really good at identifying cars.'

'I see. Recent model?'

'Brand new.'

'Company car?'

'No, her own. She's the head of a very successful communications firm, you know.' He beamed.

'And she lets you drive around in an old Ford?' Marjorie laughed sarcastically as she directed him towards a small group of cars on display and slowed her pace to execute a cleverly planned slalom among the vehicles. 'Don't you think that's a bit unfair?'

'Not really,' the client admitted. 'All I need is a reliable car that will get me wherever I want to go.'

'And where might that be?' Marjorie asked softly as she went to stand on the other side of a shiny bright green Peugeot and leant over the bonnet. Her hands clasped together, she rested on her elbows. The white silk of her blouse created a stark contrast against the newly repainted steel, and she knew that this exact shade of green set off her flamboyant mane perfectly. But, more than that, it was the opening of her blouse that attracted the client's gaze. She saw him hesitate before replying, not missing for a second his quick but obvious glance towards her cleavage.

'I don't go out much,' the man admitted. 'I need a car to take the kids to school and to do the shopping. The rest of the time, we take my wife's car.'

'Must be quite a thrill to find yourself behind the wheel of such a powerful car –' Marjorie began.

'No,' he interrupted quickly. 'She does all the driving.'

'What a shame.' Marjorie pouted. 'Still, I'm sure we have something here that would suit you better.'

'I'm quite happy with my car –'

'Yes, of course you are! But for how much longer? Besides, think of your children's safety. An older car is much more likely to give up on you when you least expect it, you know.'

'Really? I have mine inspected every year, you know.'

'I'm sure you do. But you never know what can happen, do you?'

As she spoke, Marjorie straightened and walked back to the other side of the car to join him. Again she slipped her arm around his shoulders to direct him from one car to the next, each time giving the little speech she knew so well about each car's specifications: horsepower, independent suspension, disk brakes, and all the jargon that men were usually so unfamiliar with. Eventually they went back to the Peugeot, the only car the client had manifested any interest in.

'Look at that body,' Marjorie purred as her hand slowly glided over the shiny curves of a wing. Her fingernails, perfectly manicured and painted bright red, lightly grazed the finish, more of a caress than an attempt to scratch it. She let her fingers trail almost lovingly, knowing what kind of effect the move often had on her male customers. And she was pleased to see that this one was no different. When she glanced at the man, she saw him blushing. Directing her gaze downward, she couldn't miss seeing the bulge in his trousers that betrayed his arousal. He saw what she was looking at, blushed further and turned away, pushing his hands deeper into his pockets.

'Tell me more about the Mazda . . .' he said in a trembling voice.

Marjorie smiled, unable to contain her satisfaction. She knew he didn't care for the Mazda at all: that was just an excuse to create a diversion, to get away.

'That would be the perfect car for you,' Marjorie stated as she came to join him. Again, he stepped back hesitantly as Marjorie came closer, then immediately went to the next car. Marjorie decided to have pity on him and let him off the hook.

'Why don't you take some time to think about all this?' she suggested. 'You know where we are and, if you decide you do want to change your car, I'm sure we have something here that will suit your needs.'

'I would have to come back with my wife,' he said sheepishly.

'Of course,' Marjorie said with a tinge of condescension. She had seen more than her share of this type of man: the house-husband who has yet to hear about the men's liberation movement and can't make a single decision without consulting the wife. If he did come back with her, however, Marjorie would have to be on her guard, deal with her at a higher level and not try to pull a fast one on her, like she usually did with male customers.

'Now,' she said, 'why don't we go see what Giovanna managed to find?'

But as she led him towards the garage, a wicked idea rose in Marjorie's mind. Rather than stopping at the counter and calling out to Giovanna, she gestured for the man to follow her all the way to the back where she knew Giovanna was probably still busy looking for that oil filter. She walked fast, even in high heels, skilfully dodging the discarded tools scattered all over the cement floor. She knew her assuredness never failed to impress men and she didn't need to look to know the client was probably utterly embarrassed by the sight of all the posters of naked men plastered on the walls of the garage.

As they entered the supplies room, Marjorie was pleased to see that the sight offered by Giovanna was better than anything she could have expected: the young mechanic was bent over, rummaging through an old grease-stained cardboard box. The top buttons of her overalls were undone and revealed the upper part of her plump breasts. Marjorie stepped to one side to let the client in, watching him from the corner of her eye to see his reaction.

Giovanna raised her head slightly, saw the client, then quickly glanced at Marjorie. They exchanged a brief, knowing look.

'I can't find anything,' she said as she continued looking through the box. 'The order sheet says we should have one more, and it should be here.'

'It's quite a big box,' Marjorie said as she placed her hand in the client's back and slightly ushered him forward. 'Why don't we help you look for it?'

The client, mesmerised by the sight of the beautiful Giovanna, didn't seem to quite realise what was going on. Yet Marjorie could feel a palpable tension in the air, and she knew that Giovanna not only was very aware of it, she was also fostering it by pretending to keep looking in the box. Marjorie could see that the man was only pretending to look through the box as well: his eyes constantly came back to Giovanna and he seemed in awe. Now and again, he delicately took one of the items in the box with trembling hands, briefly glanced at it and then put it back, as if uncertain what he was actually looking for, and visibly under the spell of Giovanna's raw beauty.

Marjorie observed them for a while, hoping that Giovanna would soon make a move, knowing she herself was so excited that she wouldn't be able to stand this tension much longer. She could hardly contain her satisfaction when she saw him licking his lips and noticed that Giovanna had seen it as well. Obviously, it was the cue that the mechanic had been waiting for. Bending forward still, she brought her head near the client's and pretended not to notice that their cheeks were just inches away from one another's. Marjorie saw the client close his eyes and breathe deeply, and she guessed he could probably smell Giovanna's scent, a typical mixture of female sweat and old car oil.

At some point Giovanna stopped what she was doing, raised her head, stared at the man – who was just an inch away and staring back – and gave him a seductive, inviting smile. He held her gaze for a moment then quickly looked down her overalls. From where he was now standing, he had a full view of her beautiful breasts. Pulling her hands out of the box to grab the man's head, Giovanna kissed him roughly, parting his lips with hers.

Marjorie felt her heart pound and her sex moisten as she watched the man timidly reply to the kiss by sticking out his tongue to meet Giovanna's. She had often been witness to sexy encounters in this garage, and each excited her even more than the previous one. She bent down, grabbed the edge of the box with both hands and forcefully pulled it away from them. It was heavy, almost full of a variety of metal bits and pieces but, at that point, she was so excited by what was going on that the strength came to her naturally.

As soon as nothing stood between them, Giovanna and the man moved closer. Giovanna didn't waste any time and grabbed hold of his buttocks to fondle them roughly with her grease-stained hands before moving round to feel his crotch. Already Marjorie could hear her grunting with passion. Giovanna's hips swayed as she ground her pelvis against the man. Her left hand was on his buttocks, her fingers digging deep, while she strongly handled his genitals through his trousers with the other hand. The man let her have her way with him, at times demurely putting his hands on her biceps and caressing her arms and shoulders. His lack of resistance and his panting betrayed his excitement.

Knowing she had to help matters, Marjorie came to join them, took his hand and placed it inside Giovanna's overall, inviting him to fondle the soft mounds. He obeyed readily, and Marjorie knew he had just put himself completely at the mercy of the two women. She stepped back to watch, eager to see Giovanna in action and already knowing she wouldn't be disappointed.

Giovanna quickly unzipped the man's trousers and retrieved his prick, which was already hard and erect. She fondled him in an up and down motion until he moaned with excitement. Then she let go of him, stepped aside to pull over an empty plastic crate and turned it upside down before making the man sit on it. She then promptly got down on all fours between the man's parted legs.

Marjorie was content to watch them for a while, enjoying the sight that the couple offered. She knew how good the mechanic was at providing oral gratification. Already the man was wincing with delight as Giovanna's head bobbed over his cock, her wet lips gliding up and down his shaft and her cheeks caving inward as she increased her suction. His hands, buried in Giovanna's curly mane, delicately caressed the softness of her hair.

Soon enough, Marjorie's level of excitement increased to the point where she couldn't just watch any more. Unfastening her blouse and bra as she stepped forward, she exposed her voluptuous breasts and presented them to his mouth. He let go of Giovanna's head to grasp Marjorie's mounds instead. Now she could see his hands from up close. She enjoyed the way they looked on her pale skin: quite large but delicate, caressing her with visible eagerness but not too roughly. His mouth, however, betrayed the full force of his desire as he hungrily licked and suckled her stiff nipples. It made her even hotter. But, much as she liked what he was doing, she wanted more.

She took his hands again and this time placed them under her skirt, instructing him to fondle her thighs. That was the last time she had to tell him what to do, however. He grabbed hold of her knickers and lowered them before attacking her flesh with both hands. Marjorie gasped as his fingers penetrated her and rubbed her hard bud at the same time. Her sex, already dripping wet, clenched around his fingers and she couldn't help moaning loudly.

Her cry of pleasure seemed to stir something in Giovanna, who let go of the man's dick and turned to Marjorie. Rapidly, she helped Marjorie step out of her knickers, then guided her to part her legs, straddle the client's lap with her back turned to him, and impale herself upon his prick. Marjorie lowered herself slowly, enjoying the sensation of his cock filling her. Still on all fours in front of them, Giovanna took to licking Marjorie's bud as she powerfully grabbed her thighs to help her bounce slowly on the man's lap.

The client reached round and grabbed Marjorie's breasts, kneading them while tweaking her nipples with his thumbs and forefingers. She bounced faster, unable to hold back as she whined and panted loudly. Between Marjorie's legs, Giovanna's soft hair brushed and tickled the soft sensitive skin of her thighs.

So much stimulation was too hard to withstand and, after only a few minutes, Marjorie let out a loud cry as she came.

Giovanna kept relishing her, none the less, and pleasure swept through her again and again. Soon, unable to take any more, Marjorie pried Giovanna's head away and made her stand. She also stood to help Giovanna undo her overalls and slip them off her shoulders and down to her knees. She was not surprised to see that Giovanna was completely naked underneath and the sight of the gorgeous taut and naked body pleased her even more. She helped Giovanna climb a couple of steps of a small ladder and made her sit on the workbench fixed to the wall. Giovanna readily parted her knees apart as Marjorie turned to the man. He was stirring nervously on the plastic crate, obviously in awe of the Italian's exposed flesh, and impatiently waiting for Marjorie's cue before stepping towards it.

He braced himself by placing one knee on the stepladder, then bent forward to kiss Giovanna's flesh. Standing next to him, Marjorie grabbed hold of his dick and slowly fondled him, cupping his balls with her other hand. She loved watching him pleasure Giovanna, who had grabbed her own breasts and pulled them up to bring her nipples as close to her tongue as possible.

When she felt the man was getting too excited, Marjorie ceased to work his shaft and circled it at the base, squeezing him tight for a moment to make his erection subside slightly. She didn't want him to come first. She wanted him to pleasure Giovanna before receiving any sort of reward. Then she would again resume her caresses on his member until he moaned.

The man didn't seem too annoyed by Marjorie's ritual. Working Giovanna's red and swollen slit with both his hands and his mouth, he brought her to her peak several times. And, just as Marjorie had done, Giovanna pried his head away when she couldn't take it any more. He straightened up, moved up the step ladder until his hips were level with Giovanna's, then put his hands on her thighs. Marjorie guided his prick inside the mechanic's entrance. Then she stepped back and slipped her hand under her skirt to softly caress herself as she watched his hips thrust at an amazing speed.

Giovanna climaxed again, and her cry generated so much

excitement for Marjorie that she increased the movement of her hand on her own flesh to bring herself to orgasm as well. Then it was his turn to come. He gave a few powerful thrusts, then seemed to freeze before giving one ultimate push. At the same time, he threw his head back and let out a strangled cry before falling forward into Giovanna's arms.

The three of them remained silent and motionless for a while. Their loud breathing subsided with a few last moans of delight. Marjorie couldn't tear her eyes away from the tableau, the sight of which only served to enhance the sensation of the aftershocks that still travelled through her abdomen as pleasure receded. Against her hand, the last remnants of her climax still made her flesh contract, albeit with decreasing intensity.

Giovanna was the one to put an end to the spell. She pushed the man away and stepped down, then slipped back into her overalls and buttoned them up. Nonchalantly, she reached up to retrieve an oil filter from a shelf over the workbench.

'That's the one you need,' she said as she handed it to the client.

The man looked at each woman in turn, then seemed to regain his senses. He quickly zipped up his trousers without looking at them any further. He made his way out of the garage as fast as he could, but Marjorie, who had stepped out of the small supplies room to watch him walk away, couldn't miss the opportunity.

'You come back with your car any time,' she said loudly, her voice echoing in the near-empty garage. 'If your wife can't fix it for you, we'll be happy to.'

The man didn't reply, much less look at her. Fretfully, he fished out a fistful of bank notes from his pocket and dropped them on the service counter without saying a word. The receptionist, who was back from his tea break, looked at him in bewilderment but didn't have time to ask him anything.

Marjorie couldn't help but smile when she noticed the man hesitantly walking into the showroom. She had known he would be back, but she didn't think it would be after only a couple of days. Mechanically, she checked herself in the mirror. Not that she really needed to: the simple fact that he had come back was enough for her to know that the game was already won.

She smiled again before stepping out of her office and into the showroom. 'Maybe this time I can actually sell him something,' she muttered to herself.

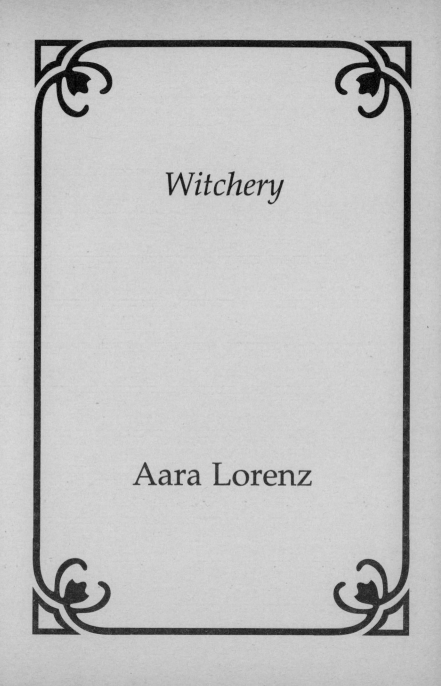

Witchery

Aara Lorenz

Witchery

❖ ❖

He came towards me, riding out of the dusk, the sky streaked heather-purple and saffron, fronds of mist rising out of the lake in the chill air. The last rays of the sinking sun glanced off his armour, turning it to beaten silver and his hair to copper-gold. Tall, he was, and young. He rode his horse like a prince. Perhaps he was; I knew not. Only that I wanted him, and would have him, no matter what.

Standing in the doorway of the hut I waited, pressing icy palms against the sudden fire in my cheeks; the echo of my heartbeat was like a drum-roll in my ears.

The meadow was knee-high with the dry grasses of late autumn. A breeze rose from nowhere, rattling the stalks like dry bones, lifting my hair softly from my neck. The thin silk of my gown grazed the beads of my nipples. With every heavy footfall of his horse, my blood thickened with desire.

He had not seen me yet. I remained motionless, drinking him in, like the finest Rhenish wine. Between my legs a pulse throbbed. Honey droplets of moisture were sticky-damp where I cupped my hand over my mound of Venus. Already, I ached for him to fill me.

When I moved, deliberately, his head jerked high in surprise and his hand gripped his sword. But it fell away in the instant, his wariness replaced by wonderment. He stared at me, eyes blazing admiration, his innocence transparent. Little more than a youth, he was, but a man grown none the less: broad in the shoulders, his thighs strong.

I made no move towards him.

Let him come to me.

And he did, halting so abruptly that the stallion jumped sideways and threw up its head, snorting.

Power and certainty made the blood sing in my veins; my lips curved into a sweet smile of welcome.

'My lady? You are alone in this place?'

He could not understand how this could be. Frowning, his gaze swept the valley, resting on the hovel to the rear, then back to me. Bewilderment and admiration jostled in his eyes. I could have laughed my triumph in that moment, but his beauty distracted me. Thick, wheaten-coloured hair, russet-streaked, hung almost to his breastplate. The blue of his eyes was smoky-violet. Hard, high cheekbones were carved clean as though by a master sculptor. The rich tenderness of his lips made me long to taste them.

Half-turning my head away, I swallowed a tide of impatience and lust, and hid behind the curtain of my hair.

'Have no fear, my lady, I will not harm you. Only tell me how I may serve you.'

He knelt and laid his broadsword at my feet. Then he kissed the hem of my gown.

I heard myself groan, soft and low.

He looked up at me, startled. Beneath the fringe of gold lashes, the blue of his eyes darkened to grey.

I held out my hand.

Still kneeling, he kissed my fingertips.

At his touch, I shivered.

'Lady, command me however you choose . . .'

The huskiness of his voice matched the tightness in my own throat. I drew him to his feet, then led him over the threshold of the hut and into the darkness beyond.

Once inside, I felt him hesitate – recoil, almost. Even in the gloom the low roof and the rough daubed walls were much in evidence. All was bare and rude. It might have been a prison.

Gently, I made him sit. The furs heaped on the floor were

thick and soft, luxurious beyond any he had known. He sank against them with a look of surprise.

Quickly, I threw a log on the fire. Along with it I scattered a handful of dried herbs. The smell of incense, exotic, cloying, eddied about us.

When I held out the goblet to him, he would not take it.

'I must see to my horse,' he muttered, and made to rise.

'No need, sir knight,' I whispered. 'There is a boy, my minion, who will see to your destrier.'

'What is it?' His hand reached for the goblet, curled over mine, gripping it tightly.

'Mead, mixed with herbs and spices, to warm and relax you, my lord.' Slowly I tilted the goblet and drank from it. The liquid ran down my throat, hot and sweet. I licked the sticky residue from my lips with the tip of my tongue, tracing their outline.

This time, when I offered it, he did not refuse the goblet.

My fingers were still pinioned beneath his. The floodtide of heat coursing through his hand told me the draught had done its work. A ruddy flush spread across his hard, high cheekbones and down the cords of his throat.

'Now, rest, my lord. Take your ease. I will be your squire and undo your armour.' I bent down to him, letting the silk of my sleeve trail across his wrist while gently, gently, I slid my fingers away and set aside the goblet.

I freed his torso first. The firelight caressed the smooth planes and hollows. He was all muscle, but lean and sculpted, his skin golden with the faintest sheen of sweat. I darted my tongue along his collar-bone and tasted each moisture bead, then down and across his breast. First one nipple, then the other, circling and butting my tongue-tip against the heated nubs. My hands explored the width of his shoulders, tangled in the ends of his hair. When I stabbed my tongue against the hollow at the base of his throat, he groaned.

His mouth took mine with a violence that sent coils of pleasure spiralling from the pit of my stomach. He tasted of mead and the wild herbs I had brewed. His lips and his teeth bruised me and pleasured me, until I cried out, panting with need.

My fingers were clumsy with haste to pull off the rest of his armour. As I tugged at the leg pieces and flung them aside, he

arched forward and slid his hands inside the bodice of my gown.
He gathered up my breasts, lifting them to his lips in a wild and
hungry ecstasy; his teeth grazed my skin and plucked my
nipples as though they were sweet ripe berries.

Desire vibrated through me, consumed me. The mead sang in
my veins and its fire flared white-hot. I shook in a frenzy of
need. He was naked, but the silk of my gown clutched and
impeded me.

'Unlace me, free me,' I instructed, and he hurried to do my
bidding.

The gown pooled around my knees, a crimson cloud, and I
kicked it away and drew him to me in the same moment. We
lay entwined in heated stillness for a mere heartbeat before I
pressed him back against the furs so that I was atop and astride
him.

His magnificent cock teased and enticed me. My skin was hot
and taut, my nipples jutting from heavy breasts as I rubbed
myself against him like a cat, feeling the muscles of his belly
clench and his shaft, thick and high, pushing at the cleft between
my legs.

Quivering, impatient, I almost let him impale me. But instead,
I rolled sideways on to my back, raised my knees and spread
my legs wide.

'Taste me!' I urged, raising my buttocks and lifting the wet
petals of my sex towards him, so that he was in no doubt of my
meaning. He came towards me slowly and I seized his head
with both my hands and cradled it between my thighs. His
tongue slid into me, stroking, feathering, exploring. With each
lush undulating movement, I writhed and gasped, pushing
myself closer and closer against his mouth, rolling my hips,
driving his tongue against my clitoris, that centre of exquisite
sensation. He needed no guidance now. As he ministered to the
swollen nub within me, flicking and circling it, teasing and
withdrawing, I grew frenzied. Arching, bucking, I flew into the
abyss, riding wave upon wave of pleasure-pain.

I lay still, savouring the ebb tide of delight, crooning the final
strains of ecstasy. Yet I was not sated. My limbs were heavy and
relaxed but my heartbeat was like a drum; I throbbed with

desire. This was but the prelude. My every sense, now aroused, clamoured for release, for fulfilment.

He raised his head and looked at me. Desire was hot in his eyes, their depths liquid brilliant. Wriggling sinuously against the furs, I showed him that I wanted more, wanted it now. At once. He needed no second invitation.

I let him caress me with his tongue. He worked at me eagerly, swiftly, and I was soon moaning in time with each skilful stroke.

When I pushed him away I saw surprise and shock chase themselves across his features in rapid succession. With both my palms on his chest, I urged him down so he was beneath me. Quickly, I straddled him and seized his cock. It was silken-sleek and staunch as granite. Inch by inch I lowered myself upon it, gasping as he filled me. Driving him deep within me, I swayed and circled, obeying the dictates of my own need. Fast and still faster I plunged against his rigid cock, feeling him push into my furthest recesses, polishing the jewel within my folds so that I was once again on the brink of ecstasy, moaning and shuddering.

Yet he held back from his own release. The muscles along his jaw were locked as he fought for control. The thick hanks of his wheaten-russet hair were wet with sweat where they touched his face. I knotted my fingers in those strands and bent my back, bow-like, as I rocked frantically on the edge of dissolution. As the first waves caught me and flung me into the whirlpool, I felt him surge beneath me, his penis swollen and urgent, plundering and violent as he too was swept away.

His arms held me fast against his chest, his mouth met mine and his tongue mimicked the rhythm of his shaft as he pushed into me. As he came, the dark heart of me flowered again. The vibrations were rich and intense, stronger than before, and I cried out over and over, wailing like a lost child. Even when he grew still and I lay collapsed across his chest, the shuddering refused to subside and the folds of flesh between my legs shook with the aftermath of our joining.

When his hand cupped my mound of Venus and then slid down to the wet cleft beneath, I groaned. He had only to touch me and desire flared bright-hot again. Languid, yet feverish with anticipation, I waited.

He was in no hurry, now. His fingers traced the outline of my sex, caressing the folds, parting them, skimming and stroking the tender flesh within. My clitoris welcomed his touch, unfurled, rose high and hard. I gasped, wanting him again, badly.

He covered me, breast to breast, knee to knee, and I felt his shaft, hard as the Toledo steel of his broadsword, pressing into me. My throat constricted with surprise, with the awareness of his arousal. Never before had I known the drug have such an effect. And yet his eyes were clear, deep and brilliant in their intensity as he gazed at me. He smiled, suddenly. The sweetness of it was like honey, and it curdled such bitterness in my stomach I almost gagged. Darkness swirled before my eyes; I was numb, ice-cold. I fought the backward rush of memory, but still it overtook me, dragged me down, down . . .

The wedding feast went on and on, in my father's castle. The sounds of drinking and dancing and merry-making echoed in the dank, draughty corners of the fortress. The hounds lapped up spilt wine and fought over trodden food scraps on the floor of the great hall. At the centre of the high table my father, red-faced and drink-sodden, pulled his mistress into a rough embrace and fumbled grotesquely with her breasts. My mother, seated beside her lord, ignored him and remained motionless, straight-backed and cold-eyed, her gaze focused on some far-off thing, like a nun at prayer.

I thought we would never escape. My husband's friends surrounded him in a revelling drunken phalanx, spluttering ribald jests and acting out a pantomime of animal coupling, grunting and shrieking, entirely for my benefit, as they wondered aloud about the pleasures awaiting me in my bridal bed. I kept my own silent counsel, features immobile, eyelashes lowered like the demure virgin which indeed I was. Only my hands, hidden beneath the table, could not be stilled. Fluttering like restless birds, my fingers picked and worried at the thick velvet gown bunched in my lap.

'Come.'

I was not sure if he had really spoken. With a start, I looked up and saw a bemused expression in my lord's eyes. He drew close to me and his warm, supple fingers circled my wrist.

'It is time we withdrew. Or would you stay, my love, to enjoy these revelries longer?'

I felt heat stain my cheeks. I shook my head, and swallowed at the sudden dryness in my throat.

'Let us away then, to our chamber.' He rose in one fluid movement, elbowing aside his craning, snickering comrades, knights-at-arms now so drunk they were beyond lucid speech. Or so I had supposed.

'Mind you remember which way to drive your battering ram this night, Ranulph!' Half-guffaw, the words still echoed clear down the table, and an explosion of laughter shook the assembled henchmen.

My lord Ranulph's hand left my elbow and came down abruptly on the shoulder of the man who had mouthed the jest, if such it was. The burly oaf winced. Slack-jawed, he dribbled spit and wine down his chin and began to babble something.

'You offend me, Harald.' Silken menace threaded Ranulph's voice. His hand slid upward; lean, tensile fingers bit into the flaccid skin of the man's neck. 'Were I not in a forgiving mood I would cut your tongue out with your own dagger and feed it to the dogs.' Ranulph forced the man's head down into a puddle of slop on the table. 'But next time you cross me, I'll not waste time with talk.'

Returning to my side he offered me his arm. 'Forgive the interruption, my lady.' He inclined his head. 'We have dallied too long. Let us retire.'

Halfway up the winding stone stairs I began to shiver involuntarily. Ranulph paused and let his arm slide around my waist, gathering me against his warmth.

'Be not afraid, Ysotta. I promise you, I will be gentle, love.' His breath whispered along my cheek and his lips brushed softly against my jaw.

I turned so that I was looking up into his eyes. But in the faint, flickering taper light they were unreadable; opaque. We stood so, in silence. Then he grasped my right hand and raised it to his lips.

'Trust me, Ysotta.'

There was a rushing sound in my ears. Pulses thudding, I could scarcely form the words I so desperately wished to say out loud, at last.

'I do trust you, my lord. With my life. Ranulph, I love you with all my heart and soul.'

He was silent. But in his eyes I could see a softness that had not been there a moment before.

'Sweet Ysotta.'

It was enough.

Ranulph kept his arm about me as we ascended the final curve of the stair. Our chamber was only a score of paces ahead.

The deep alcove of the doorway lay all in shadows so that, when a shape detached itself from that mottled darkness, I gasped.

Ranulph's squire bent his knee, dipping his head so that his face was entirely hidden. The red of his hair was the same shade as a fox's coat, and looked as thick and soft.

'Guy. You should be abed. Did I not tell you –'

'My Lord Ranulph, I stayed but to wish you and Lady Ysotta God's benediction.'

Ranulph put his hand on the boy's shoulder.

'So be it. Go now, Guy, with my thanks.'

He slipped past without so much as a glance in my direction.

The door swung shut behind us and we were truly alone at last. The great bed with its embroidered hangings dominated the room. The candlelight cast a soft glow that masked the cold stone walls and floors in honeyed hues.

I was unaware that I was twisting my hands together until Ranulph captured them gently in his and made them still, pulling me close. As the tip of my chin angled towards his shoulder blade, the whole length of my body curved into his. Beneath the soft stuff of his doublet was heat and hard muscle, a broad warrior's chest tapering to narrow hips and long legs. The points of my breasts, grazing his torso, swelled and hardened with the contact, yet the rest of my body grew soft and tingling.

Ranulph studied me with hooded eyes and I returned his gaze intently. That he was my husband I could scarce believe. He had never seemed a man made for hearth and home. There was too much wildness in him. He was dark and finely made, like nothing so much as a hawk, born to take flight and to kill with ease and grace. Even the raven fall of his hair was like the perfect wing-set of a hunting bird. The deep brilliance of his eyes held the same unblinking, impenetrable stillness of the predator. And I was drawn into their power, mesmerised.

Suddenly he smiled. The taut line of his mouth became sweetly tender as he bent down to me. The darkness in his eyes kindled to heat and transferred itself to my veins like molten gold. Slowly, his lips met mine, their touch so light, it was like a dream. Yet I breathed in the sourness of wine, felt the warmth of his mouth, and opened mine in response, testing that softness.

In an instant, everything changed. Like a summer gale that blots out blue skies with indigo clouds, my body awoke, every sense clamouring, and I surrendered utterly in that kiss.

I clung to Ranulph. My lips caught fire and melded with his, our tongues joining, tasting, exploring. I could not get enough of him. My hands moved of their own accord over his back, my fingers digging into the muscles across his shoulders. Straining forward, I pressed myself into him. We two would become one body, one flesh. I wanted that transformation. I wanted Ranulph as I had never before wanted anything in my entire life. Instinct alone guided me when I arched upward, undulating my hips in a rhythm that came from every pulse-beat in my body.

When Ranulph stepped backward, abruptly, to hold me at arms' length, I exhaled a half-moan of surprise and loss. His expression was tense and somehow remote. His fingers bit into my shoulder blades so that I had to smother a cry of pain.

'Forgive me, Ysotta.' He released my shoulders, letting his hands fall to my waist. 'You take me by surprise. No longer the frightened child, but someone else entirely . . .'

Cupping my cheek in his hand, Ranulph tilted my face towards his. 'Is it sorcery you practise, then?' With his dark, cool gaze he scrutinized me. Then his lips softened and he smiled, gladdening my heart. 'For I must tell you, my Lady Ysotta, you work magic upon me. Never have I been so impatient, so full of need. You hold me in your thrall.'

I could not speak. It seemed as though I would be consumed by the fire that coursed through me.

Ranulph's smile deepened. He raised my hand, hanging limp at my side, turned it over and pressed a kiss into my palm; and, without another word, lifted me in his arms and carried me to the great bed.

Fingers moving with deft, practised ease, he undressed me without haste. The sheer veil with its fine gold circlet and the rich, heavy velvet gown were stripped away. When I was clad only in my linen undergarments, he unplaited my hair, stroking the lengths free, twining them around his fingers. Releasing the tresses, his hands slid down my throat to my breasts.

For a moment all was still: I, motionless, feeling the warmth of his palms covering my breasts and bringing my nipples to hard peaks; Ranulph, so close that his breath whispered against my lips, waiting.

His thumbs began circling lightly, oh, so lightly, first the areolae, then closer and closer to my sensitive nipples until the linen of my shift, dragging across my skin, was both delight and agony. I was beginning to lose myself, a prisoner of some strange desire I could not name. It grew and swelled within me so that I swayed back and forth, my breath catching roughly in my throat as I let my head fall back, thrusting my breasts further into Ranulph's grasp.

He eased the shift over my head and I lay back, naked.

For a long moment he was still, his gaze sweeping the length of my body. Somewhere inside me, a tendril of fear grew and clutched, born of uncertainty that I could please. My limbs turned to lead; the breath froze in my nostrils.

'Ysotta . . .' Ranulph's dark head lowered as he whispered my name, his lips like silk on mine, but hot and demanding, so that the fear dissolved, the need in me rising to meet his, all else forgotten.

His mouth – urgent, caressing – descended my throat to my breasts, his tongue darting liquid fire, his hands stroking and kneading until I shook, fevered and panting. His hands moulded my waist and slipped lower, brushing out across my hips, sliding to my buttocks, kneading them until I heard myself make strange mewling sounds that belonged to someone else, the other that I seemed to have become.

Ranulph began to strip off his clothing, casting it hurriedly aside. The bare skin of his torso and legs was paler than the dark hue of his face, but still sallow against the egg-shell whiteness of my body. Fine dark hair feathered across the hard planes of his chest, almost hiding the tracery of scar tissue from old wounds.

'I am a fighting man first and last, Ysotta,' Ranulph said gently, following my gaze. 'If I were not, your father would never have given me you, and the lands and wealth that you bring me.'

I knew he spoke the truth. My father had no sons, and but one daughter. He had wedded me to the fiercest warrior in the land, a man whose fortune was his sword. That I loved Ranulph de Guise, more than my own life, had been my secret from the beginning.

And when he rose over me, naked and magnificent, I did not fear him. I trembled with longing and impatience. I had waited for this moment from the day of our betrothal.

He pushed me back against the bolsters, running his hands down my thighs, spreading them wide, raising my knees so that I arched towards him. I thought that he would enter me then and there, for his phallus stood swollen and erect, as huge to me as any broadsword, masculine and uncompromising. But instead his fingers parted the tight scrolls of my sex and stroked the petals within so that I started with surprise and sudden delight. It was like a rippling melody, sweet as honey, the way he touched me. The pleasure of it lapped over me, blotting out everything but radiant sensation. And yet, at the centre of the pleasure there was a nameless hunger that grew and grew until I was imprisoned by it, undulating my hips frantically, ready to beg for something, but I knew not what.

He sank down, down, his weight so heavy upon me I could scarce draw breath. All the while his eyes held mine, never wavering. They pulled me into their depths, a velvet blackness, soft and enticing, while our tongues entwined, foreshadowing the dance of our bodies.

Flung wide, like the gates of a citadel that surrenders without even a token resistance, my body welcomed Ranulph as he slid inside me. He was gentle, tender, careful. How could he know that when I gasped it was with pleasure, wonderment, not with pain? In that moment, I felt him hesitate, withhold the sleek, stroking thrusts, even as I craved not his gentleness, but the warrior's strength, the final assault.

I could not, would not, wait. I wound my arms tightly around his neck, writhing with desire, surging against his rigidity, until he plunged to meet me. And now there was no drawing back. In one violent, fervent movement he took me, driving strong and fast, filling me. I was taut and arched like a bowstring, striving, panting. Climbing Ranulph's back with my feet and hands, I felt a tide of something like anguish overtake me. It roared over me and I drowned in wave upon wave of ecstatic release, passion and fulfilment combined.

I knew that I cried out, over and over, triumph and joy giving my voice wings. I was frenzied, possessed.

Cocooned in Ranulph's embrace, my rough breathing was the only sound in the sudden stillness of the room. Tendrils of my damp hair knotted themselves against the back of my neck. My legs, sprawled wide and high across my husband's waist, trembled with a delicious weakness. Sighing, I moved a fraction and tilted my head, rubbing my cheek against Ranulph's jaw. There was no response. He lay motionless, heavy as death upon me. Yet I thought no more than that he was sated, drained of passion and desire.

I allowed my hands to move gently across Ranulph's shoulders. My fingers circled and slid, testing the damp satin of skin and the solidity of muscle and bone. Sliding them downward to his buttocks, I marvelled at their strength, following the curves all the way to his thighs. And there, with my fingertips, I explored the inner recesses of his legs, wondering at the heated, hair-roughened apex wherein was all the magic of his sex.

I could not stop my questing fingers. They insinuated themselves into that recess, encountering the twin sacs resting heavy against the place where we still lay joined. I tested their weight, stroked and massaged them, until Ranulph made a sound like a groan, half-smothered. He pulled away from me, to lie on his side, his hands clutching my shoulders as though to keep me away from him.

I knew I wanted him again, now. The feel of him inside me was the greatest happiness I had ever known, the very rhyme and reason of my existence. My throat was suddenly dry, and my breasts ached with fullness, needing the touch of his hands upon them, the wetness of his tongue grazing my nipples.

I reached for him, my hands going straight to the place between his thighs where his phallus rested, wet with the juices of both our bodies. Tentatively, I stroked his softness with my fingertips, sliding down to the flared hood at the base and then all the way up again, gliding against the sticky satin grain of his skin, all the while feeling my own excitement gathering.

Ranulph shuddered. His hands gripped my shoulders tighter and tighter as I continued to stroke him, feeling him harden and swell against my fluttering fingertips.

This time, he was not gentle at all. He took me with the raw energy of a stallion covering a mare, thrusting deep and fast into me, his teeth nipping and tugging on my breasts, dragging on my nipples until they burned. Like a sudden draught of strong spirits, the pain made me drunk, set me free. I met him full-pelt, driving back, shuddering and bucking as he rode me. Wanting, wanting, wanting. It possessed me. A great-bellied black storm cloud. I flung myself against Ranulph. And then the sudden, shattering release. I dissolved and was reborn in ecstasy.

Afterwards, I watched the guttering candle flames send spider shadows leaping into the recesses of the room. A chill wind rattled and worried at the casement, lifting the bed-hangings. But I drifted into sleep, secure in the arms of my husband, his heartbeat melding with mine.

I woke in the grey dawn. The wind no longer wracked the casement. All was still, silent. I was alone in the great bed.

At first, I thought only that Ranulph had sought the privy and would return soon. But as the minutes passed and the light seeped further into the room, somehow I knew his absence was not recent. Shivering as my feet touched the cold flag stones, I fumbled into my shift and gown, leaving the laces half done and my bodice gaping.

The revellers of last night snored drunkenly in the great hall. I crept past them to the further staircase, lifting the hem of my gown to avoid the puddles of spilt wine and vomit.

Some instinct led me down the narrow, ill-lit passageway atop the spiral flight. Here were rooms I never frequented, dank closets for minions. Rank and musty, the smells were thick as the dirt that lay in every crack and crevice. At the very end of the passageway, two mastiffs sprawled across a doorway. When they saw me they stirred and sat up, tails threshing as they whined their greeting.

I called softly to the hounds and they came to me, sniffing and rubbing around my legs like great lumbering cats. I stroked their muzzles and caressed their ears, and then I bade them lie down again and they obeyed at once. Ranulph had trained them well.

The door would not open and, thinking it bolted, I turned to go. Yet something made me try again and this time I put my shoulder to the wood and it gave, suddenly. I stumbled over the threshold and found my husband.

The narrow cot was too small for one, let alone two. The absurdity of it struck me first, before I could begin to feel anything else.

They lay tangled together, naked, staring at me. A coarse blanket had been cast aside and there was naught to hide them. Even then the beauty of Ranulph's lean, muscled torso and legs riveted me, so that I gazed at him, worshipping, while my heart turned to stone. The boy, his squire, stretched languidly like a cat in sunshine, and smirked. In his narrowed amber gaze, there was venom and triumph. He rolled on to his side, turning his back to me, and I saw that he was smooth and soft as a girl, white-skinned as I, the thick russet of his hair bright even in this dim hole.

Ranulph crossed the floor with all the fluid grace that was his alone. His eyes, blank, shuttered, pinioned me.

'Get back to your chamber, Ysotta. We'll speak of this later.'

I shook my head. Searing, bitter words flooded my throat, so that I almost gagged.

Ranulph's fingers, ice and steel combined, fastened on my wrist. He propelled me backward.

'Get you gone!'

'No!' Like a harridan, I clawed at his hand. Bright crimson beads gathered beneath my nails. 'No! No! No!' I screamed a denial and a plea. The words, unspoken, echoed inside my head: *Don't send me away. I love you, love you!*

The blow was open-handed; hard. It caught me across the

cheek and knocked me backward. I stumbled and fell in the doorway.

'Bitch!' Ranulph wrenched me to my feet. 'Have a care, my lady wife, that you do not push me beyond the limits of my patience. Know you not that I kill any hound of mine that so much as growls out of place?'

'Then kill me now,' I flung at him. 'I will not share my husband with a boy – with anyone!'

'You will obey me as your lord. Did you not make that vow before God and his priest?'

'Did you not promise to cleave only to me?'

This time Ranulph's hand grabbed not my wrist, but my throat. I saw now the cruelty of the warrior, the harsh line of his lips, white with rage, and the coal-black furnace of his eyes, full of contempt.

I would he had killed me, then. But his grip slackened, leaving me gasping and bruised.

'Get you gone from me, whore. Else I will denounce you before your father and all the household here.'

I could not breathe; my head swam. Blackness gathered, swirled. Ranulph's face, the parody of a lover's features, drew close.

'Think you I did not know? When you showed yourself so wise in the ways of the flesh? So full of lust! Where was your virgin modesty? And where was the virgin blood?'

From within the room a low, honeyed chuckle broke the thick silence.

'Witchcraft. You thought to use the black arts to ensnare me in your lust. I'll have you burnt, witch – whore!'

'My lady, what ails you?'

I tried to speak, but the shivering took hold of me, like an ague. Huddled in the furs, I felt him reach for the goblet of half-drunk mead and press it gently to my lips. I swallowed it to the last dregs and sank back into his waiting arms. My vision cleared and I was again in the hut, this place of refuge and power, and the man crouched over me, glowing with the sweat of desire and his own golden beauty, was mine to use or discard as I chose.

Long, long ago, in another life, I had been forced to flee my husband; my only love; my hated betrayer. Falsely accused of sorcery, I found strength in the practice of alchemy and natural magic. Outcast, alone, I wandered in search of my own death. Fate brought me to this place and to the woman who gave me back my life. Call her witch, wise-woman or sorcerer, it matters not. She taught me all, gave me power. I steeped myself in knowledge rich and arcane, the black arts and the white. There was nothing I feared to learn, no boundary I would not test. Like a butterfly emerging from its dark and cramped chrysalis I shook my rainbow wings in brightness. Ysotta did truly die. But it was only the death of fear and ignorance and limitation. I was reborn in wisdom, into the ancient lineage of priestesses and seers who hold the world in their thrall.

And I learnt the rites of the body and the wellsprings of all sensual pleasure. I could command worship, exact vengeance. I had the power of life and death. What more is there? Countless times, with countless men, I had exacted my retribution.

Stretching out my hand to the man beside me, I fingered the russet-gold of his hair, seeing, as I did so, the smoky haze gather in his violet eyes. In answer, I undulated my hips and felt him shift into the cradle of my groin and draw my legs up around his waist. The moment of joining was sweetly fierce. As he began to move in me, I knew that this was all, everything.

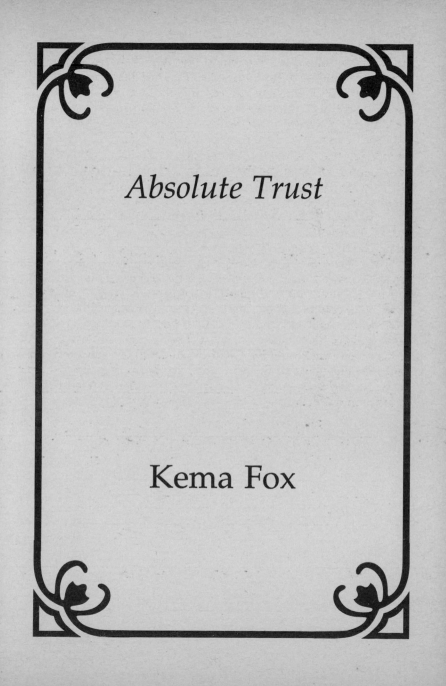

Absolute Trust

Kema Fox

Absolute Trust

❧ ❧

Kate stood in front of the mirror and cast a critical eye over her appearance. She had chosen a striking red dress – short but fitted – and black stockings with suspenders. It had taken her a great deal of time and effort to find the perfect outfit for tonight but she was satisfied with herself now. This wasn't just a normal date with Connor; it was one of their special evenings. The sort where she never knew quite how it would end.

She debated for a moment as to whether or not she should put on any underwear. It would be sexier not to but, on the other hand, it would add to the fun later if she were fully dressed. Kate walked over to her underwear drawer and rooted through the collection of briefs. After deciding against a couple she found a red-and-black lace pair with a matching bra. Slowly she undressed herself again, being careful not to disturb her hair. She slipped the underclothes on, enjoying their softness against her bare skin and, semi naked, she again considered her reflection. Her black hair fell against her shoulders, waving down her back in loose curls, and her body's curves were emphasised by the severe colour and the sleekness of the material. On her feet were a pair of wickedly high-heeled boots. She again slipped the dress over her head and allowed it to hug her breasts and thighs. She wondered if anything else was needed. No, the outfit was fine as it was and she just needed her long black coat for the walk to the pub.

As she pulled the front door shut behind her, Kate felt a sudden rush of nervous excitement. It was rare for her to wear clothes like this, clothes that felt sensuous and exhilarating even when she was alone. Normally her clothes reflected her work; she was a smart young receptionist for a prestigious advertising agency. Even when she went out for the evening she was smartly dressed. That is, until about three months ago.

Kate had met Connor in a bar. She had gone with some people from work and he had been drinking there. As soon as she had seen him, she had sensed that he was out of place. His clothes were smart but he didn't look like an office worker; his body had a streamlined power that looked slightly incongruous in a suit. He had looked up and regarded her with a sort of neutrality that she was unused to, then had started to talk to her a little while later.

The sexual tension had been obvious to Kate from the moment that she laid eyes on him. She had been unable to concentrate on any of the conversation going on around her, but he had seemed more amused by her obvious attraction to him than responsive to it. For half an hour or so, he had blown hot and cold at her: one minute flirting and the next seeming to lose interest, until she was almost begging him to go back with her. He had let her do the running but had gone home with her eventually.

Kate had been worried, after the initial liaison, that his behaviour might suggest a casual attitude, but he had never stood her up or turned a date down. In the rather short period that they had spent together, Kate had developed very strong feelings for this man. It wasn't love, or anything like it; Connor satisfied her and had taught her that she had very specialised tastes. The lack of emotional content to their relationship was compensated for by their absolute honesty, when it came to physical intimacy. She knew without a shadow of a doubt that she trusted him.

She walked out on to the road, carefully at first but then with increased confidence. The route to the pub was short but involved a long alley. During the daytime, she always used this route because it was easier than going along the road. Now, at nine o'clock, she hesitated for a moment. She glanced along the alley, trying to see in the twilight whether or not it was deserted. She could see no one and so she began to walk along it, trying to ignore the constant tapping of her shoes. She was concentrating on the end of the alley, drawing closer and closer with every step when, without warning, a hand reached out from the shadows behind her and grabbed her arm.

'Don't make a sound,' a voice snarled in her ear.

Kate had no time for anything more than a muffled gasp of shock, but a strong hand covered her mouth and held her still. Gradually it let her go but, as she turned round, she saw that the man was holding something in his other hand. Her heart missed a beat as she took in the barrel of the gun that he held. She looked up at him with eyes dilated with fright. He brought it up to her face and pushed her chin up, the barrel digging into her throat.

He held her so for a moment and Kate looked up into his face. It was darkly handsome with a strong jawline and sensuous lips. He ran his tongue over them as she watched and then stepped back, his attitude more casual and confident as he pointed the gun at her.

'You look like you're dressed for a date,' he said, a question in his voice.

Kate nodded mutely.

'Well, you seem to have found yourself a new one. Take your coat off.' She did not instantly obey and his tone sharpened. 'You do as I tell you to. Take your coat off.' He moved a couple of steps towards her, so Kate obeyed, gingerly slipping her long evening coat off and allowing it to fall to the floor. The man looked her up and down for a moment and then smiled.

'Was this supposed to be for someone in particular?'

Again Kate nodded. She felt unable to speak; words crowded in her throat but her muscles seemed to have frozen.

The man walked around her slowly, examining her from all angles. He suddenly pushed the gun into her back. 'What are you wearing underneath this?' he asked.

'Just stockings and underwear.' Kate stuttered slightly with nervousness.

The man walked back to face her. 'I like my dates to wear just stockings,' he said softly. 'Would you take the rest off? Now.' It was politely phrased but the words sounded like an order.

Kate pulled up her skirt.

'No, I want you to do it slowly. I want to see what you're doing.'

Trying to control her trembling hands, Kate slid her skirt up to her waist. She carefully fitted her fingers into the elastic of the lace and satin panties and began to pull them down. She moved her thighs rhythmically to draw them to her ankles and stepped out of them. Only then did she push her skirt back down.

The man moved forward and picked them up. As he did so, he caught her off-guard and pulled her towards him. For a second, she thought he was going to force her to the ground, but he pulled her skirt back up so that his fingers could feel underneath. He pushed her thighs a little way apart and his fingers felt her groin, briefly touching her clitoris and fingering the soft skin. He pulled away again and stroked her face with his damp fingertips.

'Your pussy's soaking,' he gloated. 'I could fuck you here and you'd love it. You're just a dirty little tart.'

Kate flinched inwardly at the words, knowing their truth. She could feel all of her body's responses to his touch, now that there was nothing between her wet skin and the night air. She wondered if it was going to happen here: now. She looked back up into his face.

'What are you going to do with me?' she asked. Her voice had gained a little more confidence, now that the initial shock had worn off.

'I'll decide that when I've found somewhere a little more private,' he replied. He caught her arm and pulled her towards the end of the alleyway, the gun pressed firmly into her side. 'Don't do anything stupid,' he recommended.

They walked a little way down the street until the man stopped next to a black car. Kate saw that its windows were darkened. He opened the passenger door and beckoned to her. Gingerly, she got into the front seat and sat with her legs tightly crossed. He leant over her and opened the glove compartment, pulling out a pair of steel handcuffs.

'Put these on,' he ordered. She slipped them first over one wrist then the other, leaving her hands manacled in front of her. He tossed the gun into the glove compartment and shut it, and then went round to his own side of the car. Kate looked at the manacles, knowing that there was no way to get them off without the key. She wondered if that too was in the glove compartment but, as he opened his door, she saw them gleaming in his hand. He held them out to show her and then laughed as he slid them down the front of his trousers. 'That should make getting those cuffs off a great deal more interesting,' he said, leering.

He settled himself into the driver's seat and turned the key in the ignition. The car leapt into life and they pulled away from the curb. For a moment or two he concentrated on getting out of the narrow streets on to the main road, but then as the car sped along the dual carriageway he caught her eye in the mirror.

'Open your legs,' he demanded. Kate slowly uncrossed them, wondering what he wanted her to do. 'Now pull that dress up again. I want to get a proper look at what's under there.' He adjusted the rear-view mirror until it reflected her hands pulling up her dress; he smiled as it slid over the top of her thighs and around her waist.

'I want you to rub yourself. To make yourself come. Get yourself ready for the cock that is going to be inside you later.' His eyes gazed into the mirror, flicking back to the road when necessary, and watched her as she obeyed him.

Kate moved her hands, feeling the cold of the handcuffs against her thighs. Her fingers prodded gently at the flesh between her legs – but the insistent burning of her desire made her quickly start to push into herself; her nerves already felt raw and desperate for something to satisfy them. She pulled her dress even further up, caressing her belly and thighs with an intensity which made her back arch and caused groans of pleasure and need.

She knew that he was watching her, gaining a sadistic enjoyment from her increasing excitement and yet doing nothing to quench it. Gradually, her body began to peak, and the last wave of passion flooded through her. She collapsed back against the seat.

They drove for perhaps twenty minutes. The route took them along winding country roads and Kate did not recognise where they were going. She half-lay against the seat, not moving or speaking but studying the man covertly as his attention was fixed again on the road. He was a tall man, dressed entirely in black. The muscles on his arm were clearly defined and physical power seemed to permeate his movements. His hair was dark and clipped severely into a crew-cut. On his face was an expression of cruel lust and arrogance. They swung round one last bend and stopped in front of a house, set a little way back from the road. The man leant across her again and pulled open the glove compartment. He took out the gun and slipped it into his pocket.

'Get out.'

Kate fumbled at the lock on her door and then tried to keep her balance as she got out of the car. The night air caught at her bare arms and sent a shiver down her back. There was no one in sight but her captor; he was holding the front door of the house open for her. Nervously, she entered.

He guided her into a living room which was beautifully furnished in dark wood, with the soft furniture covered with red material. As they entered, he pushed her into the centre of the room and then shut the door. She stood still and watched him as he sat down on the sofa.

'Now these are the rules.' His voice was calm and quiet, but still held that undercurrent of threat. 'You don't speak unless I tell you to. You don't move unless I tell you to. You do what I say, when I say it – and then everything will be all right. Do you understand?'

Kate nodded. She was no longer terrified because excitement had replaced her fear.

She stood still, waiting for him to speak.

'I'm afraid I need those handcuffs for something else now, so I'm going to need the key. Come over here.' Kate moved forward slowly until she stood directly in front of him.

'Kneel down.' Kate obeyed, slipping down on to her knees. The man sat back, his legs open, and pulled the gun out of his pocket.

'I want you to find me those keys, and I want you to do it gently,' he said. Kate felt the cold metal against her forehead. She leant forward, her hands still manacled, and unfastened the front of his trousers. She loosened them slightly from around his waist and then pushed her hands into his groin, feeling for the keys. As she touched it, she felt his cock harden and his sharp intake of breath. She felt further down, around his balls, until she could feel the shaped metal under her fingers. Gently, she eased them out.

She glanced up and found that he was smiling. He took her hands and unlocked the cuffs. Picking up the gun again, he gestured to the door.

'I think that we need a little something to get us both in the mood.' He got up and led her through the door and up a winding staircase. At the top there was a single doorway. He flung it open and Kate stepped inside.

It was a room with a bed in it. The walls were painted black and the light came from lamps placed on various surfaces. It was impossible to call the room a bedroom because no one would ever sleep in it. On the surface beside the bed there was a bottle of champagne in a cooler and two glasses. The bed itself took Kate's breath away. It was a four-poster with a black silk canopy and black covers. There appeared to be no other colour in the room.

The thing that shocked Kate completely was the panoply of chains and manacles that were attached to the bed. The silver of the metal stood out sharply against the surrounding black material and gleamed threateningly up at her in the muted light. She stood still for a second, her heart pounding with adrenalin, and waited for the man to speak.

He moved behind her to a chest of drawers and drew something out of one of them. He held it up and Kate saw a strip of velvet with a leather strap.

'I want you to take your dress off now,' he said softly, eyeing her as her hands fumbled with the zips. She slid out of the red satin and let it fall around her ankles. He walked over and stood towering above her. She caught her breath in anticipation as his fingers began to play with the straps on her bra. He pulled the straps down her arms so that her breasts were bare and gently started to fondle them, making the nipples tight and firm. Gradually, his touch became more aggressive, until she was moaning again with a combination of pain and desire. He skilfully unhooked the strap of the bra and ripped it off, throwing it to the ground.

They stood for a second without moving, the man still fully dressed and Kate naked apart from her stockings and boots; her hair was dishevelled and fell down her back. The moment of stillness broke and he picked up the velvet collar from the bed. She stayed still and passive as he fastened it around her neck and then he picked her up, his strength making her feel as light as a doll, and put her on the bed. Without speaking, he attached one of the chains on the bed to her collar and another two around her wrists. The chains were not tight but they meant that Kate could not move from the bed. She sat still as her captor surveyed her, his eyes gleaming with lust and power.

'Get on your hands and knees.' His voice was still perfectly controlled, in spite of the betraying tension in his posture. Kate moved obediently into the position, but he moved behind her and pulled her legs open as wide as they would go. She felt her pulse quicken with the sudden physical contact and gasped as he began to stroke the insides of her thighs with one finger.

'Would you like a drink before we start – something to get you in the mood?' he asked softly.

Kate nodded, her mouth dry with nervousness. She went to move back into a sitting position but his hand held her down.

'No, stay as you are.' He moved away from her to the champagne and poured himself a glass. He sipped it as he looked at her meditatively, and then poured some of the bubbling liquid into a saucer. He placed it in front of her and pushed her head down towards it. 'Now I want to see you lap that up and lick the saucer clean.'

Kate leant down and tentatively tasted the champagne. She lapped gently at the liquid, keeping her eyes lowered but letting her tongue display the sensuality of the act. She allowed her tongue to linger against the hard cold surface of the saucer and then delicately licked her lips. She looked up and saw him in front of her; his trousers were now undone and he was holding his cock in one hand, gently stimulating it.

'I could have you right now, couldn't I?' The man's tone was quietly contemptuous. 'I could have had you in that alleyway and you wouldn't have given a damn. You like being tied up and given no choice. Well, I want you to beg me to touch you – beg me to do anything I want with your body until you can't take any more.' His hand tightened round his penis. 'Come on,' he demanded. 'You're on your knees, now beg.'

Words crowded in Kate's throat but refused to be spoken. Even through the feeling of humiliation a burning desire held her in its grip and the sight of him, so hard and sensual and yet not touching her, was like torture. She tried to calm her breathing sufficiently for speech.

'I want you,' she stammered, her voice constricted but her eyes burning with a desperate need.

The man moved closer to her. 'I told you to beg.' His tone was losing its control, growing more ragged as his desire rose.

'I'm begging you to touch me!' Kate nearly shouted now, her voice freed by the desperation of her feelings. The whole scenario of the gun and the abduction had faded from her memory, in the excitement and passion of the moment. Her body strained at its bonds: not with the need to escape but instead to move closer to him. He stood before her, his eyes boring into her face for a few long seconds, before he succumbed to his own need and moved swiftly towards the bed.

Kneeling up behind her, he mounted her roughly: Kate felt no pain because her body had been wanting this for what seemed like hours. The act of penetration became aggressive for them both as they moved together. Kate felt him inside her body, with his hands scratching at her back and then coming round to clutch at her breasts. His grip would normally have hurt her but Kate revelled in the combination of pain and pleasure as his fingers pulled at her nipples and hardened them under his touch. They moved steadily faster, their bodies in perfect motion until, just as Kate was climaxing, he pulled out of her, making her nerves jangle with the shock.

He stumbled off the bed and got in front of her. He pushed her down with her back against the cool satin sheets and, without speaking began to rub his cock against her lips. His hands were moving between her legs, sending shimmers of ecstasy through her spine. Slowly, trying to retain some sense of control, Kate opened her mouth, letting him in inch by inch and allowing her tongue to taste the fluids with which he was covered. She allowed her teeth to drag along the skin gently, knowing that, in spite of the chains that bound her, she was now in control.

His body seemed to be racked with barely controlled lust but he remained motionless, allowing her to define the movement and velocity of the act. She tried to simulate penetration by moving her tongue and muscles against him to increase the responsiveness and sensation. She could still feel his fingers moving against and inside her, no longer teasing but hard and ruthless, so that her own satisfaction would match his. Again, at the last moment, he pulled away.

For a second or two, they stared into each other's eyes and then slowly he began to push her back; the chains that were fixed around her wrists fell loose against the bed. As she lay back he came forward and again entered her, but gently, this time, almost lovingly. Kate still gazed into his eyes, seeing the hint of a smile in them, and lost herself in the sensations of nearly sated lust. Her body was only a second away from climax and they matched each other perfectly, feeling the tell-tale quivers of the final moments running through their veins. In a moment it gave way and he fell against her, his head hitting the pillow next to her head. Kate lay still, her body refusing to move or function. She felt the sensation of floating fill her and her mind drifted into a state of semi-consciousness so that she was barely aware of what was happening around her.

The man moved himself gently away from Kate and stood beside the bed, looking down on her. She was lying sprawled upon the bed, with her hair ruffled and spread across the pillow in a cloud of waves and ringlets. Her face was peaceful and happy, the expression showing a seemingly unshadowed innocence. He gazed at her, realising again that this girl was the only one that he had ever wanted. He carefully unlocked the manacles that held her wrists and detached the collar. She moved slightly but didn't seem to wake, so he left her and walked over to the side where he had left the gun. He opened the chamber and twisted it, watching the empty cartridges spin before his eyes. Snapping it shut again, he allowed his hands to caress it, feeling all of the risk and danger from the look of it. This gun wasn't a weapon: it was a representation of their relationship.

He carefully placed it down again and moved back to the bed. As he leant over the sleeping girl, her eyes opened and she smiled.

'Connor,' she murmured, her voice still heavy with sleep.

He smiled back and poured them both another glass of champagne. As she heard the sounds of activity, Kate struggled back into a sitting position and took one of the glasses. As she sipped at the delicate liquid, Connor handed her the pistol.

'It will be your turn, next time,' he said.

Kate took the gun and ran her fingers over it. She enjoyed the feeling of the metal in her hands and the power that it represented as much as she had enjoyed its threat before. The fluttering submission which had played upon her face throughout the evening drained away and her smile was now hard and cruel. She turned the gun towards him and pressed it against his chest.

'Kiss me.'

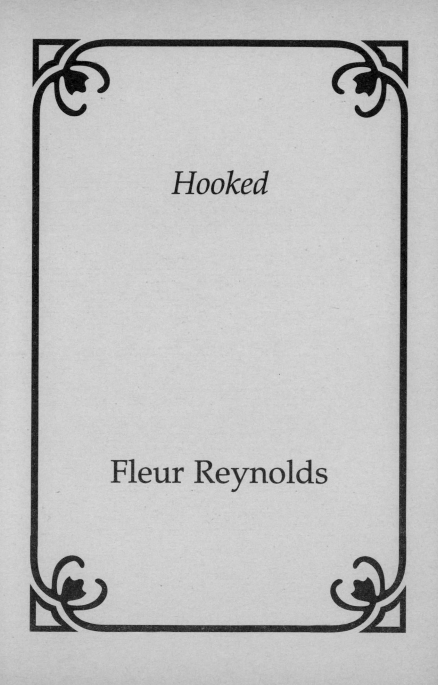

Hooked

Fleur Reynolds

Hooked

❖ ❖

*S*hit! she thought, rebellion surging through her body the moment she saw him. 'Here I am trussed up and only capable of watching.'

With no alternative but to submit to her predicament, Mary Fountain had been gazing idly at the people passing by. Black and white, yellow and brown, fat and thin, loose and wobbly, uptight and tense, smiling and happy. She had been indolently reflecting on the infinite variety on the basic pattern of two arms, two legs, a torso and a head when the man captured her attention.

Tall, thick-set, broad-shouldered and long-legged, he strode assertively, two at a time, up the steps to the raised ground floor of the gabled house opposite. She watched him pat the pocket of his fashionable jeans. Couldn't he remember where he'd put his keys? He started back down the steps, stopped and lifted his head. Then she saw his face. Handsome. Black-haired, clean-shaven, with a wide fleshy sexual mouth.

Nice one, she thought, the rebel within her suddenly itching to get out.

The man put his hand inside the pocket of his designer jacket and pulled out a key. He went back up the stairs, opened the heavy black door and disappeared within a cool magnolia-painted hall.

The sight of a well-dressed, good-looking man had engaged

her interest but, with the closing of the door, her initial spurt of mutiny quickly faded. Once again she felt listless, resigned to her condition.

The room Mary Fountain occupied was classically well furnished. Too classically; too perfect. All mod cons. There was even a fan attached to the centre light, which seemed to her to be droning on and on relentlessly. Too much good taste showing little originality, thought Mary. She found it boring. The state she was in she might have found anything boring – but, from her brief glimpse, she knew there was nothing there to excite her imagination.

She dismissed her impersonal surroundings and looked out of her first floor French window. In this part of central London the streets did not consist of identical terraced houses. Here there was a cluster of four or five similar buildings, separated by a tradesmen's delivery passage. Then another cluster, totally dissimilar, and so on until the end of the road. These houses had been put up one hundred years ago by speculative builders, using their own plans and ideas and frequently going bankrupt in the process. The houses were as diverse as the people who occupied them but, from the shape of its windows, Mary realised that the house opposite mirrored hers.

Vaguely, she wondered which apartment belonged to the handsome stranger. She could see from the array of bells by the door that the four-storey house had been converted from a family home to flats. But – and this she thought odd – all the windows that she could see had the same expensive cotton lace curtains.

'Most probably,' she mused, 'one landlord owned the whole house but let it off in furnished apartments.'

Mary's eyes flitted from one floor to the next, hunting for signs of life. Moments later, she was rewarded by the view of a white but lightly sun-tanned bare back, close to the lace curtains. Her man? Could be. He had broad shoulders. Concentrating, she willed herself to see beyond the drapes specifically designed to stop people peering in.

Her effort was unnecessary. He was backing up against the glass. More of his naked body came into view. His waist, his buttocks. Neat, a good shape. Now what? What exactly was he doing? His head was inclined to one side. Was he talking or listening? Listening. Definitely listening. To a radio, perhaps? No. Something about his body betrayed an intensity. Somebody was saying something that directly affected him.

Then he turned his head. Mary held her breath. Would he reveal more of his body? If he did, what else would she be able to see? But why was he naked? Mary answered her own question. Because it was a hot and sultry afternoon. And, of course, people change their clothes when they arrive home, especially when it's humid. But was it his home?

Then she saw his cock.

He'd turned sideways and, as clear as if there was no curtain, she could see it standing upright, excited.

Mary swallowed hard. She could feel a tightening in her belly and a loosening, a moistening, in her cunt.

This surprised her for a number of reasons. Paramount was the shock of suddenly seeing an erect prick. Not what she had expected at all. Not there. Not through a window. Secondly, and wrongly, she had thought in her severely restrained condition she could not possibly have been turned on by it. She realised it was having the reverse effect. Her very constraint had kindled her excitement.

Mary's mouth felt suddenly parched and her lips dry. With difficulty, she pushed her tongue past her teeth and licked them wet. The vicariousness of the situation excited her. She trussed up – a hidden watcher; him unknown, with a large hard prick. The sight of a stiff cock at a distance was ineffably stimulating. Like seeing a photograph of a beautiful man with half-closed sexy eyes and his phallus raised. Raised proud and thick, desiring. But not originally for you.

For whom? What or who had been the fount of his erection? Who had turned him on? That didn't matter. It was up and hard. In the instance of turning the page, the beautiful man was hard for you. And seeing it could spin a web of lust through the veins of the onlooker – as the sight of the stranger's cock did to Mary. It was perilously exciting by inference, not by actuality.

Oblivious of Mary's voyeuristic involvement in his activities, the man remained by the window, his large upright prick in silhouette. A *frisson* of danger whipped through Mary. If he noticed her watching, what would he do? Ignore her? Move deeper into the room, well away from her prying eyes, or come after her?

He was free to leave his apartment. He could easily make his way into hers. Not by the front door – she doubted if that would be allowed. She had a feeling there would be intense restrictions on who could obtain access to the building she was in. The people in control wouldn't let just anybody past its portals. They wouldn't want outsiders to see her trussed up.

Nevertheless, they had left her by the open window. But then, it was rare for passers-by to look upward. Most people kept their eyes on the ground or stared fixedly into the middle distance. But what would the man do if he noticed her looking? Climb the leafy elm tree in the tiny front garden, then leap on to the small but sturdy wrought iron balcony? It would take his weight, Mary was sure of that. And her French windows were wide open. She had no lace curtains to hide behind. Should he choose that route, access was immediately available. And she would be powerless.

Mary kept her eyes ranged on the man. He leant his small neat bare bottom against the window and inched his body down very slightly. Mary saw his shoulder blades flatten the lace curtain against the glass. His elbows were pushing out sideways, as if he were gripping the low window sill.

An extrordinary thought entered Mary's head. Was somebody sucking his cock? The angle of his body suggested that was exactly what might be happening. Mary garnished her imagination – seeing a rosy mouth giving him head, enveloping its cap. A tongue sneaking down to the rim then along its hard shaft.

Mary's curiosity was growing stronger by the minute. The man stood up. Again sideways, his cock quite distinct. If someone had been sucking him, they hadn't made him come. Mary found a certain satisfaction in that. She didn't want her peepshow to end that quickly. His prick was as large and as stiff as it had been before.

Then she thought she could see a hand moving along his cock. One hand. Up and down. Was it his own? It was difficult to tell. It could be. His body was bent slightly backward. Damn the lace: it was foiling her attempt to see if there was anyone else in the room.

Mary forced her tongue past her own lips again, enjoying the feel of the friction on her mouth. She would have given anything to be able to move her hands and place them down between her rigidly held-apart legs. She was swelling, opening. No coaxing necessary. She was ripe for a fuck.

She closed her eyes in something akin to panic. What a stupid thing to do. That was playing into their hands. Mary had the feeling they were trying to elicit a reaction from her. She would not give them that pleasure. She would be calm. She must be calm. The noises from the lilac bush close by her window lulled her stirring passion.

Birdsong. A sweet harmonious sound. A blackbird? Yes. And perhaps there was a nest nearby. Mary was always surprised by the variety of birds in London. Not just the usual smattering of starlings, pigeons and sparrows, but robins, chaffinches, and thrushes. The coarse call of the jay assailed her ears, shattering her pleasant thoughts. Mary had no love of jays. They were sleek, handsome and dangerous. They were nasty predators. Pests.

An involuntary shudder sped through her as a heavy truck trundled along the quiet street. It screeched to a halt, braking suddenly. Startled, and briefly opening her eyes then closing them again, Mary trembled in futile apprehension. Raised voices. Shouting obscenities.

'I could've fucking killed you.'

'You didn't, OK?'

Screaming curses.

'Fucking cyclists.'

Anger. Please, no anger. She was pleading inwardly. No anger. Let it go. Let it be. Desperately, she tried to block out the hysteria, but the harsh shrieking duet continued unabated until the truck drove away. Mary's fear subsided but the episode left her unsettled and anything but calm.

Disgruntled, she opened her eyes and abstractly looked straight at the window opposite. Was that a body shape beside the man? Was it another person? Suddenly alert and curious, Mary scanned the window hard, endeavouring to work out whether it was shadows and sunlight playing tricks or if there really was someone else there. Was that a flash of long blonde hair?

She cursed inwardly. She shouldn't have shut out the view. She shouldn't have allowed her own self-indulgent desire and the unseen strangers' screaming anger to overcome her watching brief. And now she'd most probably lost the opportunity to discover who was in that room with him. What sort of a female? Tall, short, fat, thin? That was an interesting piece of conjecture. It might not be a female. Up and until that moment, the hand and the imagined mouth had been disembodied. Not belonging to any sex, or any person.

Then the naked man moved beyond her interested gaze.

Mary became aware of someone moving behind her but she couldn't turn her body. Couldn't see who it was. There was silence, apart from the constant droning of a machine. Not a word was spoken. She couldn't and whoever was in there with her wouldn't. Wouldn't? Well, didn't. Mary felt cool hands on her head, then on her face. They were checking on the leather straps. Making sure the steel rings were in position. She caught a glimpse of man's hands. Clean, long-fingered, well manicured. His arms must be leaning over her shoulders but he was standing back from her, out of sight. It was impossible for her to see any more of him. Which one of the three men in the establishment was it?

Whoever it was, had he noticed her arousal? Surely not. She was too well trussed. But he would know if he touched her. Would he do that? Would he kneel between her strapped-up legs and lick her bare rosy cunt? Would he put his long fingers along her sex-lips and squeeze them gently, allowing her juices to ease out? Would he spread her wide open and reveal her rigid aching clit? Would he let his tongue slurp along her delicate and tender flesh and hear her exhale, in a moment of deep satisfaction?

The very thought made her buttocks quiver and contract. The unexpected hankering for sex was now supreme. Everything else was erased from her mind. Mary Fountain wanted to fuck. The man in the room with her was a good start. But did he realise that was what she was wanting? Mary thought he did but was pretending he didn't. Was he deliberately teasing her? She closed her eyes and inhaled.

Noiselessly, the man departed. Mary was conscious of his going, felt the lack of his presence in her room. She reopened her eyes and again focused her attention on the window opposite.

The curtains hung straight, no movement discernible. Lazily she surveyed what she could of the street. A tall wiry black man, arm in arm with a short slim black woman, stopped at the house. They climbed the steps and rang a bell. There was no answer. They rang the bell once more.

The black man stepped back from the door and looked up at the window which was the object of Mary's fascination. He shouted, 'Chris, Chris.'

Moments later, the window was raised. With a towel around his midriff, the man called Chris – her man - stuck his head out.

'Hi, Gary; hi, April,' he said.

'Hey, man, can we come up?' said Gary, waving a bottle of champagne.

'Er, no, sorry . . .'

'We just got engaged,' said April.

'Congratulations! See you later in the Parrot.'

'Don't need the Parrot when I got the fizz here,' said Gary, a note of petulance in his voice.

He was, thought Mary, obviously somewhat put out by his friend's reticence to celebrate with them.

'I'll buy you some more later,' said Chris and began to lower the window.

'Hey, man, you got pussy in there?' asked Gary perceptively. He snorted a laugh.

In reply, Chris laughed too.

'I said you'd never go more than a week,' shouted Gary. 'Man, I won my bet. That's two bottles of champagne.'

'OK,' said Chris, bringing the window down but not completely shutting it.

The couple walked away, smiling. Gary punched the air.

'I knew it,' he said to his fiancée. 'I knew it. Telling me he was real sore when Katie left for no good reason. Gutted, man, he said he was gutted and never gonna screw again. Yeah, yeah, I told him. Give it a couple of days . . .'

Mary watched the two lovers laughing and giggling until, bound by the confines of her condition, she could no longer see or hear them. Then she raised her eyes back to the window, waiting.

Extraordinary, she thought, how much you could learn by being still and watching. Not participating in deed but in thought, in imagination.

So the handsome well-dressed man's name was Chris. He drank in the Parrot, wherever that was; he'd had a relationship with a woman called Katie; he had a couple of black friends and he liked sex. Liked sex a lot, that much was obvious.

But did he have a woman in there with him? He could be by himself. He could be enjoying his own body. Having a wank. The body he'd been given was a good one. Why shouldn't he enjoy it as much as anybody else? He'd most probably spent years perfecting the art of making himself come, giving himself endless enjoyment. At that moment, Mary would have loved to feel herself, fondle and caress her wet cunt. But her hands were imprisoned at her side. Imprisoned and immobile.

She wondered, if the man did have a woman with him, what she was like. Blonde. Yes. There had been that flash of blonde hair. Mary was convinced he was not alone. She had seen another body in the room and she decided it was female. Mary asked herself why Chris hadn't let his friends in. If Gary and April and Chris were on such intimate terms, being able to take a bet on him not screwing for a week, then why did he not open the door?

All the woman had to do was put a towel round her, the same as he had done; then sit and drink and wait until the newly engaged couple had gone, before resuming their love-making. Perhaps it was somebody Chris didn't want Gary to see. Perhaps they were doing something Chris didn't want Gary and April to know about.

Suddenly there was movement at the window. Mary was quickly alert. Breasts. Tits flattened against the glass. Dispassionately, Mary assessed them. Rounded, upright and pale, with large dark-red nipples. Nice tits; a good shape, though not as good or as full as her own. The woman raised her hands above her head, her palms flat on the glass. Mary couldn't see her face. Her head was bent, her long blonde hair tumbling over her shoulders. Mary smiled inwardly. A sense of triumph overcame her. She had been right.

Then the man stood beside the woman. He must have touched her somewhere because her tits moved slightly; her flat palms dragged downward on the window. Mary gave a sharp intake of breath as she imagined his hand on her bottom, then feeling between her legs, feeling for her cunt, feeling her wetness, opening her juicy red lips, playing with her, exciting her.

Involuntarily, the muscles in Mary's bottom clenched. She wanted to close her eyes, float into her own sexuality; but, frightened she might miss something, she kept her eyes fixed on the window.

The man took hold of one of the woman's hands and placed it on his prick. For seconds, the two of them stayed as a tableau. He must have commanded her to remove her other, steadying, hand. The next moment, her breasts were out of view as her top half moved backward and her slim thighs suddenly appeared, pressed against the glass. Mary watched in growing sexual turmoil as the woman's other hand snaked its way over her belly until it found the mound of light-brown hair at the top of her thighs.

Brazenly, blissfully unaware that she was being watched, the woman began to fondle herself with a careful determination, using deliberate and slow caresses on her cunt-lips. At the same time, and in perfect rhythm, her hand began to move on the man's cock. Up and down, up and down; every movement visible through the lace curtain.

Mary was captivated, enthralled, by their behaviour. She was hooked. Couldn't bear to tear her eyes from the gently gliding hands on their relentless voyage backward and forward. The not knowing made it more exciting. The disembodiment of the parts made the scene infinitely more thrilling than if she had been watching sex on a screen, or being played out before her in the full glare of lights and knowledge, let alone participating in the act.

Mary's own body was responding to their obvious mutual

affection and to their licentiousness. She could feel her nipples quickening. As they stiffened, held back by their restrainment, they chafed. It was not unpleasurable. It increased her arousal.

The couple moved away from the window. As they did so, a portion of the curtain flowed out into the room after them, giving Mary a full view of the man standing and the woman kneeling in front of him, her mouth level with his cock.

Mary's belly tensed, her buttocks tightened again and her cunt swelled more. She was moist now and ready to receive. She wanted a cock inside her. She had made space for it. The whole of her was aching, trembling with the desire to pull a cock into her cunt. In and up. Up, and further up, gliding, thrusting. Its shape and ridges blending with hers, easing to the tip of her womb. Mary was yearning for sex. She closed her eyes in an effort to contain her imagination.

When she reopened her eyes, the curtain was blowing out in the breeze. The two had moved. She couldn't see the man, only the woman's well-rounded bottom. Mary's eyes were level with it, mesmerised by it. Then something protruded between the woman's legs. Just beneath her arse. Disappeared. Protruded again.

Mary's eyes were out on stalks, staring. It was the head of his cock. A supremely sexual sight. A sight full of promise. Promise and anticipation. Anticipation coupled with sweet torment. He was gliding his prick between her thighs, along her cunt-lips. And Mary felt the sudden intense swoop of rampant sexual desire. The remembered excitement. The teasing. The fine nerve-endings on the soft inner thigh and the sense of satisfaction as a stiff hard prick rubbed against it, its ridges miraculously soothing that place, but heightening the craving within.

The curtain flapped back and down. The couple retreated into the shadows, well away from Mary's searching eyes.

She was left with a forlorn tension in her body but a fresh awareness of its capabilities. That awareness was augmented by the small muscle movement in her buttocks, the shimmering tingling, the wetness in her own aching cunt.

The pain of her restrainment was forgotten, overcome by desire. Mary could feel her own heartbeat. The blood coursed through her body fast, aided by her lascivious thoughts. Sex, a fuck, sucking: every fibre in her body screamed at her. Caress, touch me, take me. Fuck me.

Soon somebody would come in. Would they notice her plight? Would they guess what she was now wanting? Would it be one of the men or the woman who realised she was ready?

How many men were there? She had seen three. A small fat one, quite jolly; he'd smiled a lot. A young lanky one, with untidy hair, a bit precious. And one middle-aged, grey-haired, slightly supercilious. Yes, she'd like to see him with his trousers off. Not necessarily naked. Just his prick stiff. None of them inspired her as much as the man opposite. But would one of them oblige? Or would they continue to pretend?

She thought about the woman. She was quite young and pretty. Mentally, Mary stripped her of her uniform. Big tits, small waist. Round face, round legs. Soft yielding flesh. Woman to woman. Would she do it? Would she position herself between Mary's legs and slide her fingers along Mary's glistening cunt-lips and put her long red tongue to Mary's clit and lick her?

Mary's breath was coming in short fast bursts. Somewhere in her body she felt pain but that was taking second place to her craving for sex.

She looked back at the window. Somebody had opened it further, wider. She had been so lost in her own thoughts, she had not noticed that happening. There must, she thought, be a fan in the room, because the curtain was waving wildly. Now the man had the woman standing in front of him. Their bodies appeared still, fused in harmony. Affectionate as well as sexual. His mouth was against her neck. One arm was crossed over her naked body, holding a breast; his fingers had captured her nipple. His other hand was down between her legs. The woman began moving her hips, round and round with a languid, flowing dancer's motion.

Mary suddenly realised what it was the woman was doing, and knew she had done it many times. The man's hand was quite still; it was the woman's dulcet movement that allowed his fingers to slowly penetrate.

It was a slow love-dance usually made by two people who knew each other's body extremely well. So had the recently departed Katie returned?

Then something changed. Suddenly the sense of affection between the two of them was lost. Mary tried to assess what it was, but she knew their oneness had dissipated. Piqued by the loss, Mary stared at them quite blatantly, not caring whether they noticed her not. She was trying to figure out what had altered. Their stance seemed the same, but it wasn't. He'd moved slightly back and yet his hand remained rigid in place.

Yes. It was his hand on her cunt. It no longer said enjoyment but possessiveness. *I own you. You are mine.* Rage welled up inside Mary. Fool! she wanted to shout at him. You fool. You own yourself, no one else. Take responsibility only for your own love and life. And a turbulent anger overwhelmed Mary.

In exasperation, the woman swerved violently away from the man. She knew, too. She had realised what Mary had sensed. Possessiveness. Jealousy. Every curve of the woman's body seemed to have become angular with fury. The lace curtain flapped down, shutting out the woman and the man from Mary's sight.

Mary was shaking with uncontrollable anger and resentment. For them, for her. There was a mingling of emotions. Rage and sex, curdling. And pain. The pain was eking through, taking over, filling up her consciousness. A bright sharp pain. She wanted to call out but couldn't. Closing her eyes, she endeavoured to find the source of that pain. Take it, grab it, expel it. The pleasure in her womb, in her cunt, had been overtaken by the piercing, the stabbing somewhere else. Around her there was a flurry of activity, then a dull sullenness enveloped her.

Through a fog, Mary heard a young woman saying, 'I thought so but now you're quite sure?'

'No doubt about it,' replied a deeply masculine but clipped voice.

'Mary, Mary, can you hear me?' asked another male voice. A more soothing sound.

Mary didn't want to respond. She lay quite still, keeping her eyes closed. Her brain was whirring. Thinking. Wondering. Listening.

'Quite remarkable,' said the first voice, his words measuring his surprise. 'We can unplug that contraption now. She's past the worst. Touch and go – but she's definitely turned the corner.'

Mary felt strong hands loosening the leather straps around her face.

'In a few days' time,' the first voice continued, 'the plaster and the other bits and pieces can come off and then we'll work on those limbs.'

'Who shall we get?' asked the woman.

'Chris Dalby,' replied the man.

'Oh, but . . .' interrupted the woman. 'I thought he was taking a break. Going on holiday. A second honeymoon. That's what he said yesterday.'

'That was yesterday,' said the man, an assured arrogance making his voice more clipped as he sounded each syllable. 'He rang ten minutes ago. Apparently, the reconciliation didn't work.'

'Oh, dear – and I've cancelled all his appointments. I'm sorry,' said the woman. 'I liked Katie, thought they were well suited. Still, it's like many things – only the people concerned know what really goes on. Handy, though, him living opposite.'

'Just as well. This one's going to need a lot of attention. Between you and me, when they brought her in, I didn't think she'd pull through.'

'Wasn't that why they sent her here?' asked the woman.

'Ssh,' hissed the second man angrily. 'I'm going to wake her now.'

Mary sighed. A sense of relief flooded through her as the paraphernalia attached to various parts of her body was removed. She turned her head for the first time in days and watched the young technician roll away the apparatus that had been beside her bed. Then she raised her eyes up to the two men and the woman staring indulgently down at her. Mary tried a smile. They nodded, understanding that she already knew she could live without a machine. Mary was fully aware she was hooked on life.

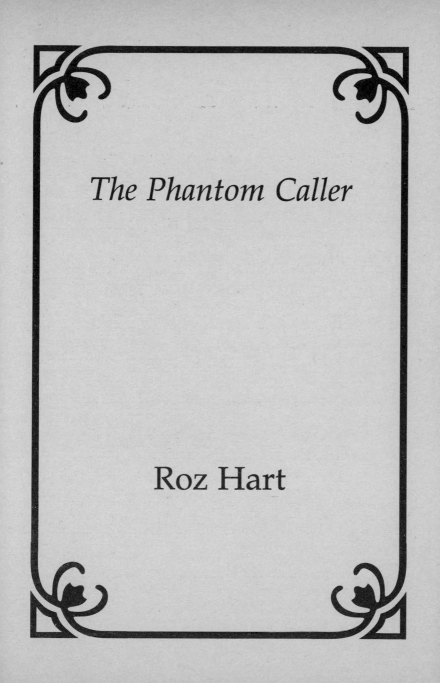

The Phantom Caller

Roz Hart

The Phantom Caller

❧ ❧

'*A* re you in bed? What are you wearing?'
Marnie groaned and sank back against the pillow. Him again: that was the third time this week.

'Is it a nightie?'

Well, what else would she be wearing at two-thirty in the morning?

'Not pyjamas, I hope. I hate pyjamas.'

She didn't answer. The first few times she had: challenge him, the experts advised, give as good as you get. But that had only encouraged him; she'd learnt that the best approach was just to say nothing and wait till he'd finished his little performance. Even hanging up achieved nothing; he called back immediately, and kept calling until she let him have his say. The obvious solution was to unplug the phone; but she was a keyholder for the clinic and, after the break-in earlier that summer, she didn't dare. Next time, they might not be disturbed before they could get away with anything valuable.

It had been going on for a month or more now. The calls only came when she was alone: when Chris wasn't staying the night. At first they had scared her, sent the adrenalin on a frantic dash round her veins, keeping her awake for the rest of the night.

'It must be someone who knows you,' Chris said. 'Tell the police; they'll pin him down in no time.'

But Marnie couldn't take the hassle – or the embarrassment,

for that matter. Fancy describing the sexual fantasies someone wove around you to some burly middle-aged sergeant. In any case, it soon became plain he was all talk; and there were security locks on all the doors and windows and the front gate of the apartment complex was like a bullion-store entrance.

'. . . and then, when your arse is glowing red, I'll hand you the cane, and slowly take my trousers down and bend over the back of the sofa, and wait for you to take your revenge . . .'

The voice was muffled, obviously disguised but without a single familiar note. It was cultured, too: soft, almost caressing. She never meant to listen, but it was hard not to, especially when he was spinning the very fantasy she had ached to whisper to Chris just a few hours ago when he phoned to say goodnight.

How did he do that? Read her thoughts, and know exactly what turned her on? Last time, he had described the way he planned to remove all her clothes, slowly, item by item; and the time before, he gave her a detailed account of the blow-job he wanted from her, and how he would use his tongue on her in return. The more she thought about it, the more likely Chris's theory became: that it was someone she knew.

Sometimes he seemed to know more about her libido than she did herself. Last week, for instance, when he described her walking down a busy street wearing nothing but a mink coat worth thousands of pounds. However obscene and politically incorrect real fur was, the thought of it wrapped round her naked skin made her thighs rub together of their own volition.

'And then I'll come up behind you and hustle you into a narrow alley,' he had gone on, 'and we'll fuck against the wall, both wrapped in the mink, just a few feet away from half the city on its way home from work.'

That call had left her breathless: the combination of the scenario her fantasies had never envisaged, the thought of the fur on her body and the risk of getting caught carried a powerful erotic charge.

This one was almost as potent. Her nipples began to tingle as he continued to describe the swish of the cane, and the way it stung his bare flesh into arousal.

'And then, when I can't take any more, when my cock is hard as concrete and throbbing like an engine, I'll snatch the cane from your hand, fling you down on the carpet and shag you till you explode.'

A faint moan escaped Marnie's lips as the phone line clicked softly and the dialling tone began to purr. She slammed the handset back into its cradle. It wasn't fair, leaving her up in the air like this. Every single time, she became aroused against her will and was unable to sleep till she had appeased her hungry body. Trust Chris to choose this week to catch up on his leave and visit his mum; where was he when she needed him? She'd never get back to sleep unless ... Her hands were ahead of her, one plucking at an already erect nipple and the other seeking the swollen nub of flesh between her thighs. A picture rose in front of her eyes: a pair of taut male buttocks arched towards her, the skin slightly reddened.

She groaned as the spasms shook her body, and sank back into the mattress, feeling the tension flow out of her muscles.

Sex shouldn't be like this, she thought. An orgasm should be the culmination of something special, of the ultimate in human contact – not like scratching an uncontrollable itch. Trouble was, it took so little to turn her on. Her libido was a force to be reckoned with – as Chris had discovered a few months ago. So far he had kept up with her, and they were good together; he pressed all the right buttons instinctively and was game for anything. She'd been faithful to him, too – well, almost, if you didn't count the taxi home from the night club after Penny's hen night – and it hadn't really been a struggle. Maybe it was time she let their relationship move on; he'd been dropping heavy hints for a couple of weeks about moving in, ever since she told him about the phone calls, in fact.

I'll talk to him, she promised herself, as sleep began to claim her again. Over lunch tomorrow.

'So what do you wear under that sexy little tunic?' Rob March said conversationally, putting out a hand and just missing her thigh.

'Knee-length bloomers and a woolly vest,' Marnie riposted brightly, digging her fingers into the firm muscle of his upper back more vigorously than was strictly necessary. 'Oh, I'm so sorry, did that hurt? Still, if you want to be back in the team by Christmas . . . No pain, no gain, eh?'

Physiotherapist to the stars, her sister called her, and Rob March was certainly the darling of the sports writers, not to mention upward of thirty thousand loyal fans who paid to see him every Saturday. She could see why; his grin had a cheeky twist to it and there was a wicked sparkle in those slate-blue eyes. He had torn some knee ligaments in a cup match last month, and was visiting the clinic every day for treatment. When he asked for massage as well, Marnie had drawn the long straw.

Specialising in sports injuries had been a smart move, she reflected; there weren't many jobs which would allow her to lay hands on the naked body of one of the country's most talked-about young footballers. Between Rob March's firm flesh and the dirty phone calls, Chris had been on a promise twice a night for weeks.

She slapped Rob's tautly muscled bottom and moved away from the massage couch. 'That's enough self-indulgence for one day. Full-body massage isn't going to help your knee one bit.'

'No, but it's more fun than heat treatment. And you're prettier than the guy with the beard – what's his name again?'

'Chris. He's not here today; I'll be doing your heat treatment as well.'

He was doing it on purpose, standing there beside the couch and making no attempt whatsoever to cover himself up, plainly aware of what a magnificent physical specimen he was. He knew damn well the effect he was having on her.

'Friend of yours, is he, old Chris? I bet he doesn't wear a woolly vest under his tunic. Actually . . .' He took a step towards her. 'I bet you don't, either.'

He was right. She wasn't wearing anything at all. Ever since Chris had mentioned a couple of weeks ago that it made him hard just to think of her without underwear, she had worn her work tunic with nothing underneath. And when he found out, things had got pretty steamy in the little treatment room next to the hydrotherapy pool.

And now Rob March was looking at her as if he knew she was naked under the thin cotton. His cock, a good five inches long in flaccid repose, was beginning to stir. He slipped his hand under it and held it up for her inspection.

'I've been fancying you ever since I first came here. How about it? Something to tell your friends in the wine bar?'

Marnie swallowed hard and licked dry lips. 'Sorry. That's not part of the treatment.'

He shrugged and reached for his towelling robe. 'Your loss.'

His eyes met hers and held them. Arrogant little prick, Marnie told herself, trying to be cross; he's far too used to getting his own way. But even as the thought was flicking across her mind, she knew she wasn't about to help him break the habit. Not because he was a well-known footballer: fame didn't do a thing to turn her on. Plenty of sports celebrities crossed her path, and she was constantly surprised how unattractive they proved to be without their clothes. Mostly they seemed to hang up their brains in the changing room, alongside their boots. But Rob was different; he took an intelligent interest in the work they did here at the clinic. Besides, a pair of well-formed gluteals made up for a great deal, not to mention a penis that was well on its way to nine inches.

It was hard to take her eyes off it. Her nipples were tingling and she felt moisture running between her thighs. She slid the bolt on the door and moved towards him. Sorry, Chris, she thought; it's a one-off, I promise.

She unbuckled her belt and dropped it on the floor, and he made short work of the buttons down the front of her tunic. His eyes opened wide as it fell apart, revealing her naked body underneath.

'*Love* the vest and bloomers, babe,' he said huskily, reaching for her breasts. He pinched her erect nipples, shooting tiny barbs of sensation all over her body. He stroked her from neck to ankles, then plunged a hand between her legs.

'You weren't really going to say no, were you?' he chaffed. 'What a waste of all this lovely honey if you had.'

He swept an arm behind her knees and lifted her on to the couch. His cock had continued swelling; now it was her turn to stare as he knelt in front of her, stripping the wrapper off the condom he had taken from his robe pocket.

'You planned this!'

'Let's say I hoped,' he said, grinning. 'I like to be prepared.'

He unrolled the condom over his penis, and Marnie spread her legs wide and closed her eyes. He pushed into her, stretching and filling her, and began to thrust.

'Know what I'd really like?' he said after a few moments, already a little breathless. 'I'd like to do this in the middle of Wembley Stadium, in front of a Cup Final crowd. Imagine the roar when we . . . aaaaah, Jeez!'

His back arched and he pounded into her furiously. Her nails dug into the flesh of his thigh as goose-pimples prickled down his hip; his whole body convulsed and he clutched her shoulders and buried his face in her hair. 'Sorry. Took me by surprise. You shouldn't be so bloody sexy!'

He slid out of her and eased down the couch, sliding expert fingers over the burning flesh between her legs. With two fingers in her channel, he began to rub her clit from side to side with his thumb; it only took seconds for a fire to ignite and spread through her whole body in a series of sizzling spasms. She opened her eyes to find his slate-coloured ones glimmering puckishly at her.

'You are one gorgeous lady. I'll be recommending this establishment to all my friends.'

'Don't you dare tell them why!'

'Don't worry; our secret is safe.' He swung his legs to the floor, wincing a little. 'I've put the knee back a day or two, I guess. Worth every twinge, though. Next time, you'd better go on top.'

'Next time?'

He reached for his robe and tossed her tunic towards her, grinning. 'I can keep hoping, can't I?'

The smile was infectious; Marnie felt the corners of her mouth curling in response. His treatment wouldn't be over for a while, and what Chris didn't see wouldn't hurt him. Who knew what tomorrow might bring?

'Are you in bed? What are you wearing?'

Two nights in a row. Didn't this joker ever sleep? Thank goodness Chris would be back tomorrow.

'I can picture you in a Newcastle United shirt. Nothing else, just black and white stripes and a big number 69 on your back.'

He was doing it again. Marnie jerked awake and pressed the handset closer to her ear. That voice . . . perhaps it was familiar, after all.

'You can keep it on if you like. Just as long as there's nothing underneath to get in the way. Unless you'd rather be naked, feel the cool grass on your skin as I lay you down in the middle of the pitch and . . .'

She listened closely as he described every thrust and tremor, searching every phrase for familiar intonation. When she replaced the handset, she had almost convinced herself it was Rob March's voice. The evidence was circumstantial, but it existed. The calls had begun round about the time he first came to the clinic, he could find her number in the phone book, and he had revealed only today how much he fancied her.

She pulled the duvet around her shoulders and closed her eyes. She still couldn't be absolutely certain. Rob's accent betrayed his East End origins, and the caller's was almost upper-crust. But if it wasn't him, something distinctly weird was going on.

She decided to play it cool in the treatment room next day, responding to Rob's banter in monosyllables and determinedly ignoring the erection that began to burgeon as she smoothed massage oil into his pectorals.

'What do you do when you leave here in the evening?' he asked her, lifting a hand in the general direction of her hip.

She moved out of reach. 'Go home and crash out, usually.'

'There's no devoted significant other waiting by the log fire, then?'

'No comment. Why, are you offering?'

'Who, me? No way. I'm not ready to settle down. Wouldn't want to cramp my style.'

'So what is your style?' Making dirty phone calls in the small hours, she added silently.

'Oh, you know. Wine, women, clubbing the night away.'

'Is that what you did last night?'

'You bet. Every night, if I can escape the club coach's eagle eye. He seems to think I should drink mineral water and go to bed at ten. Alone. Boring old fart.'

'Where did you go last night, then?' And what time did you get home? asked the silent voice in her head. The call had come at a quarter to two.

'The Ice Box. I recommend it. Live music till midnight and a comedy cabaret afterwards.' He yawned widely, showing even milk-white teeth. 'It's a wonder I made it on time this morning; didn't get home till gone three. Bloody paparazzi caught us as we left. *Daily Globe*, he said; expect I'll be all over the back page tomorrow. I hate those bastards – don't give you any peace. Ow, watch it; that hurt.'

'Sorry.' Marnie stopped pummelling his calf muscles and slid her oil-slicked hands up his thighs. Bang went a good theory. Then again, maybe he'd never been a serious suspect. East End accent aside, his voice was pitched higher than the caller's, and that was difficult to disguise. So it was back to the drawing board.

'Night, babe. Pleasant dreams.'

Chris was such a sweetie; whenever he didn't stay, he called to say goodnight. She hadn't really expected it tonight; he'd been out to a club with a crowd of his mates on someone's stag night, so she'd dropped him off at the pub, all prepared to poke fun at his hangover in the morning. But here he was, not long after midnight, sounding far from pissed. She was almost tempted to tell him to get a cab and come straight over.

She still had a few reservations about letting him move in but, the more she thought about it, the more it seemed like a good idea. 'And when my Calvins are nestling close to your Victoria's Secret, we'll celebrate with an early night,' he had said yesterday, brushing her earlobe with his beard in a way that made her tremble from head to toe. 'I'll undress you one garment at a time, and then I'll . . .'

Her face grew hot as she recalled exactly what he had said. What was it about so-called dirty talk, bad language, four-letter words, that reached inside her and massaged her libido into instant and relentless arousal? As Chris went on whispering the words into her ear, her hands began to fumble at his clothes of their own accord, until his jeans were on the floor round his feet and he was backing her towards the sofa.

What a night they had had. She snuggled under the duvet, pulling the second pillow close to her. Monogamy could turn out to be fun.

She was on the edge of sleep when the phone rang again; she leapt a foot in the air and gazed around wildly, unsure where the sound was coming from. When she identified it, she snatched the handset up and barked the number.

'Are you in bed? What are you wearing?'

'Oh, it's you.' She subsided on to the pillow and let out a long breath.

'What a big sigh. Missed me, have you? What shall I do to you tonight? No kinky stuff – let's just shag ourselves senseless. Think of it: my prick sliding in and out of your cunt, fucking and fucking and fucking. I'll pull out at the last second and spray your lovely tits with come, then I'll slip down the bed and spread your legs wide, and push a finger right inside your pretty quim and wrap my tongue around your clit until it erupts like a volcano. All night long we'll fuck and shag, cock to cunt, prick to twat . . .'

The stream of four-letter words was defused of its violence by the creamy, soothing voice. Marnie lay back and let it flow over her. How did he do it? How could a complete stranger know so much about her?

She sat upright. No. It was impossible. Why would he? What did he have to gain? He knew the phone calls didn't frighten her; if he did move in it would be because she wanted him to, not as some kind of knight protector.

The voice flowed on. The more closely she listened, the more like Chris it sounded. His was practically accentless, and pitched so low it was almost gravelly when he put his mouth close to her ear and made her shiver. This voice lacked that husky, sandpapered quality, but there was something . . .

It was obvious, now she thought about it. The calls always came when Chris wasn't here; and nobody knew better than he did what turned her on. The football field incident which had pointed the finger at Rob March must have been nothing more sinister than a coincidence.

She smiled. As well as keeping up a lavish supply of the best sex she'd ever had, Chris was a good friend. He made her laugh, too, and knew exactly which romantic gesture would melt her knees: a midnight call to say goodnight beat clichéd red roses out of sight. She wasn't wildly in love with him in the sense that she'd rush into a burning building to rescue him, but she liked him a lot: certainly enough for the thought of having him around all the time to fill her with pleasure, at least for a while. And who knew what the while might lead to if it were carefully nurtured? He was obviously nuts about her; it was rather sweet, the lengths he was prepared to go to to persuade her to let him move in with her. Dirty phone calls in the small hours, for instance: just a suggestion of danger and a need for an extra line of defence – like a man about the place.

The dialling tone was purring in her ear; she cradled the handset and settled herself for sleep. OK, big guy, she thought; you win. But not because you've scared me: just to make sure the phone doesn't wake me at two in the morning.

She'd spent most of the day clearing a shelf in the living room for his CDs, and sorting out her wardrobe to make space for his clothes. Chris had arrived in the hired van shortly after four o'clock. And now they were lying languorously on the sheepskin rug, naked limbs entwined and tinted pinky-orange by the firelight. Planning ahead had never been Marnie's style up to now; but the promise of months, perhaps even years, of glorious nights with Chris were beginning to stretch out in front of her like a golden carpet studded with stars.

She disentangled an arm and ran her fingers through his chest hair. 'Are you falling asleep on me? On our first night as a live-in couple?'

'Would I?'

'You'd better not.'

He opened his eyes and raised himself on one elbow. 'When's bedtime in this establishment?'

'Depends what you mean by bedtime. I'm ready when you are – as long as you weren't planning to nod off.'

'Well, even if I was . . .' He took her hand and guided it to his crotch; he was already hard again, after less than twenty minutes.

He scrambled to his feet and pulled her after him. 'Did we finish the wine?' He opened the fridge. 'Good, there's nearly half a bottle left. I'm going to paint your tits with it and lick it off.'

What would the phantom caller make of that? Marnie wondered. Except that there was no phantom caller; he was a real live person, with one hand laced into hers and the other wrapped around a bottle of Chardonnay. There wouldn't be any more calls, now that they had achieved what he wanted.

She followed Chris into the bedroom and lay down obediently. At times like this her entire body turned into one big erogenous zone, with her breasts the most erogenous of all – something Chris had discovered very early in their acquaintance, and used for their mutual pleasure ever since.

He poured wine into the hollow in her throat and let it trickle downward, using his fingers to direct the tickly flow towards her nipples. She gasped as cold liquid met tender skin, then cried aloud and he lowered his mouth on to her and began to flick his tongue across the sensitive nub. His teeth closed gently around it, and her fingers raked up and down his back. Suddenly she was ablaze, and sensed that he was too, and was holding back.

'Fuck me!' she commanded. 'Fuck me hard and fast.' She took his cock between her hands and pulled him towards her, lifting her legs on to his shoulders. Her orgasm had already begun to mount before he pushed into her, and soon the tension was filling her to bursting point. Was this how living together was going to be?

His chest hair brushed her nipples as he pounded into her again and again. Just when she felt she could take no more of that volcanic pressure, a dam burst inside her and hot champagne seemed to erupt, deluging her legs and torso with an effervescent flood. An inarticulate shout heralded the approach of Chris's climax and his buttock-muscles clenched under her hands. A thought trailed over her mind from a distance: Rob March isn't the only one with a nice bum.

He fell back on the mattress, a long gust of breath escaping him. Marnie's hair stuck to her forehead in damp tendrils, and every muscle ached deliciously. She would sleep like the dead tonight.

After a while, they straightened the sheet and retrieved the duvet, which had somehow sprawled itself across the chest of drawers. They finished the wine, taking turns to drink from the bottle, and she nestled against him. This living together was OK, she decided. Good, in fact. She pulled his hand over her breast and began to drift towards sleep.

On the edge of a dream about a football match, she became aware that repeated blasts on the referee's whistle were actually something else. The phone. She groaned and leant over the side of the bed to pick it up.

'Are you in bed?' crooned a familiar voice. 'What are you wearing?'

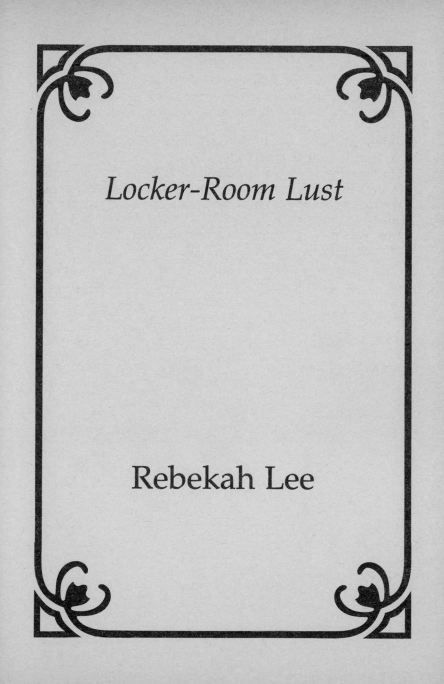

Locker-Room Lust

Rebekah Lee

Locker-Room Lust

✤ ✤

Jessica wrinkled her nose as she stepped into the chlorine-fresh atmosphere of the public baths. As always, she inhaled the warm air greedily, a little ripple of excitement running the length of her spine. Pushing a book of saver tickets under the glass window, she luxuriated in her secret pleasure. There was something incredibly sensual about swimming semi-naked among strangers. As she made the short walk to the pool, she anticipated the caress of her lycra costume; as always, it would mould her curves like a possessive lover. The scent of chlorine filled her nostrils as she headed for the women's changing area.

As she undressed, she remembered how the new starter from accounts had been shadowing her all day. The women in her office had struggled to suppress their sniggers until he was out of earshot.

'He's after you, Jess,' Linda announced dramatically, arching her eyebrows.

'Don't be ridiculous. I bet he's half my age,' Jessica said dismissively. Only privately did she wonder whether he might find her attractive. As she eased herself into the second skin of a swimsuit, she cast a critical eye over her naked body. Not bad for thirty-six, she thought, running a hand upward over a still trim waist to the swell of her pert breasts. The golden tan she had acquired in Turkey still accentuated her long limbs.

She smiled as she remembered the holiday and, of course,

George. Dark and brooding, he had fucked her mercilessly beneath the stars as she moaned quietly into the curly hairs of his chest. At her request, he had spoken to her only in his native tongue as they made love. Her need for the exotic had been totally fulfilled, as George possessed incredible stamina and an imagination almost as kinky as her own.

Disturbed by a conversation taking place just outside her cubicle, Jessica's daydream shattered into fragments. She blushed slightly as she removed her hand reluctantly from its warm nest between her thighs. Her memories had been so absorbing that she hadn't even realised she had been pleasuring herself. Flicking her unruly dark hair back over her shoulders, Jessica stuffed her clothes into a locker and sauntered towards the pool. The floor tiles were damp and cool beneath her bare feet.

She had finished work early, knowing the baths would be quieter in the middle of the afternoon. Of course, it hadn't escaped her attention that Dex would be on pool duty today. As she was a very frequent visitor, she had got to know most of the pool staff by name. Unlike the simpering boy from accounts, Dex was very much a man. Although she guessed he was only in his early twenties, Jessica had had many chances to admire his well-developed body in the lifeguard uniform of shorts and T-shirt. As he patrolled the edge of the pool, she continually glanced at his strong chest and firm thighs.

Jessica noticed the pool was almost empty as she descended the steps at the shallow end. It had been a good idea to come earlier. The water, she noticed, was warmer today. To her goose-pimpled skin, it felt like a caress. Little waves lapped at the pool's tiled edge as Jessica slipped easily into her first length. As she neared the middle, she felt a little self-conscious when she realised that Dex was studying her from his high chair at the side of the pool. Curls of tousled blond hair fell into his eyes in a way that she found dangerously suggestive. He could have been a surfer, a bad boy: someone your parents wouldn't like. And those eyes . . . As blue as the ocean on a sunny day and just as inviting. How easy it would be to dive into their depths.

She smiled at him as she swam by, wishing he would break the tense silence between them.

The lifeguard returned her smile with one that hinted at eroticism; his eyes burnt into her. Parting his lips, he mouthed the words, 'I want you.'

Jessica gave an involuntary shudder and swam on quickly. She must have imagined it. Yet, even without looking up, she knew he was still staring at her. She tried to concentrate on her surroundings: the high domed ceiling and spectator balcony below it. An enclosed water slide for the children. I wonder what it would be like to have him in the slide, Jessica thought. All that running water beneath our buttocks, jets of water spraying us from above as we struggled not to slide down into view, and the humidity building as our bodies thrashed together. His penis would move inside me as I sought his tongue hungrily. And what if someone caught us?

Jessica moved through the water mechanically, her cheeks blazing as her imagination ran wild. She was acutely aware of him but refused to look in his direction. What if he could somehow read her thoughts? Hadn't he said that he wanted her? Of course, she could have been mistaken. Perhaps he had mouthed a completely different message. The tingling in her body seemed real enough, though.

'Can't take his eyes off you today, can he?' asked a middle-aged man she often saw here, nodding in Dex's direction. The man gave a knowing wink, a sly smile, and front-crawled his way out of earshot before she could reply.

At the end of her session, Jessica paused by the steps and looked up at the lifeguard. He was now walking along the side of the pool towards her, each step bringing him closer until she could see the generous bulge in the front of his shorts. She watched, fascinated, as the protuberance swelled before her eyes, straining to be free. Dex saw her reaction and grinned mischievously, but this time his eyes were glued to the hard pegs of her nipples as her body responded to his excitement. Jessica, suddenly uneasy, climbed out of the pool and shivered as she went back into the women's changing area.

Wild thoughts bombarded her mind as she fumbled with the locker key. Hadn't she wanted something like this to happen? Didn't she need a really generous portion of uncomplicated sex? The answer to both was a definite 'yes'. Since George, there had been only the predictable hum of a vibrator to satisfy her need for penetration. She was feeling frustrated and very, very horny. Fantasising about their lovemaking had awakened a desperate carnal hunger. What if she showered and changed, only to find the lifeguard had taken his break, leaving her to relieve this pent-up longing with her own nimble fingers?

At that moment, Dex was striding through the changing area purposefully, his heart racing beneath his well-developed chest and perspiration beginning to stain the regulation lifeguard's T-shirt. He could hear the sound of a locker opening just around the corner. She was so close to him now that he could almost smell her, taste her. He allowed himself a second or two to remember her seductive smile and the perfect shape of her lithe body cutting through the water: and then he was there, behind her.

She stood with her back to him, still dripping wet and not yet out of the red one-piece costume, but he knew instinctively that she sensed his presence. Turning quickly and clutching a large towel to her chest, Jessica opened her mouth and began to form words that refused to be spoken. Dex, painfully aware of the hardening between his legs, reached forward and took the towel roughly from her, brushing his hand against both nipples as he did so. At this, she gasped, and he could see in her eyes the beginning of a scream; although her flushed cheeks and the pert erectness of her nipples denied such fear.

'What the hell do you think you're doing?' she gasped.

'I'm going to fuck you. Right here. That's what you want, isn't it?' the lifeguard asked teasingly.

Dropping the towel on to the tiled floor between them, Dex swallowed hard and reached for her, knowing the next swimmer could arrive in the changing rooms at any moment. His penis throbbed painfully, fully erect now and almost poking out of the waistband of his shorts. Jessica began to back away into the dead-end of a tiny changing cubicle, her long dark hair dripping into the generous cleavage he so desperately wanted to explore.

The lifeguard covered the distance between them in a stride and, without a word, lowered his face and sought her mouth hungrily. Parting her lips with his flicking tongue, he probed the sweet cavern of her mouth and pressed his hot body against her dampness. Taking her hand, he guided it quickly over the front of his shorts and felt his member twitch eagerly at her touch.

Jessica gasped at the size and strength of his erection as she wrapped her slender fingers around his knob. Impatient with her hesitance, he moved his hands over her taut buttocks and then gently down between her legs. As his fingers caressed her smooth thighs, she responded generously with the sticky secretion of her sex. Now she shuddered and her grip became firmer on his penis. Dex was, on some distant level, aware of echoing voices as new bathers entered the locker room.

'People will see us, for God's sake,' Jessica whispered, her hand still gripping his cock.

Dex could tell that, despite her protestations, she was thrilled by the threat of discovery.

'I'm going to bring you so much pleasure, you won't care who watches. You keep giving me raging hard-ons, Jessica. I'd like to share this one with you.'

'I can't wait to feel it inside me!' She purred, stroking her way down his cock and cupping his balls in the palm of one hand.

Dex gave a long guttural moan and brought his head down, down, to her breasts. As he ran his tongue along the soft flesh, he pushed long thick fingers into the moist bush between her thighs, pushing aside the dampened gusset of her costume. Jessica's fingers worked quickly on him, drawing the flesh of his prick rhythmically up and down and pulling him closer to her own belly.

As two long fingers reached deep inside her, Jessica lost her balance and staggered further back into the cubicle. They both disappeared from open view just seconds before the next swimmers approached; the cubicle curtain flapped open, in defiance of their privacy. Thrilled by this, Jessica squirmed down against Dex's hand, grinding on to him and squeezing fiercely with her internal muscles. The lifeguard groaned and gently bit into her soft breast. His fingers wriggled and thrust deep inside her pussy, then Dex pulled down the shoulder straps of Jessica's wet costume to reveal the generous curves of her breasts. Sucking greedily at each nipple in turn, he was aware for a moment that this was madness, that anyone could walk by and look in on them.

As Dex sucked, Jessica arched her back, knowing she was on the point of orgasm. The familiar feelings flooded in until the lifeguard suddenly withdrew his fingers and pushed her back on to the small seat at the rear of the cubicle. For a moment, she looked bewildered and confused; her cheeks burnt and a mass of dark hair tumbled around her shoulders with wild abandon.

'Flagging already?' she breathed. 'Frightened we'll be discovered?

She was silenced quickly as he knelt before her, ripped the swimsuit completely off and lifted her tanned legs over his broad shoulders.

'I love your musky scent,' he whispered, his nose nestling between her labia. 'It makes me so hungry, I'm going to eat your wet pussy before I fuck you.'

Jessica tensed as each delicious word played a light warm breeze across her throbbing clitoris.

Although Dex was desperate for full intercourse, he couldn't resist licking her out first. How could you possibly know a lover without tasting them? Savouring the freshness of her skin, he used his practised tongue to part the tight curls; it slipped between her swollen lips and into her sex as far as it could reach. Jessica cried out and pressed her thighs against his ears, all the time driving her sex down, down on to his face and working his tongue deeper inside her. Her fingers struggled urgently to find a hold in his blond curls as she guided him against her.

Footsteps. Mumbles of conversation. Whispers that became words as women approached the lockers.

'– and I said he could bloody well go and –'

'– don't blame you, he's been asking for it.'

They haven't seen us, Jessica thought, her mind swimming deliriously. How on earth can they miss his feet sticking out from the cubicle?

That they might be discovered imminently only heightened her already intense arousal.

Sensing her orgasm nearing, Dex pulled his tongue from her pussy and began to flick it over the hard knob of her clitoris again and again until she shuddered into her climax, bucking against his face until his cock felt as if it would explode.

Knowing his need, and partially satiated, Jessica unwrapped herself from him and stood up, inviting him to do the same. The cubicle had become a sauna; its end-of-row position ensured semi-darkness and their coupling maintained its humidity. From somewhere in the distance came the sound of water gushing from a hose. Smiling contentedly, her body flushed with the afterglow of sex, Jessica pulled down the lifeguard's shorts, letting her fingers catch teasingly against his hardness as she did so.

His penis jumped fully to attention and twitched excitedly at her scrutiny. Still people chatted as they changed ready to swim, oblivious to their presence. Jessica gave Dex a wicked look and squatted before him, pressing her chest against him. He moaned as she took his length between her breasts and used both hands to contain him completely in her soft flesh. He watched as she bent her head and circled the tip of his straining prick with her tongue.

'I could tease you for ever,' Jessica said, smirking, knowing that his breaking point was near but enjoying the game.

'Enough!' Dex gasped. 'I need to be inside you. Now.'

Needing to quench the animal within him, Dex moved quickly. Tousling Jessica's hair, he kissed her passionately before bending her face down over the bench seat until her firm milky buttocks brushed against his penis. Jessica pulled away, wanting him to take control and feed another of her fantasies. Dex felt her wriggle from him and his excitement became unbearable. Taking her hips firmly between his hands, he took a deep breath and buried the full length of his penis inside her. She stiffened against him, trying to deny him her pleasure, but still he possessed her; he fondled her pendulous breasts firmly as she started to rock beneath him.

Harder and faster he burrowed into her, with short deep strokes. His pubic bone smacked against her, each thrust taking him closer to his own climax. Dex panted thickly, the most primitive of urges guiding him on.

Jessica answered in quiet whimpers. Never had she known intercourse like this, or a lover as needful of sex as she was. As his orgasm approached, she yielded totally. Reaching a hand behind her, she took hold of his testicles and dragged the tip of her long nails against the sensitive flesh. With this, he groaned and made a last deeper thrust inside her, coming harder than he ever had before. She, too, cried out as Dex fondled a plump breast with each hand, pulling her tight against him as he climaxed. This heady combination of stimuli pushed Jessica over the edge, into a second, stronger orgasm which surprised and delighted her lover.

The lifeguard slipped his penis from her and kissed the chlorine-tasting skin at the back of Jessica's neck. Just the sight of her and the memory of their incredible fucking session was arousing him all over again. He passed the discarded towel to her and dressed quickly, already late for his next duty at the pool. Then he looked at her. She had wrapped the towel around herself like a sari and looked more beautiful than he remembered. Dex couldn't remember ever having been so turned on. Of course, there were always opportunities . . . but Jessica was so different. She positively smouldered. On impulse, he pulled her to him and kissed her tenderly.

'That was . . .' Dex offered, unable to put his thoughts into words. Sleek as a dolphin in the pool, adept as a gigolo in the cubicle. Struck dumb when he really wanted to make it count.

Jessica smiled reassuringly and took his hand. Guiding it under the towel, she placed it against the warmth of her pussy. As she looked into the fathomless depths of his eyes, she realised he was searching for something appropriate to say. As if in reply, she pushed his thumb into her sex and wriggled against him seductively. Patience might well be a virtue, but how very dull!

'Why don't we skip the small talk and fast forward to something we'll both enjoy?' Jessica breathed, her voice husky with renewed desire.

Dex didn't need to be asked twice. His thumb had already started moving in ever increasing circles deep within her. 'You're a very greedy girl,' he admonished seriously. 'Whatever shall I do with you?'

'Absolutely anything you want,' Jessica replied eagerly. 'A little punishment might be just what I need.'

And, with that, she let the towel slip to the floor.

Sleek and Dangerous

Lilith Dupree

Sleek and Dangerous

❖ ❖

*U*ndercurrents. That was it, undercurrents. That's why I was so uncomfortable around Judith. Undercurrents between Judith and her brother, Leif, that I couldn't ignore; between Judith and me – we had nothing in common, so why did she continue to pursue my friendship? – and between Leif and me, overshadowing everything else.

Judith was all soft curves and soft colours; honey-brown hair, soft hazel eyes, peachy complexion. She and I were the same height, but she was far more voluptuous. Leif had hair the colour of an antique gold ring I'd seen once, neither white gold, nor yellow, but somewhere beautifully in between. His face was classically angular: straight nose, wide cheekbones, with ice-blue eyes. The only thing soft about Leif were his richly sensuous lips. All of that on a very tall 6'6" frame, sleek, but elegantly muscled.

My hair is red, my eyes the expected green. Quite well-endowed, my willowy frame sometimes looked as if it weren't made to carry all that, needing my Audrey Hepburn shoulders to bring it all into balance. Taken together, the three of us would look like an advert promoting variety.

I hadn't really noticed Judith before I met her and her brother at a club one night. Rhys and I had been leaning against the railing at the edge of the dance-floor, enjoying the music. I'd felt

259

someone watching me, and had seen the head and shoulders of a beautiful Viking rising out of the crowd of dancers. Even from across the room, I could feel him inventorying my assets. That was a challenge I could meet; I stood proudly, my feet braced a little apart, daring him to look his fill.

He nodded his approval and smiled at me, as his eyes glided up from my feet to measure the length of my legs, pausing where they joined. I could very nearly feel him there like a warm hand through my clothes. He raised his eyes to my breasts, as though he measured them each by cupping their weight in a sinewy hand. A stroke of his eyes acknowledged the width of my shoulders, then finally moved up to my face. I felt stripped bare, but I enjoyed his explicit admiration.

My lover, Rhys, couldn't help but feel the scrutiny, too, but didn't comment. We were both attractive people. If we hadn't been able to accept seeing our partner being admired even as blatantly as this, we'd never have stayed together.

Eventually, a woman I hadn't noticed had come over to introduce herself. 'Simone, my name is Judith.' I wondered how she knew my name. She smiled and put out a hand to stroke my arm. I looked down at her hand, thinking that caress a bit over-friendly from a total stranger.

'We both work at Lanvale Microelectronics,' she told me.

I remembered then that I'd seen her around the complex, but we'd never had any professional contact. Now she seemed somehow ardent and breathless. I had expected her to focus that ardour on Rhys; instead, Judith seemed to refer continually to the beautiful Viking beside her.

Rhys and I both registered the not-so-subtle interchange between them as we looked curiously at each other. It wouldn't be the first time some unknown couple had sought to join us at one of the clubs or at a party. What was it that these two wanted?

The man's impact was devastating close up. He watched me in silence, with an occasional dismissive flick of his eyes towards Rhys. I was powerfully aware of him but assumed he was Judith's date. Rhys, not used to being ignored or treated with such disdain, was becoming angry. To smooth over the awkwardness, I hurried to introduce him.

'Oh, Judith. This is Rhys. Rhys, this is Judith and . . .' I paused, looking up at the tall man, waiting for one of them to fill in the blank.

'My brother,' and 'Leif,' they answered at the same time.

His voice was so deep and warm you could drown in it. I looked at him blankly, thinking he'd said, 'Life.' He must have been used to the reaction, because he gave a lazy grin. 'L-e-i-f.' He spelt it out slowly, ever so slowly, forming the letters with those lush lips, his eyes caressing me with each syllable.

Rhys brusquely took my arm. 'Well, nice meeting you –' this was addressed only to Judith '– but we have to be going.' I was too bemused to argue, allowing him to shuttle me through the crowd and out of the door.

'Why did you say that?' I asked, once we were outside and the spell of Leif's presence was broken. It wasn't a complaint, just curiosity.

'You didn't really want to spend the evening with them, did you?'

'No.' I shook my head and leant forward to brush a kiss along his lips.

I had enjoyed the feel of Leif's desire, but I hadn't really wanted to include the two of them in our plans. When Rhys and I were together, we both counted the moments until we could be alone. Like many men of similar deceptive physical type – delicate-featured, a bit less than medium height, and whipcord-slender – he was intensely male, and a passionate and demanding lover.

I had first seen Rhys in the library. I was reaching to withdraw a book from the stacks, when I had been held by a pair of eyes so deep a blue they were almost purple, framed by thick dark lashes, staring intently at me over the tops of the row of books. My first thought was, what a lucky woman. Then several volumes slid down the shelf to reveal an unmistakably masculine person on the other side.

We had eyed each other silently and lustfully until I forced myself to break away. However, my visits to the library increased in frequency – as, apparently, did his. We performed our literary mating dance over several nights, before he sat down opposite me one evening and said, with an intensity unsuited to his words, 'We've got to stop meeting like this.'

The only solution: we left together. He led me to his flat, offered me a glass of wine, then shook his head and pulled me into his arms. We were almost frantic to get each other's clothes off.

That first time, we'd made love standing there, half undressed, too eager to observe the niceties. Looking back on it now, it's rather frightening to think of what could have happened if Rhys had been some maniac whose kink was picking up women in libraries, but instead that encounter was the genesis of a passionate relationship that would redefine me as a woman.

I'd never been so aware of a man as I was of Rhys, and I'd never had such a hair-trigger libido. I only had to think of him to find myself moist and eager. He said it was the same with him: my image would flit through his mind at a meeting, turning him hard and draining all the blood from his brain to his sex.

After that first encounter at the club, Judith seemed to be everpresent in my life, calling me at the office to see if I'd join her for lunch, planning little girlish outings to shop, or inviting me to her club for a game of tennis. At first I had agreed simply because I had nothing better to do or could come up with no convincing reason for refusing.

However, the more time we spent together, the more painfully obvious it became that we had nothing in common. Judith was always eager and excited and mentioned her brother often. I felt guilty for disliking her, when she was so desirous of my company. I'd discussed it with Rhys, when one of her calls had interrupted our precious time alone.

'Perhaps she's just lonely, doesn't have any other women friends.' Tolerant and sympathetic, that was his attitude.

Then she had invited Rhys and me to dinner at her home. Now let's see how tolerant he feels, I thought. But he agreed, at the last moment stipulating that it was to be a dinner-only invitation.

'Tell her we have tickets to that sold out show at the Orpheum,' he suggested.

'I can't do that; we'd have to leave before dinner even started to get there in time. If you're so eager to accept, then you can think of some way to get us out of there at a reasonable hour.'

'Well, if she delays us, she'll just have to put up with her dinner guests humping each other silly right before her eyes,' he said with a leer, just before he pounced on me to love me into forgetfulness.

His wiry strength and sureness as he took me in his arms overwhelmed any desire I had to do anything but feel him over me, inside me. We tasted each other, explored every inch of that familiar territory, our bodies melting together like some sensuous caramel of pleasure.

On the night, we were both surprised to see Leif there. Judith hadn't mentioned him when she'd proffered the invitation. I knew Rhys would have refused, had he known. He didn't mind another man leering at me on neutral territory, where he had the option of calling a halt by the simple expedient of asking me to leave with him, but Judith's home was definitely not neutral territory.

All through the meal, Leif's eyes had been on me, repeating his caressing appraisal of as much of me as could be seen while at the table. In turn, my eyes had been drawn to him and the spectacle of his torso lovingly caressed by the cling of a silk turtleneck. I may have felt naked and vulnerable under his intent gaze, but I was hardly blameless myself, imagining those satiny muscles under my hands. Rhys drew my attention by stretching to rub his leg against mine from across the table, reassuring and claiming me.

When I got up to go to the powder room after we'd finished dessert, I heard Rhys begin to make our excuses. Coming back out, a few moments later, I was mentally preparing to second his goodnights, but Leif was waiting there in the hallway for me, leaning next to a doorway across the hall. I felt my heart in my throat at the sight of him, his casual posture displaying his body so that I couldn't help but run my eyes over every sleek contour.

He suddenly moved, reached out to take my wrist and pull me into the room behind him. I was in his arms there in the dark before I realised what was happening. Pressed up against the great length of him, I felt his sex hard against my abdomen.

Leif's kiss was proprietorial, taking my lips and tongue and all my consciousness and claiming them for his own.

I did finally remind myself that it was Rhys I loved, Rhys I wanted, Rhys I had come with, but I had to fight myself as much as Leif in pulling away. We were standing about a foot apart – I with my hand pressed against his chest, Leif with arms out-stretched to draw me back – when the door was flung open, bathing us in the light from the hallway. It was Rhys and Judith.

Rhys was angry and ready to fight even that much larger man. I barely noticed Judith in my rush to forestall Rhys and get the two of us out of there without bloodshed. It wasn't until later that I recalled the horridly avid expression on Judith's face as I had pushed Rhys past her.

If I had expected that episode to finally halt Judith's pursuit, I would have been mistaken. She called me the next day for lunch, as though the whole thing had never happened. As the days passed, we went back to our routine of pointless companionship.

One Friday, Judith told me how much she wanted to see where I lived, how we'd been 'friends' for so long, but she'd never been to my home. I felt invaded, but my guilt over resenting her so forced me to bow to her pressure, and I invited her for lunch the next day. Rhys would be coming over later in the afternoon, which would put an end to what was bound to be a tedious visit.

I prepared a simple meal: steamed fresh tuna, chilled and dressed with olive oil, lime and freshly ground black pepper. This was accompanied with a green salad, a loaf of crusty bread, and sliced tropical fruits for desert. I'd just finished putting it all on the table when the doorbell rang.

I dawdled over to the door, sighing, wishing it were already over, but when I opened the door, it was Leif standing there. He stepped past me, ignoring my surprise. I turned my attention from him to look around outside for Judith, but he was alone.

I closed the door and turned to face him, leaning back against it for support. My knees were wobbly and my heart was pound-ing. 'Where's Judith?' My voice betrayed my agitation.

He didn't answer, but calmly removed his jacket and gloves, placing them on the arm of the chair by which he stood. When he moved towards me, I didn't even try to evade him. I couldn't deny it; I wanted him to make love to me.

His kisses would have drained any will I might have had to resist. I had the sensation that I was whirling in space, trailing a vortex of stars. His hands were everywhere, touching and teasing and pulling away my clothes.

This was so different from making love with Rhys. We were equals, I as much of an aggressor as he. But Leif was so big, so powerful; I felt helpless lethargy, letting him undress me, letting him strum my body into a singing vibrating instrument.

When he paused to slowly remove his own clothes, I held my breath, savouring the beauty unfolding before me. I could only stare hungrily at him, long and hard and waiting for me. He cupped his testicles and offered his cock to me. I reached out to grasp his penis, to slide my hand along its hot and silky length. He sighed at my touch.

Wavering like a sleepwalker, I let him draw me towards him. When he picked me up, I wrapped my legs around him, lowering myself on to him. I gasped at his length and thickness; he truly filled me up.

Holding my hips when I tried to draw away to begin our intimate dance, Leif carried me to the bedroom. He bent to lower me to the bed, still holding my hips up, keeping himself inside me. That moaning: was that me? It was almost painful, that continued pressure, but such exquisite tension, as I teetered on the edge between pain and pleasure.

I clutched his cock with my sex, twisting my hips, and releasing and clutching once more. Writhing, with his big hands holding me against him, I felt myself begin to throb; then I was gasping, frantically forcing myself harder against him over and over, as my body spun out of my control.

When I fell back against the mattress, spent, Leif loomed above me with what I could only feel was a sinister smile, but he only lowered his body to cover mine, warmly possessive. He began kissing me again, and I responded passionately. Then he slid off to lie beside me, bending that silver-gold head to capture my nipples in his lips. He licked and sucked my breasts, stroking me.

I tried to turn my body towards him, needing to feel him

against me again; but, instead, he rolled me on to my side, away from him, moving his lips to my neck and shoulders. His kisses moved down my spine, causing me to arch my back, savouring the tingle it sent down to my sex.

When I felt his hands at my hips, I was ready – more than ready. The thigh he pressed between mine, spreading me for his entry, was hard with muscle. I trembled with anticipation as he entered me. This time he moved inside me, slipping his hands from my hips, across my belly to spread my sex-lips and tease my hard little bud until I thought I would scream. His panting, thrusting climax set off my own raging waves of release.

I lay there, nestled back against him. Both of us were languid with satisfied lust, oblivious to the soft sounds coming from the living room. Leif's lovemaking had completely driven the recollection of Rhys's expected arrival from my mind. How long had Rhys been standing in the doorway, before I raised heavy eyes to see him?

He must have come in and, seeing no sign of Judith, assumed I was waiting in the bedroom for him. He had undressed and come down the hall, expecting to see me waiting eagerly for his lovemaking. Instead, he found me and Judith's Viking of a brother nestled against one another, the air ripe with the aroma of sex.

Rhys was naked, hard, and ready for battle. He'd never looked more beautiful, and my traitorous body wanted him.

'Rhys.' A whisper as I held my arms out to him.

I felt Leif move away from me and glanced round apprehensively, for fear of what he might be going to do. He was sitting up and looking inscrutably at Rhys.

Leif ran his eyes up and down my lover's body. Rhys returned his scrutiny, watching the big man angrily. Then Leif moved over to rise from the bed. When he strode slowly towards Rhys, he was erect again, as if the challenge of another sexual male turned him on.

Rhys's head went up, and he stood his ground. I should have been afraid that they would fight, but something about Leif's slow, deliberate stride and Rhys's frozen posture told me that this was not to be a battle of blows.

The taller man reached out a lazy hand and trailed it along

my lover's jaw, stroked a finger across his lips. Rhys stood unmoving, but I felt those caresses on my own face, on my own lips. And I still wasn't sure what Rhys would do.

Leif put his hands on Rhys's shoulders and pulled him forward so that their bodies almost touched. Indeed, if they'd been closer in height, their hard penises would have been bobbing and rubbing against each other. Then Leif bent to press his lips to Rhys's mouth. I held my breath; I knew what Leif's kisses could do. Would my lover surrender or would he fight free?

When Rhys still didn't respond, Leif straightened up and looked at him calculatingly.

Then I smiled. I knew then what Rhys would do. He was never one to be overpowered; he was an equal or a conqueror, never a submissive partner. He moved towards Leif until their bodies touched, reached up and pulled the big man down to him.

Their kiss was powerful, two strong male animals battling with their bodies in a most sensuous arena. At first it was tempestuous, Leif seeming determined to take control. But, as they fought their mastery, I could see them both begin to settle into the kiss; their bodies moulded together as they unconsciously began to stroke and caress one another.

When Leif pulled back this time, it was to kneel down in front of Rhys and take him into his mouth. Leif was so large, it looked as though he could swallow my lover's entire sex, but he worked him gently at first, gradually pulling harder with his lips, engulfing him completely.

Rhys was nearly helpless under this onslaught. He tried to pull back a little, as if the bigger man's lips and tongue were claiming too much of him, but Leif grasped Rhys's buttocks in his powerful hands, halting his retreat. I saw the motion of Leif's fingers teasing at him, even as his lips and tongue licked and sucked Rhys's distended member.

When Rhys came, it was violently, with a cry of total abandon. He had to brace himself on Leif's shoulders to stay on his feet. I felt protective of him, knowing how it felt to be recovering from such powerful sensations. I got up and went over to the two men, taking Rhys in my arms to lead him to the bed.

We lay down together, feeling strangely close in that moment

– we'd shared an experience that few lovers ever do. When Leif lay down on the other side of Rhys, I reached out to take his hand, but he held it back from me. Leaning against my lover's body, he reached across to slide his hand between my thighs and into my sex.

His touch was so sure and strong; I spread my legs to him. But he soon withdrew his hand and moved to slide it between Rhys's cheeks. He was using my fluids to lubricate him. At first Rhys didn't seem aware of anything except renewed pleasure, but when Leif tried to slide his huge erection into him, Rhys balked.

'No!' He pushed back on the bigger man. Leif ignored his protest, seeming determined to have his way.

I sat up and grabbed him by his silver-gold hair, pulling with all my strength. 'Leave him alone!'

The look he threw me frightened me, but not enough that I'd let him force Rhys. While we glared at each other, Rhys slid from between us and moved across the bed. He knelt, sitting back on his heels, and shook his head at Leif.

'If you want to play with Simone and me, you have to play nicely.'

I laughed at that description, and the tension was broken. Leif relaxed and joined in the laughter. Then the two men turned their heads to stare at me with dark lust-filled eyes. The breath caught in my throat. What would happen now? I felt almost afraid, but so excited, my heart was pounding like a wild thing.

Rhys fell forward on to all fours and crawled towards me. I knew that playful expression. I lay back against the pillows, bending my legs and spreading my thighs for him. When he nuzzled his face into my thatch, I raised my hips to him.

His tongue was hot and expert at teasing me into a frenzy. My eyes were half-closed in pleasure when Leif straddled my torso. He had grasped my hands to hold them out at my sides, before I realised what he was going to do. He wanted me to take him into my mouth: but he was too big, and I was afraid.

Rhys must have felt my tension in the tightening of my sex. He was beside us, pulling Leif's hands from mine, angry and once again ready to fight. 'I told you to play nicely. You don't force Simone any more than you force me!'

The two of them battled it out with their eyes and their wills while I lay there, helpless. Finally, Leif moved off me, casting petulant looks at both of us, and moved to the other side of the bed, looking pointedly away from us.

Rhys and I exchanged looks. Leif had given both of us pleasure, but he was still rigid and unsatisfied. It wasn't really fair, was it? There must be some way we could pleasure our new playmate. And he was so beautiful – we would both enjoy exploring that large and elegant body, teasing him into a state of helpless ecstasy. We grinned at each other, then pounced.

The big man was taken unawares. We pushed him back against the mattress, Rhys spreading Leif's legs and kneeling between them, while I straddled his hips. Leif looked back and forth between us, a rather uncertain smile on his face. When he reached towards me, I reached for his hands, shook my head at him when he would have put them on my waist, and laid them out at his sides.

When his eyes closed and he moved under me, I looked over my shoulder to see what Rhys was up to. He was licking and nibbling his way up the insides of Leif's thighs, stroking and kneading those long muscles with practised hands as he went. While our captive was thus occupied, I moved to fetch silk scarves from my bureau.

When I returned to the bed, Leif was lying there, smiling weakly, brows drawn down in the sweet pain of his mounting excitement. Rhys still knelt between Leif's outspread thighs; his head was bent, now, to lick at Leif's testicles.

When I trailed the silk over Leif's wrist, he started, turning his head and opening those icy blue eyes wide in surprise and confusion. Their blue was now just a gemlike ring around his dilated pupils, and his breathing was shallow and rapid.

I tied the scarf around his right wrist, pulling it up over his head, and laying it against the pillow. When I repeated the game with his left wrist, and he realised that it was only a token binding, his expression was meltingly submissive. I sat astride him again, admiring the beauty of his face. His torso was warm and smooth, the muscles defined and hard as I ran my hands over them.

I leant forward to tease at his nipples with lips and tongue;

they were tight but soft and warm. When he gasped as I nipped at his breasts, I worried that my fascination had driven me to be too enthusiastic, but one glance at him told me that it was a gasp of pure joy.

His eyes were closed. My breasts felt heavy with the need to feel someone relish them as I was relishing his. I leant forward to dip one breast down to his lips, until I had his attention once again. He raised his head to reach for my breast with his lips, but I leant back, pulling it away from him, then bent to touch the other breast to his mouth.

He moaned and I felt his hips moving under me, as he raised his head and licked out with his tongue to try to capture me. That tiny tantalising touch, coupled with his total lack of resistance, melted me. I bent again, resting my breast against his lips.

When he realised the treat was not to be withdrawn this time, he pulled my nipple into his mouth and suckled, sending a flame straight to my sex. I felt Rhys's hand on my arm, as he motioned toward Leif's still hard member.

I moved back to capture that hard cock and fill myself with him once again. The big man and I sighed as we came together. I had barely started to move on him when Rhys pushed me to the side. I toppled slowly over; Rhys pushed Leif towards me so that we lay on our sides, clasped together.

He and I both hesitated momentarily, locked together by my enclosing thighs. Then Rhys pushed against Leif, silently indicating that he was to cover me. One more roll and Leif and I smiled at each other, beginning to move in our own sexual rhythm. His movements were surprisingly leisurely, considering how long we had made him wait.

When he gasped and thrust into me hard, I eagerly absorbed him: all of him. His breaths were shaky and his thrusts spasmodic, as if in climax. It was Rhys, up on his knees behind him and thrusting into him in time with our coming together, that had affected him so.

Leif braced himself, elbows locked, hands to either side of me, gasping and shaking his head from side to side. The three of us had reached a mutual rhythm, slow deep thrusts passing from Rhys into Leif then into me. When I clenched to hold him, I felt the power of the two of them filling me with glory.

When Leif came, it was truly earth-shaking. His breath whooped in his chest; he trembled with the force of it. For my part, I was lost in the grip of a giant hand whose clasp wrung me out and left me gasping. Rhys came at last, wringing further gasps from poor Leif before our Viking collapsed on to his side.

I curled into Leif's arms. They felt heavy and limp as he placed them around me. I kissed him gently, tasting his lips and tongue with just the tip of my own tongue. I felt a surge of protectiveness towards him; I stroked my hands through his sweat-drenched hair and kissed his eyelids.

When Rhys lay against Leif's back and reached his arm around the bigger man to touch me, we hugged him between us, warming and protecting him with our bodies. Leif's breathing deepened and became regular. He slept in our embrace; soon, we slept, too.

When we all woke later, I was famished. I left my two lovers to go to the dining room and rescue the tuna, discarding the wilted green salad and putting the bread and fruit on a large platter with the fish. I brought it back to the bed, and we lay there, the three of us feeding each other, savouring the tangy dressing of the tuna and the sweet moistness of the fruit.

The inevitable dribbles were duly and with great pleasure licked from wherever they fell. We had nearly finished our meal, when Leif let out a whoop of laughter.

'Poor Judith!' he exclaimed.

Rhys and I looked at him in a query.

'She wanted to be here, to join us, and the two of you drove her completely out of my mind.'

'Poor Judith,' Rhys and I said in unison, chuckling and moving into our new lover's arms.

BLACK LACE NEW BOOKS

Published in November

FORBIDDEN FRUIT
Susie Raymond
£5.99

Beth is thirty-eight. Jonathan is sixteen. An affair between them is unthinkable. Or is it? To Jonathan, Beth is much more exciting than girls his own age. She's a real woman: sexy, sophisticated and experienced. And Beth can't get the image of his fit young body out of her mind. Although she knows she shouldn't encourage him, the temptation is irresistible. What will happen when they have tasted the forbidden fruit?

ISBN 0 352 33306 5

HOSTAGE TO FANTASY
Louisa Francis
£5.99

Bridie Flanagan is a spirited young Irish woman living a harsh life in outback Australia at the turn of the century. A reversal of fortune enables her to travel to the thriving city of Melbourne and become a lady. But rugged bushranger Lucas Martin is in pursuit of her; he wants her money and she wants his body. Can they reach a civilised agreement?

ISBN 0 352 33305 7

Published in December

A SECRET PLACE
Ella Broussard
£5.99

Maddie is a locations scout for a film company. When a big-budget Hollywood movie is made in rural UK in the summer, she is delighted to be working on-set. Maddie loves working outdoors – and with a hunky good-looking crew of technicians and actors around her, there are plenty of opportunities for her to show off her talents.

ISBN 0 352 33307 3

A PRIVATE VIEW
Crystalle Valentino
£5.99

Successful catwalk model Jemma has everything she needs. Then a dare from a colleague to pose for a series of erotic photographs intrigues her. Jemma finds that the photographer, Dominic, and his jet-setting friends, have interesting sexual tastes. She finds their charms irresistible but what will happen to her career if she gives in to her desires?

ISBN 0 352 33308 1

SUGAR AND SPICE 2
A short-story collection
£6.99

Sugar and Spice anthologies mean Black Lace short stories. And erotic short stories are extremely popular. The book contains 20 diverse and seductive tales guaranteed to ignite and excite. This second compendium pushes the boundaries to bring you stories which go beyond romance and explore the no-holds-barred products of the female erotic imagination. Only the best and most arousing stories make it into a Black Lace anthology.

ISBN 0 352 33309 X

To be published in January

A FEAST FOR THE SENSES
Martine Marquand
£5.99

Clara Fairfax leaves life in Georgian England to embark on the Grand Tour of Europe. She travels through the decadent cities – from icebound Amsterdam to sultry Constantinople undergoing lessons in pleasure from the mysterious and eccentric Count Anton di Maliban.

ISBN 0 352 33310 3

THE TRANSFORMATION
Natasha Rostova
£5.99

Three friends, one location – San Francisco. This book contains three interlinked and very modern stories which have their roots in fairy tales. There's nothing innocent about Lydia, Molly and Cassie, however, as one summer provides them with the cathartic sexual experiences which transform their lives.

ISBN 0 352 33311 1

If you would like a complete list of plot summaries of Black Lace titles, or would like to receive information on other publications available, please send a stamped addressed envelope to:

Black Lace, Thames Wharf Studios,
Rainville Road, London W6 9HT

BLACK LACE BOOKLIST

All books are priced £4.99 unless another price is given.

Black Lace books with a contemporary setting

MÉNAGE £5.99	Emma Holly ISBN 0 352 33231 X	☐
THE SUCCUBUS £5.99	Zoe le Verdier ISBN 0 352 33230 1	☐
FEMININE WILES £7.99	Karina Moore ISBN 0 352 33235 2	☐
AN ACT OF LOVE £5.99	Ella Broussard ISBN 0 352 33240 9	☐
THE SEVEN-YEAR LIST £5.99	Zoe le Verdier ISBN 0 352 33254 9	☐
MASQUE OF PASSION £5.99	Tesni Morgan ISBN 0 352 33259 X	☐
DRAWN TOGETHER £5.99	Robyn Russell ISBN 0 352 33269 7	☐
DRAMATIC AFFAIRS £5.99	Fredrica Alleyn ISBN 0 352 33289 1	☐
UNDERCOVER SECRETS £5.99	Zoe le Verdier ISBN 0 352 33285 9	☐
SEARCHING FOR VENUS £5.99	Ella Broussard ISBN 0 352 33284 0	☐

Black Lace books with an historical setting

THE SENSES BEJEWELLED	Cleo Cordell ISBN 0 352 32904 1	☐
HANDMAIDEN OF PALMYRA	Fleur Reynolds ISBN 0 352 32919 X	☐
JULIET RISING	Cleo Cordell ISBN 0 352 32938 6	☐
THE INTIMATE EYE	Georgia Angelis ISBN 0 352 33004 X	☐
CONQUERED	Fleur Reynolds ISBN 0 352 33025 2	☐
JEWEL OF XANADU	Roxanne Carr ISBN 0 352 33037 6	☐
FORBIDDEN CRUSADE	Juliet Hastings ISBN 0 352 33079 1	☐
ÎLE DE PARADIS	Mercedes Kelly ISBN 0 352 33121 6	☐
DESIRE UNDER CAPRICORN	Louisa Francis ISBN 0 352 33136 4	☐
THE HAND OF AMUN	Juliet Hastings ISBN 0 352 33144 5	☐

─ ─ ─ ─ ─ ─✂ ─ ─ ─ ─ ─ ─ ─ ─ ─ ─ ─ ─ ─ ─ ─ ─ ─

Please send me the books I have ticked above.

Name ....

Address ....

....

....

.... Post Code ....

Send to: **Cash Sales, Black Lace Books, Thames Wharf Studios, Rainville Road, London W6 9HT.**

US customers: for prices and details of how to order books for delivery by mail, call 1-800-805-1083.

Please enclose a cheque or postal order, made payable to **Virgin Publishing Ltd**, to the value of the books you have ordered plus postage and packing costs as follows:

UK and BFPO – £1.00 for the first book, 50p for each subsequent book.

Overseas (including Republic of Ireland) – £2.00 for the first book, £1.00 each subsequent book.

If you would prefer to pay by VISA or ACCESS/MASTERCARD, please write your card number and expiry date here:

....

Please allow up to 28 days for delivery.

Signature ....

─ ─ ─ ─ ─ ─✂ ─ ─ ─ ─ ─ ─ ─ ─ ─ ─ ─ ─ ─ ─ ─ ─ ─